Explanation from Physics to Theology

Explanation from Physics to Theology

AN ESSAY IN RATIONALITY AND RELIGION

Philip Clayton

YALE UNIVERSITY PRESS
New Haven and London

Published with assistance from the foundation
established in memory of James Wesley
Cooper of the Class of 1865, Yale College.

Designed by Sonia L. Scanlon
and set in Caledonia and Baskerville type by
The Composing Room of Michigan, Inc.
Printed in the United States of America.

Library of Congress Cataloging-in-Publication Data

Clayton, Philip, 1956–
    Explanation from physics to theology : an essay in rationality and
religion/Philip Clayton.
        p.   cm.
    Bibliography: p.
    Includes index.
    ISBN 0–300–04353–8
    1. Religion—Philosophy.   2. Science—Philosophy.   3. Social
sciences—Philosophy.   4. Rationalism.   5. Religion.   6. Theology.
I. Title.
BL51.C56   1989
121—dc19
                                                                88-39306
                                                                CIP

Contents

Preface

This book explores the often hazy intersection between two radically diverse fields: the nature and justification of explanatory claims in science, and the nature and status of religious explanations. Scientists have long recognized the lines that run from certain features of religion or metaphysics toward their own disciplines. If anything, recent developments have softened the contrasts. But we shall be moving mostly in the other direction, from the natural sciences and toward religious explanations. It is my thesis that the recent debate in religious studies and theology on the status of religious beliefs cannot make significant progress without careful consideration of the nature and testing of beliefs in other disciplines.

The title of this book by itself does not convey what I think has been the missing link in many science/religion discussions: the problem of meaning in the social sciences. As I show, direct epistemological connections between the natural sciences and theology commit a type of category mistake. Only when the discussion of scientific rationality—which too often has meant natural scientific rationality—has been stretched to include the semantic perspectives of both researcher and researched will the field be clear for a productive treatment of the links between explanations in science and religion.

The first chapter of this book is introductory, specifying several important types of religious explanation and relating these to the faith/reason debate in western religious thought from Tertullian to Lindbeck. Chapter 2 examines the reasons for moving from a formal or structural treatment of scientific explanations to a stress on contextual factors. With the aid of the work of Imre Lakatos, I steer a middle course between purely formal and purely contextual treatments of rationality. Chapter 3 represents the turning point in my argument. The philosophy of social science has been torn between those who wish to equate natural and social scientific explanation and those who wish completely to rid the social sciences of their explanatory goal. The work of Jürgen Habermas offers hope of a significant mediation in the discussion and, though I am ultimately critical of his compromise, it merits our close attention.

After an excursus on philosophical explanations (chapter 4), I turn to the problem of explanation in the study of religion and theology. In chapter 5, the centrality of the question of meaning in religion reveals some important continuities with the discussion of the social sciences. Strong discontinuities, however, must also be acknowledged. I attempt to draw some science/ religion connections based on the role of reason and of doubt in religion; the outcome is a defense of the *secular believer*, for whom faith and a fundamental openness to criticism are no longer incompatible. In the final chapter, I enter into the much disputed realm of theological methodology. I argue against facile attempts to equate theological method with that of the natural or social sciences; theology's tie to a believing community does indeed set it apart from those fields. However, if theology wishes to take its place as an academic discipline concerned with reasoned explanations, it must share in the privileges and responsibilities pertaining thereto.

The present manuscript has undergone a threefold gestation period. A first draft was composed in Munich, Germany, during a period of study under Wolfhart Pannenberg and Lorenz B. Puntel. I am grateful to those two scholars for their advice and friendship and to the Deutschen Akademischen Austauschdienst for the two-year grant that made the stay in Munich possible. Those who know Wolfhart Pannenberg's work will recognize in these pages significant similarities to, but also important divergences from, his understanding of the philosophy of science and theology; I happily acknowledge the influence of my German mentor.

The manuscript then received a complete reworking in the course of Ph.D. work at Yale University. In this case, as in most, the influence of my former advisors, Louis Dupré in the Religious Studies department and Karsten Harries in Philosophy, is too pervasive for me to footnote particulars and can only be hinted at through this blanket acknowledgment. Ultimately, though, it took several years of further reading and reflection while teaching at Williams College to bring the manuscript to its present form. The generous research and administrative support provided by Williams, and the conducive atmosphere of the Berkshire hills, contributed to the rewriting process. I am also happy to acknowledge a generous publication subsidy provided by the President and Trustees of Williams College.

Numerous discussions and critiques of earlier drafts have shaped this text; all those who have attempted similar projects know how indispensable such criticism is. Especially I wish to thank Dustin Anderson, R. I. G.

Hughes, Steven Knapp, George Lindbeck, Peter Lipton, Steven Mill-hauser, John E. Smith, and Kevin Vanhoozer. These friends and critics have drawn my attention to a multitude of sins; many I have corrected, though the work is still *simul justus et peccator*.

The most gracious critic this manuscript encountered was Hans Frei, whose untimely death in September 1988 represents a great loss for the American theological community. Professor Frei was an advisor, discussion partner, and friend for a whole generation of scholars, both at Yale University and beyond, and scores of former students like myself will be able to testify to his generous assistance with their work and careers. I would like to think that Hans's influence can be detected wherever I have managed to avoid extreme positions and work genuinely toward a mediation with the opposing theological positions.

All italicizing in quotes belongs to the original author where not indicated as mine. Unless otherwise noted, parenthetical page references refer to the work cited in the most recent note. Full bibliographical information on all works cited in the notes appears in the Bibliography.

Like many authors today, I have struggled with the question of personal pronouns. The employment solely of masculine forms is offensive to many contemporary readers and to me; yet "he and she" is cumbersome, "his/her" unaesthetic. Finally, I have chosen to alternate the use of masculine and feminine pronouns in the work, as is currently the practice in most social scientific literature. Though this is distracting to some readers at first, perhaps it will become less so as they encounter it more frequently.

One referent of a feminine personal pronoun deserves special acknowledgment. My wife, Kate, has borne the burden of the research and writing process through these years as fully as has this author. Without her support this book would not have been what it is, and perhaps would not have been at all.

CHAPTER ONE

Explanation in Science and Religion

For believers, religious beliefs help to explain the world and their place within it. Of course, religious beliefs do a number of other things as well. They can also function as redescriptions of the rites and practices of believing communities, as expressions in the language of faith of psychological and sociological needs and influences, or even as attempts to answer philosophical (ethical, aesthetic, literary) questions in religious terms. In addition, religious beliefs reflect a general sense of meaningfulness on the part of the believer, an existential attitude underlying particular dogmas that can be formulated and discussed. In this last sense actual beliefs may be subordinated under a (possibly ineffable) picture, mood, or *blik*, a sense of fit or meaning, which relativizes their function as explanations of the world or events within it.

Still, among the various functions of religious belief is explanation. Ideally, one would begin a comparison of explanations in scientific and religious contexts with a complete definition of *explanation*. But if a definition were specific enough to be helpful, it would be specific enough to beg some of the questions along our way. Indeed, it would be question-begging in an even more onerous way, for one of the more interesting issues implied by this book's title is whether there even is a single concept of explanation that runs from physics to theology. We will find that the bulk of our task lies in specifying how one can even speak of *explanation* in the singular when referring to a broad spectrum of disciplines. The two concepts that I treat in greatest detail, coherence and criticizability, provide at best a few necessary conditions and thus only the beginnings of a unitary theory of explanation.

Following standard usage, I use the term *explanans* for the account that does the explaining and *explanandum* for the thing to be explained. I begin with the general hypothesis that explanations are answers to why-questions. If one is asked to explain an action that she has performed, she will tell *why* she performed it, listing as explanans her reasons, her intentions, or the external forces that constrained her. Or, in order to explain the fact or explanandum that two magnets move together in a certain manner, one will give an account of why they did so, referring to the laws of magnetic attraction and the way that these particular magnets were aligned. It is sometimes argued that explanations need only answer *how-questions*, that is, that one can provide no more than a description of a series of events in order to explain the explanandum. In order not to beg this question, we must construe the term *why-questions* in a rather broad sense, such that their answers *may* be given by relatively unembellished descriptions of states of affairs. Theories of explanation in particular disciplines will then have as their goal to specify the standards for agreeing that an explanandum is explained by its explanans in their field: must the explanandum be construed as the effect of certain causes? as the action that resulted from certain reasons (as in Aristotle's practical syllogism)? or merely as the thing that a certain description describes?

In general, then, an explanation makes some area of experience comprehensible to a number of individuals, either by presenting it in terms of its components or details (analysis), or by placing it into a broader context within which its meaning or significance becomes clear (synthesis). Unless one denies that the explanatory moment has any place among the variety of functions served by religious belief, it is important for the study of religion to carry out a careful analysis of religious belief as explanation.

Religious beliefs function to make sense of the world for the believer. They tell why something within the world—or why the world as a whole— is. They provide a framework within which, ideally, life as a whole can be viewed. Prima facie, we may expect to find some connections between explanations in religion and other areas of human belief and practice. Obviously, it is in the various sciences that we find the human explanatory project in its most fully developed and reflected form. In order to set the stage for examining religious explanations, then, I look in detail at recent work in the philosophy of the natural and social sciences in chapters 2 and 3. The parallels with the sciences are both intriguing and fruitful for the understanding of religion. However significant the parallels, religious explanations have unique aspects as well: they may be all-encompassing and deeply personal; they arise from vague and elusive questions concerning the meaning of an individual's life or human mortality; as religious answers they function to provide a context of significance and security, to "make life meaningful." In most cases, at least in the western tradition, religious explanations involve positing the existence of a transcendent being or beings, who may be accessible (knowable) only to the believer or obedient follower. Both the scope and content of this sort of explanation separate it from explanations in other areas. Our task must include assessing the discontinuities as well as the continuities between religious and other types of explanation.

The approach in this chapter is largely descriptive or typological: we will consider types of religious explanation, the connection between the explanation debate and the classical faith/reason debate, and some views on explanation in contemporary theology and philosophy of religion. But, since no typology is completely neutral (a theme stressed in chapter 2), the description of the alternatives here already sets certain parameters for the chapters to follow. In order not to obscure this fact, I comment on the normative assumptions or implications as they arise in the discussion.

Types of Religious Explanation

In developing an initial list of types of religious explanation, a number of approaches can be used. If one took explanations to be no more than redescriptions of the world as the believer sees it, one could merely redescribe the descriptions. The goal would be to avoid any categories or "external" terms whatsoever, to portray only how specific beliefs and practices vary among religious traditions. (But, as I argue below, does not *any* redescription or comparison tacitly impose some framework on one's data?) Or, if religious explanations could be divided into a limited number of formal models, we could analyze these formal types, subsuming actual instances under them. (But theologians have encountered formidable difficulties in producing such formal models.)

By contrast, I will concentrate on the type and scope of the *justification* that is claimed for religious explanations. In doing so, I assume that the problems of explanation and rationality are integrally linked. Justification involves the nature and adequacy of the warrants that are given for particular explanations. A religious community may formulate beliefs of extremely broad scope that are believed to be *true* of or for all humanity; it may also view these beliefs as in principle *intelligible* to all persons; and yet it may still hold that the reasons for the beliefs are accessible to (carry weight for) the members of the community alone. It is my thesis that a rough spectrum of epistemic positions emerges, lying between absolute, universal, or objective justification claims and purely private justifications. Below, I focus on the categories of private, communal, and intersubjective explanations. If we are to draw any nontrivial science/religion comparisons in the final chapters, I must defend the intersubjective approach as at least one viable form of epistemic justification in religion.

The typology should begin with the private explanations, since a number of the options, whatever they may be in addition to being private, also make appeal to private justification. This category covers religious explanations that are held to be warranted solely by the fact that they make subjective sense of experience for the believer. It allows us to speak of the *explanatory potential* of religious traditions that are utterly unconcerned with the justification question. Tribal religions are often cited as examples of this category, insofar as they lack a consciousness of choice or multiple options and have not developed a tradition of rational defense or apologetics.[1] Where religious belief and practice are pursued as a means to individual salvation or release, as in many of the Eastern traditions, the justification of religious explanations reduces to the personal efficacy of specific spiritual disciplines for achieving the desired spiritual state. One thinks of traditions within Buddhism in which the doctrines of the endless wheel of becoming (*bhavacakra*), impermanence (*anicca*), and no-self (*anatta*) explain primarily in the sense of defining a spiritual problem and the path that the believer can follow to escape from a life of suffering.[2] Where the justification of a religious explanation is rooted in its personal disclosure value alone, I will speak of *private explanations*.[3]

An especially clear example of private explanations is provided by the emphasis on the individual in recent Western religious thought, especially during the last two centuries. Paradigmatic is Kierkegaard, who held that "truth is subjectivity," and for whom the utter paradox of the Christ event transcended the fruitlessness of philosophy by leading to "an objective uncertainty held fast in an appropriation-process of the most passionate inwardness," an "infinite passion of the individual's inwardness."[4] But the believer who claims that her sense of the presence of God in Scripture is sufficient reason for her faith fits the same model. Whatever broader epistemic warrants may be found for religious beliefs or traditions, this sense of fitting relevant aspects of one's life into a subjectively perceived coherent structure or whole remains a central component of religious explanation.

The second variety of explanation is similar to private explanation in limiting the horizon of its justificatory task. In this category the limitation in epistemic scope is not to the individual but to a circumscribed community of believers or language users. Under this model, reason-giving (for instance, appeals to the Koran) is taken as authoritative for the entire linguistic community but is not assumed to carry weight for others unless they join the community of believers. This epistemic view, which has exercised a strong influence on the philosophy of religion through the influence of the later Wittgenstein,[5] can be categorized as relying on *communal explana-*

tions, since the standards for adequate explanations are set by the particular believing and practicing religious community. Since we are considering modes of justification rather than the scope of explanations, communal explanations need not be broader in content than private explanations or more circumscribed than transcommunal ones.

Not all religious explanations can be subsumed under the private or communal types. Especially within the Christian tradition, many thinkers have maintained that religious beliefs can be given a justification that transcends the boundaries of the individual religious community. Historical movements such as the apologetic tradition, natural theology, and perhaps even the quest for a systematic theology as such, have earned an important place for the notion of transcommunal justifications within the Christian tradition. When expressed in systematic form, Christian beliefs are often held to offer a reasonable or rational explanation of the world or of particular areas of human experience, one which the believer takes to have more than merely communal validity.

Explanations of this type need not be foundational in structure; they may involve appeal to broad (intersystematic) coherence rather than to indubitable premises or intuitions upon which beliefs are grounded. Though I wish to preserve a role for private and communal explanations in religion, the central task of this book is to explore the possible nature, scope, and structure of transcommunal explanations. Because they claim to be valid intersubjectively or, in principle, without restriction, I label them *intersubjective explanations*. A more accurate label would be *pansubjective*, since these explanations often claim validity for (virtually) all knowing subjects. (Communal explanations are also, strictly speaking, intersubjective, in that they are accepted as valid among a specified group of persons.) Nevertheless, to avoid the neologism I will consistently use the term *intersubjective* with the broader sense of *pansubjective*. In epistemological contexts, intersubjective explanations are explanations whose warrant is not limited in principle to a specified individual or group of individuals.

Intersubjective explanation is at this point a term more suggestive than precise, especially since a theory of explanation only gradually emerges in the coming chapters. Intuitively, one can imagine a whole gamut of positions regarding the strength of the epistemic claims that might be made on behalf of intersubjective explanations. Are they (on the one extreme) *intelligible* to all though criticizable by none? Beyond the confines of the community, can they merely be shown to be *possible*, or can their *plausibility* be established as well? Or must the intersubjectivist be able to demonstrate the *probability* of her claims? Presumably the strongest version of intersubjectivism is the attempt to *prove* one's religious beliefs, to give them deductive warrant. Natural theology often proceeded in this way, especially in its preoccupation with the proofs for the existence of God. However, the deductivist model as a standard for religious explanation rightly finds few advocates in contemporary philosophy of religion; even the theistic proofs are today more often taken merely to predispose one toward belief or to offer a retrospective justification.[6]

In that it works toward a decision between these options, this book can be taken as a contribution to the epistemology of natural theology. As such, however, it stands in strong opposition to older, deductivist models. My thesis is that recent reflection on rationality, informed by work in contemporary philosophy of science, has effectively overcome the traditional dichotomy between *rationalism* and *fideism* in the faith/reason debate, thus requiring a complete rethinking of what a *natural theology* would entail. More specifically, I defend the quest for intersubjective explanations in the Western religious traditions by exploring their similarities to and differences from the various models of explanation that have been advocated in the natural and human sciences. Such explanations can claim to be intersubjectively or pansubjectively accessible even when they draw their content and form from a given religious community or tradition rather than from any outside discipline.

The predominant theme of the book is therefore epistemological, in that I am concerned with the nature and strength of the claim to rational justification inherent in intersubjective explanations. Ultimately, I will argue that this justification has its source both in the way that religious explanations are formulated and in the sort of discourse in which they are debated. No definitive list of standards sufficient for rationality will be provided, since the nature of the discourse and the context of the discussion play an essential role in what counts as rational. Nevertheless, four central necessary conditions serve to guide the discussion.

(1) *External reference.* To the extent that a religious explanation is alleged to be intersubjectively valid, it must be regarded as referring beyond the parameters of the believer's or community's experience. When Judeo-Christian believers speak of God, for instance, they do not intend to make a statement only about their own experience but about an actually existing entity as well. The intersubjectivist takes the objectivity, or subject-independence, of the referent—and the representational theory of language often linked to it—as providing prima facie reason for attempting to formulate religious explanations in an intersubjectively assessable manner.

(2) *Truth.* Closely linked (and perhaps equivalent) to external reference is the claim that sound religious explanations must themselves be true and not merely, for example, enlightening to a given individual. The intersubjectivist argues that the ideal of truth is relevant to explanatory warrants as

well. The concept of truth implies something about what is in fact the case, whether or not I know or believe it to be so. Likewise, a theory of rational explanation must include the distinction between adequate and inadequate justifications; explanations must "get the world right" if they are to be adequate. Epistemologists have traditionally conveyed this requirement with their definition of *knowledge* as "justified *true* belief." If anything, the link must be stronger for religion: it is easy to imagine a practicing scientist who views her theories instrumentally or as "useful fictions," less easy to imagine a religious believer who does so. Of course, the fact that the question of truth is indispensable to religious belief does not yet resolve the debate concerning which of the various theories of truth is most adequate. Conversely, depending on which theory of truth one advocates, the relationship between the various necessary conditions presented here may be altered.[7]

(3) *Validity.* To avoid the murky waters of the contemporary truth-theory discussion, I often speak neutrally of the *validity claims* that various explanations make. In light of the goal of intersubjectivity, we can grant religious explanations to be intersubjectively valid when they are accessible to rational criticism by any person who wishes to examine the reasons for and against them. They are not merely arbitrary reflections of the contents of the individual's consciousness and his will to believe. To speak of reason-giving in an intersubjective context is not a return to *objectivism*: we may still discover significant influences on the knowledge process from personal, societal, and historical perspectives. Yet it is to say that, when intersubjective validity claims are made by believers, a certain burden of proof rests with them to defend these claims.

(4) *Rationality.* It is clear from the appeal to validity that an intersubjective explanans will claim to explain its explanandum in a rational manner. Obviously there are vast differences between explanations with regard to the objects being explained and the methods used for explaining them. Moreover, there are differences between explanations formulated in one's day-to-day experience and those developed within an academic discipline. My seat-of-the-pants explanations of my neighbor's behavior are not very likely to coincide with the explanation that a psychologist would give. Likewise, the believer may go about explaining events in the world in a rather different manner than would the theologians of his tradition.

We will consequently anticipate some significant differences in types of and warrants for explanations, depending on the area of experience and on whether it occurs in an individual or disciplinary context. For instance, we will need to examine the explanatory efforts of the religious individual and of the religious community separately in chapters 5 and 6. However, I dispute that individual and disciplinary efforts at explanation are to be absolutely distinguished. A discipline includes a theoretical tradition, standards for evaluation, and testing procedures that are shared by its practitioners; as a communal effort it has a built-in corrective to the prejudicing influence of individual perspectives. But there is no inherent reason that each of these factors cannot be replicated on the individual level as well.

"Different objects, different forms of explanation" need not be the final word on the subject. The epistemic claim made by intersubjective explanations suggests that there need to be some shared standards by which to evaluate explanations, lest the claim to adequate warrant prove to be vacuous. For this reason I have held that the explanation question shades gradually over into the discussion of standards of rationality. Unfortunately, a fully worked out theory of rationality would have to incorporate all the goals of human action and thought, as well as the myriad methods employed to achieve these goals. It is not an overstatement to argue, as Hilary Putnam does, that philosophy "is almost coextensive with theory of rationality."[8] In his introduction to *Rationality To-day*, for example, Theodore Geraets argues the centrality of the rationality issue in all philosophical reflection[9]; the diversity of the issues handled under the rubric *rationality*, in his book and elsewhere, testifies eloquently to the breadth, complexity, and divisiveness of "the rationality question." Nor does narrowing the question to the rationality of religious belief improve matters much. As C. F. Delaney notes regarding the collection *Rationality and Religious Belief*, the various approaches "exhibit the fact that [the] specific question about the rationality of religious belief should be seen to be as much about rationality as about religion" and therefore faces all the complexities of the more general rationality question.[10]

Consequently, no monolithic theory of rationality will be advocated in these pages. As thinkers like Wittgenstein, Habermas, and Foucault have shown, there is an irresistible plurality of rationalities corresponding to the different goals and contexts of human action. However, this pluralism becomes slightly more manageable if we focus specifically on the explanatory goal, as it influences the methodologies of the various disciplines. For it may be possible to derive certain shared standards of rational assessment that stem from the more limited project of explaining a particular explanandum, even when the explanandum in question varies from discipline to discipline. Indeed, if the use of the term *rational* is not to be merely equivocal, it appears necessary that there be at least some commonalities between the diverse disciplines that claim to offer rational explanations.

How can these potential commonalities best be discovered? One could attempt a formal definition or criteriology of rational explanation by means of an a priori analysis of the concept of rationality itself, seeking to discover necessary conditions of the possibility of being rational. But there are less speculative alternatives. I examine instead the explanatory practices of the various academic disciplines themselves, using recent work on the methodology of the natural sciences, social sciences, and theology. What I believe emerges from such an examination is a specification of rationality as intersubjective criticizability. By comparing the rationality of explanations in various contexts, we discover differences and parallels in how they are criticized and in what makes the critical process possible.

Out of this inquiry, we can determine whether the explanations given by religious individuals, and those advanced in the discipline of theology, evidence any significant similarities with explanations in other disciplines or areas of organized human reflection. Of course, the explanatory quest represents only a part of the phenomenon of religion; still, it is a crucial part. To the extent that religious individuals or traditions share in their different ways the common goal of explaining a range of phenomena, a common framework for discussion exists. My aim is to show that this sort of comparative study yields a number of interesting continuities and discontinuities between the various explanatory disciplines.

Religious Explanation and the Faith/Reason Debate

Clearly, the debate between the various models for the justification of religious explanations is not new to discussions of religious belief; western theology has debated the question under various guises since its inception. Indeed, in some respects the question of the epistemic status of religious explanations is merely a differently specified restatement of the classical faith/reason controversy, at least if the latter is taken as the dispute between internal (re)description of a religion and its presentation or systematization in terms of a general notion of human rationality. In what follows I concentrate on the Christian theological tradition, though parts of the discussion would generalize to other traditions as well.

Tertullian (b. 160) represents an earlier advocate of *fideism*, the total separation of faith and reason and of the primacy of faith for religious knowledge: "What has Jerusalem to do with Athens, the Church with the Academy?"[11] From the perspective of intersubjectivism, Tertullian's position is not fundamentally different from the views of other theologians who maintain that divine revelation is self-authenticating. For Calvin, for instance, God has really revealed himself through nature and in the human heart, so that God is justified in holding us responsible for our unbelief.[12] However, because of sin the minds of humans are darkened, so that they do not see and respond to God's revelation. Speaking of human, hypocritical religion, Calvin writes: "From it one may easily grasp anew how much this confused knowledge of God differs from the piety from which religion takes its source, which is instilled in the breasts of believers only. . . . Yet that seed remains which can in no wise be uprooted: that there is some sort of divinity; but this seed is so corrupted that by itself it produces only the worst fruits" (ibid., I.4.4). In a direct rebuke to philosophy as the attempt to gain knowledge of God apart from revelation, Calvin asserts that only when we read the pages of Scripture are our eyes "enlightened" by the Holy Spirit, so that we know them to be inspired by God and thus true. No independent reasons need to be given for Scripture's truth because of this immediate testimony of the Spirit (though some reasons can be produced nonetheless). A number of later positions in the faith/reason controversy essentially share Calvin's belief in the immediate efficacy of God in belief, including Pascal, Kierkegaard, and Karl Barth.

The opposite position, the subordination of faith as a moment of reason, has taken as many forms as the notions of reason employed. For Hegel it was the philosophy of Absolute Spirit (*absoluter Geist*); for Kant, the requirements of the moral life; even Locke, who allowed for special revelation in principle, controlled it in practice by the demand that reason verify that the source of a given claim was indeed divine revelation. It is important to note the distinction between the *rationalism* of these thinkers and the notion of intersubjective explanation as I have defined it. The classical rationalist treatment of Christianity subordinated the content of Christian belief to the metaphysical claims of a given philosophical system. It is another matter if theologians maintain that religious beliefs, expressed in terms of canonic texts or the church's tradition, make explanatory claims that bring them into genuine contact with explanations in other areas of human experience.

If any position in the faith/reason controversy could be taken as the classical position, it would be that of *faith seeking understanding*. Anselm is most often cited as its typical representative, though the view was explicitly formulated by Augustine. In addition to underlying Augustine's *Confessions* and most of his theological work, this view can probably be found also in Clement of Alexandria.[13] Augustine taught that faith is the direct response to God. Of course, we must have some idea of what we are responding to and some reason to believe it worthy of our response. But the Christian proclamation is sufficient for Clement, the authority of the Church, whose teaching had been a reliable guide for several centuries, adequate for Augustine. Once the soul has offered its *assensus* to God, acknowledging its sin and entering into right relationship with God, the mind may—within the parameters of obedience—seek to understand matters of faith. Augustine's inquiry into the nature of time is one well-known example of insightful analysis of a philosophical question carried out within the framework of belief.[14]

Despite, or because of, its classic status, "faith seeking understanding" is a rallying cry that has attracted a very diverse group of followers. The meditational nature of Anselm's use of the phrase in the *Monologion* is reminiscent of Augustine's writings.[15] By contrast, the *Proslogion* stemmed from the conscious search for "*one* argument . . . resting on no other argument for its proof, but sufficient in itself to prove that God truly exists" (ibid.). Yet, notwithstanding the differences between Anselm's two works, the latter also was written "in the role of one who . . . seeks to understand what he believes," and Anselm even suggested for it the title "Fides Quaerens Intellectum." Aquinas also falls under the same rubric, notwithstanding the fact that he offered proofs for God's existence in a manner in which Augustine would not have. Further, his use of Aristotle's philosophy in his theological work was more essential—or at least more conscious, more emphatic—than was Augustine's use of Platonism. Revelation for Thomas was sufficient for most persons, and sure; but with the aid of philosophical categories one could come to know that a God (first cause, necessary being) exists. He thus held that one is justified in making use of philosophy, in apologetic contexts, for instance. Only revelation, however, can convey to us that God is a Trinity and that Jesus is also God.

From these few examples it appears that the faith seeking understanding position allows for significant latitude and accounts for a considerable portion of the continuum between rationalism and fideism. Though it has much to recommend it as a model,[16] it is not sufficiently precise to count as a resolution of the faith/reason debate, especially in light of our more specific question concerning the nature of religious explanations. Even less precise are the "both/and" positions, of which Schleiermacher's belief in the complementary contributions of philosophy and faith is paradigmatic (see chapter 6). That theology encompasses two very different activities or moments has been maintained by thinkers as diverse as Ernst Troeltsch and Paul Tillich.[17] Notwithstanding the effectiveness of the formulation in drawing attention to the onesidedness of some of the alternatives, "both/and" is not a resolution of the faith/reason debate as much as a statement of the desiderata for such a resolution. All attempts to integrate the two poles, however, have so far seemed perforce to shift the delicate balance in favor of one or the other pole.

Theology since Kant has been no less tossed by the controversy between faith and reason; the terms may have changed, yet close parallels with the earlier debate remain. The Kantian critiques set an agenda for theologians, compelling them either to accept their assignment in the service of practical reason or to rise up against a sea of troubles and attack the entire Kantian structure. Additionally, the growth and spread of the sciences helped spawn the methodological turmoil within theology. In the late nineteenth century and even into the 1920s neo-Kantian philosophy served alternately as friend (in H. H. Wendt) and foe (in M. Kähler) for theologians; the friendly side argued that there are formal similarities or laws between all areas of knowledge, the foes that "scientific procedure" is determined only by the object studied. The fear of reductionism, effectively implanted in theologians by Feuerbach, Marx, and Freud, as well as concern for the autonomy of their own discipline, led many theologians to counter any theological approach that did not adequately emphasize the distinctiveness of theology. Thus we find attempts to protect theology from the historical-critical method, the "threat" of which had been brought home by D. F. Strauss and W. Baur; from the methods of Harnack and the liberal theologians, who allegedly "reduced" Christianity to a glorification of European (German) culture; and from thinkers like Ernst Troeltsch, who were criticized for making theology overly dependent on a psychologistic philosophy of history.

As a consequence of these perceived threats—and somewhat paradoxically—theologians have looked to a number of twentieth-century philosophical movements to provide justification for the removal of theological explanations from competition with the various scientific explanations. Bultmann's extensive use of Heidegger, for instance, accomplished an *existentializing* of theology that freed theological statements from the demands of scientific criteria. After the threat posed by the unity of science movement and logical positivism (especially as popularized by A. J. Ayer), a number of theologians took advantage of the refuge offered by Wittgenstein's later philosophy. Once again, against those who claimed that theological explanations must meet certain minimum standards, theologians could claim that general notions of truth, rationality and epistemological methodology were vacuous; theology as a unique language game provides its own standards.[18] Added impetus against drawing parallels between theological explanation and scientific explanation was provided by hermeneutical theology (Ebeling, Fuchs), with its emphasis on the multiple horizons of history, on the use of empathetic understanding (*Verstehen*), and on the "claim of the text" as opposed to that of scientific explanation as the appropriate modus operandi for theology.

Indeed, several major theologians of this century have consciously opposed *any* approach that would treat theological explanations within some general framework of rationality. Among them, Karl Barth has certainly been the most influential. Barth advocates the position that God is known only by his self-disclosure, that his self-revelation provides the axioms for all further theological reflection.[19] God has become Word in Christ, establishing a framework of objectivity for Christian reflection, and "Christian faith as knowledge of the true God lets itself be included in this area of objectivity" (ibid.). Nor is faith only a matter of intuitive understanding that would exclude explanation. Barth speaks of the New Testament as "a continual explanation of a definite historical event—of the same historical event that began with the Exodus" (II.1, 18f). But Barth is vehement in forbidding the move from the objectivity of God's revelation to a general epistemology of intersubjective explanation; Christian explanations may not be constrained by any external canons of rationality.

In the *Christliche Dogmatik* Barth strongly opposes H. H. Wendt's attempt to specify the concept of theology in methodological terms: "the possibility of validation in every area [must] be determined by the particularity of the object rather than that, conversely, violence be done to the object by means of a previously chosen, concrete concept of method and scientificness [*Wissenschaftlichkeit*]."[20] Instead, the sufficient condition for the *Wissenschaftlichkeit* of theology is its *Sachlichkeit* or appropriateness, a criterion elaborated at length along Barthian lines in Torrance's monograph on scientific methodology and theology.[21] In the oft-cited opening of the *Church Dogmatics* Barth denies the validity of H. Scholz's three postulates for the scientific pursuit of theology.[22] The requirement that theology contain noncontradictory assertions that are coherent and criticizable Barth rejects as "unacceptable"; it suffices that theology pursues a "path to knowledge that is in itself consequential [*folgerichtigen*]" toward "a specific object."[23]

Obviously, this book is fundamentally opposed to any Barthian approach along these lines. In its strongest form, my thesis is that theology cannot avoid an appeal to broader canons of rational argumentation and explanatory adequacy. If the need to argue in a reasonable manner is accepted as essential to theology, it should be acknowledged as intrinsic to theology; it should be granted a place in theology's self-understanding. The attempts at staking out an exclusively theological arena require arguments, often drawn from philosophy of science, hermeneutics, or anthropology, that can claim to be rationally persuasive. Admittedly, many theologians argue that their use of philosophy or science is not essential, that these disciplines provide only examples, models, conceptual structures to be used and discarded. The arguments needed by theology are all internal to theology. Now *internalism*, carefully stated, is not automatically a self-refuting view. But it does have significant impact on how we judge the status of the internalist's "appeal" to other disciplines. In fact, in some cases, the limitations can adversely affect even the truth claims that internalists make within their own particular theological traditions. But these are issues to which we will return in due course.

According to my reconstrual of the faith/reason debate, to argue against internalism emphatically does not mean to defend the reduction of theology to philosophy or apologetics. The task of exploring the internal logic or grammar of one's religious belief remains a vital one. It is my contention that the comparison with scientific theories precisely insures a place for this activity. Nonetheless, explicating the inner logic of the Christian tradition does not exhaust the task of Christian theology.

Intersubjective Explanation in Contemporary Theology and Philosophy of Religion

Many of the predominant paradigms in twentieth-century theology have been drawn from Barth's theological proposal and from the philosophies of Heidegger and the later Wittgenstein. However, Christian theology and the philosophy of religion in general have by no means dispensed with intersubjective explanation in the sense in which I define it. Mentioning some of the relevant thinkers here may help to focus the treatment of explanation in the natural and social sciences.

The influence of Barth and Wittgenstein has been somewhat less marked outside of Protestant theology. Because its fundamental theology remains heavily indebted to metaphysical thought, traditional Roman Catholic theology has continued its dialogue with nontheological disciplines within the framework of a general (or generalizable) epistemology. Within non-traditional Catholic and much of Protestant theology, theologians—even many of those influenced by Heidegger—can be classified as espousing intersubjective explanation when they employ some sort of general theory that is applicable both inside and outside Christian theology. One thinks of David Tracy's *Analogical Imagination*, in which he accepts the "publics" of society, church, and academy as dialogue partners even though he is concerned with Christian truth claims in terms of their disclosure value. His general framework of a classic text revealing to the reader a mode of being-in-the-world links Christian theological statements to religious statements in other faiths. The same result can be perceived in those theologies that employ other general conceptualities such as Marxism (liberation theology), process philosophy, or a social scientific theory of human meaning-formation.[24]

The liberal tradition has turned from its confrontation with the *Kulturprotestantismus* critique and neo-orthodoxy to a reformulation of its approach and a reexamination of its roots in Schleiermacher and the early nineteenth century.[25] In general, those theologies that take universal history as opposed to salvation history as their object will acknowledge the importance of general epistemological reflection. Their credo might be summarized in the statement, "If, however, historical study declares itself unable to establish what 'really' happened on Easter, then all the more, faith is not able to do so; for faith cannot ascertain anything certain about events of the past that would perhaps be inaccessible to the historian."[26] This classical liberal position denies an epistemic role to faith; it looks instead to the development of human history or to the dialogue between the world religions for justification of religious explanations. As Wolfhart Pannenberg has argued, Christianity will inevitably remain "in dispute" (*strittig*) until the eschaton.[27]

Conservative (e.g., evangelical) theologians have continued to view theological explanations as in competition with explanations outside theology—a somewhat ironic fact in light of their not uncommon reticence to integrate contemporary scholarship and science into their formulation of the Christian faith. Documents like the *Chicago Statement on Inerrancy*, with its insistence that the Bible is without error on all scientific and historical questions, lead to (sometimes ludicrous) attempts to defend theological statements about, for example, Creation *as* science. Carl F. H. Henry, whose concern with theological statements as propositional truths motivates his extensive theological opus, surely sees himself as defending a general explanation; this is also the case with evangelical apologists such as Edward John Carnell, Bernard Ramm, and Gordon L. Lewis.[28]

The acceptance of intersubjective explanation typical of the above four categories of theologians holds also for most philosophers of religion in the analytic tradition, who make a similar assumption of generality. This was true of the self-styled "Metaphysicals" at Oxford in the 1950s and holds also for the work of thinkers like Richard Swinburne and Basil Mitchell.[29] The extensive preoccupation among analytic philosophers with justification questions such as proofs for the existence of God and the problem of evil is indicative of a similar concern with generally accessible explanations, especially since the discussion forms an implicit response to the influential falsification debate of the early 1960s.[30]

A recent school of thought in the philosophy of religion, owing much to the influence of Alvin Plantinga, argues that any system of beliefs contains basic beliefs that are generally unquestioned (e.g., the belief that there are other minds, that there is a window in this room, that I had breakfast this morning). It argues that belief in God, likewise, is "properly basic."[31] These thinkers represent an interesting middle position in the discussion. On the one hand, they claim to be working on the level of a general (universal) theory of rationality. On the other, their notion of *proper basicality*, like appeals to a self-authenticating revelation, grants a certain epistemic weight to unargued religious beliefs. Instead of taking these beliefs to be epistemically neutral, they wish to place the burden of proof on the nonbeliever to challenge any beliefs that are basic for the believer.

However, even if I am personally disposed to continue to hold a belief when I am aware of no "defeaters" for it, it is not clear to me that this should give that belief any positive epistemic weight. We seem to find a tacit admission of this fact in Plantinga's attempt (in his forthcoming Gifford Lectures) to ground the belief that our perceptual and epistemic faculties are "properly functioning" through a theological appeal. Indeed, perhaps the basic problem with the theory of proper basicality is that it remains foundationalist in orientation, even if it is a negative foundationalism, a foundationalism based on the absence of defeaters rather than on positive epistemic grounds.[32] But even this weak form of negative foundationalism is far removed from the contextualism of Wittgenstein's philosophy or the appeal to coherence defended below.

A similar attempt to use general epistemological arguments while rejecting any normative theory of rationality arises among thinkers whose epistemological case draws not from a positive theory of rationality but from the epistemic shortcomings of others. These are the famous *tu quoque* ("you too") arguments, such as the claim that scientists employ unquestioned presuppositions and therefore religious persons are justified in doing the same. By contrast, the goal here will be to supplement negative pronouncements with positive continuities as we proceed through the wide variety of explanatory contexts in the sciences and religion(s).

Alternating between the internalist and intersubjective poles are also those thinkers who take theological positions to represent a worldview (*Weltanschauung*) among other possible worldviews. Some theologians conclude that the uniqueness of the Christian worldview immunizes Christianity from external critique, whereas others lay stress on the formal parallels between various worldviews and attempt a criteriology of worldview comparison. In the latter camp are Whitehead's *Science and the Modern World*, which offers a useful historical survey and comparison of some of these modern worldviews, and Stephen Pepper, who isolates four "root metaphors" together with the attributes they share as worldviews.[33]

The question of the nature of explanation in the natural and social sciences can now be considered. This brief outline of the debate within theology and the philosophy of religion can help to orient the discussion in the following two chapters. In order not to obscure considerations important to the philosophy of science discussion—for the literature is replete with over-quick comparisons of science and religion that do painful injustice to both[34]—I will minimize direct applications to the religious phenomenon until the later chapters.

CHAPTER TWO

Explanation in the Natural Sciences
The Contextualist Shift

Many attempts have been made to draw connections between the modes of rationality at work in natural science and those employed in the empirical social sciences, the humanities, and religious reflection. As an example of the connections that have been drawn, consider the case of theology. Repeatedly in the last few centuries, science has made some important methodological or substantive advance in response to which theology has sought to employ (or to fight) the methods and truth claims accepted by the newly advanced science.[1] The latest instance to receive widespread attention came as recently as the second decade of this century. By 1930, the doctrines of *logical positivism*, formulated by thinkers associated with the Vienna Circle, began to attract significant attention; the criteria for science that they advocated gave direct impetus to the movement toward the "unity of science" (and, by implication, of rationality). Their "principle of verification" held that "a sentence had literal meaning if and only if the proposition it expressed was either analytic or empirically verifiable."[2] The potential danger for theologians[3] was manifest: not only rationality, but even meaning seemed to be dependent on the criterion of empirical verifiability; statements falling outside the purview of verifiability were neither meaningful nor rational; statements within could be clearly located within one of the scientific disciplines; and a clear description could be given of the structure of scientific arguments and theories, that is, of the nature of scientific rationality.

Today logical positivism has been as fully refuted as any epistemology in the history of philosophy. Nevertheless, its demise has only fueled the debate on the nature of scientific rationality,[4] which in turn continues to spawn applications to questions of theological method. When Karl Popper's critical rationalism was influential in the philosophy of science, thinkers advocated its use in theology; when *communicative theory* gained ascendancy, it was used as a model; when philosophers of science turned to sociological approaches, the implications for theology were stressed.[5] The debate about scientific rationality remains of no little concern for students of religion, even if the concern is only the negative one of protecting their disciplines from unfair attack on the part of overavid philosophers of science.

At first blush, the question of explanation appears to be clearly distinct from the rationality debate in the philosophy of science; they constitute two conceptually distinct sets of problems. The rationality debate—understood as the question, What makes, or would make, science rational?—considers the epistemic justification for scientific patterns of research and inference. It addresses broad issues such as the problems of induction, falsifiability, historical or cultural or institutional context, and the role of individual subjective factors in theory choice. The question of explanation, by contrast, seeks to specify wherein the explanatory force of a scientific explanans lies. Generally speaking, scientific explanations are answers to specific why-questions, posed within the context of a scientific discipline, that attempt to make some group of empirical phenomena scientifically comprehensible.

We might approach the examination of scientific explanations by searching for a general, normative theory of explanation, or we might eschew such an attempt. If we choose the latter, we will presumably limit ourselves to largely descriptive accounts of the various types of explanations that are offered by scientists, the different ways that these explanations function in scientific practice, and the procedures that scientists use for constructing and evaluating these explanations. But if one wishes to speak of explanation in the singular, one is committed to providing some sort of unified account of explanation. One strategy for achieving this goal has been to construct a single, formal model: all valid or good explanations have such and such a form, such that a specialist could examine any given explanation to see whether or not it meets the structural requirements. A theory of explanation might, for example, require that the explanandum be the deductive consequence of general laws or the necessary effect of a causal chain. The quest to produce a general model of this sort I call the *formalist* approach to scientific explanation.

The question of the nature, form, and evaluation of scientific explanations is thus not equivalent to the question of scientific rationality. I might give a detailed, normative account of the structure of scientific explanations without dwelling on the rationality of theory choice; alternatively, I could construct a broad picture of scientific rationality without developing a precise model of explanation. However, in practice one finds that, instead of clearly separating the two tasks, philosophers of science often provide wide-ranging accounts of science that address both the nature of theories as explanations and the nature of science as a rational endeavor. In at least two types of cases this link is clearly justified. If one gives a formal account of what constitutes an adequate explanation in science, it will probably entail some general standards for evaluating explanations or theories that will lead eventually to a general picture of scientific rationality. I take this to have been the case with the work of Carl Hempel and Karl Popper. Conversely, if one argues that no general account of scientific rationality can be given (as Paul Feyerabend has done) it would be inconsistent then to proceed with a normative, or formalist, account of scientific explanation.

Hence the questions of explanation and rationality, while themselves conceptually distinct, turn out to be bound by certain relations of implication. It is rational to accept a given theory in part because it provides a better explanation of the relevant phenomena than any of its rivals. Note the move from "scientific reasoning" or rationality to the problem of explanation in Clark Glymour's job description for the philosophy of science:

> The ambition of philosophy of science is, or ought to be, to obtain from the literature of the sciences a plausible and precise theory of scientific reasoning and argument: a theory that will abstract general patterns from the concreta of debates over genes and spectra and fields and delinquency. A philosophical understanding of science should, therefore, give us an account of *what explanations are* and of why they are valued but, most important, it should also provide us with clear and plausible *criteria for comparing* the goodness of explanations.[6]

In the natural sciences, whose status as explanatory disciplines is undisputed, no ultimate separation can be made between the explanatory task and the question of rationality. By contrast, we could presumably explore the rationality of many other types of human activity (e.g., sleeping) that are rational without being explanatory endeavors. In disciplines in which explanations play a subordinate or peripheral role, as in aesthetics and many of the humanities, very different models of rationality would be operative. Matters are more ambiguous in the social sciences; there I will first have to argue their nature as explanatory disciplines before returning to the explanation-rationality link. Through the examination of scientific explanation in this and the following chapter, I seek to demonstrate the central place of the critical explanatory project within theoretical discourse in general. The remaining chapters then apply this conclusion to questions of explanation and rationality in religion.

Some of the claims about scientific practice that I will advance reflect a relatively recent shift in the explanation discussion within the philosophy of natural science. In order to set the stage for this shift, we must examine the views on the nature of explanation that led to and stemmed from the pivotal work of Carl Hempel. The precision and completeness of these formalist views provide a good picture of what a full-fledged model of explanation might look like. We then explore a crucial transformation in the understanding of science that gained momentum in the 1950s. Instead of continuing to analyze the *structure* of explanations within a basically inductivist or falsificationist view of science, philosophers of science such as Toulmin and Hanson, and later Kuhn, began to focus on the role of *context* in theory choice.[7] Of course, analysis of the structure of scientific theories and explanations has continued. However, since we can no longer ignore the role of pragmatic factors in the construction and evaluation of explanations, formal analyses must now be supplemented by historical and institutional studies of scientific practice. I resist the claim that inclusion of such contextual factors entails an irrationality or "epistemological anarchism" in science, enlisting the late Imre Lakatos as my ally. Still, the *contextualist* view that we cannot even know what why-question is being raised without considering the pragmatic context does show purely formal accounts of explanation in science to be inadequate.

This contextualist shift holds special significance for discussions of rationality and religion. Given our focus on intersubjective explanations, the comparison of religious explanations with explanations offered within the context of other academic disciplines becomes crucial. If general standards for rationally evaluating theories can be detected in other disciplines, this will create at least a prima facie case for their applicability to theology as well. If criteria vary randomly as one moves through the various scientific disciplines, however, one can hardly hold theology to the criteria for explanations in any other field.

In either case, it is clear that the contextualist shift has radically changed the climate for discussions of theological rationality. For example, Karl Popper's falsificationist model of scientific rationality tended to separate, or "demarcate," the natural sciences from the humanities and religion, while Kuhn's model of science has worked to break down any separation. Popper's work tends to consign all philosophical or theological explanations to nonscientific "metaphysics," while Kuhn's suggests smoother transitions between the various disciplines. To the extent that we find a sympathy for Popper or Kuhn in contemporary philosophy of science, we can expect that the relationships between explanations in the various disciplines will be differently formulated. Below, I defend a mediating position between Popper and Kuhn regarding scientific rationality, one opposed both to unvarying, formal criteria and to explanatory relativism. The general desiderata for rational explanations then structure my discussion of the quest for rational explanations in the field of religion.

The Formalist Approach to Scientific Explanation

There is widespread skepticism today regarding the possibility of a general theory of explanation that specifies shared formal requirements that all valid explanations must share. Yet this skepticism is not a matter of course; it is born out of concrete difficulties faced by the formalists in their efforts to provide such a theory. Only in light of the earlier project can we properly understand the emphasis on contextual considerations in current discussions.

I have chosen the work of Carl Hempel as a point of orientation for this brief treatment. The canonical account moves directly from Karl Popper's theory of falsification to the criticisms of Thomas Kuhn. But it is crucial to place Popper's account within that broader tradition of thought that I label *formalism.* Hempel's position and his reactions to his critics are particularly well suited for revealing the strengths and weaknesses of the formalist school; they nicely propel us into the discussion of contextualism below.

The Birth of the Formalist Model

For an anticipatory statement of the formalist model of explanation, it is sufficient for us to go back to Karl Popper's *Logic of Scientific Discovery.* In many ways Hempel's entire program can be seen as a fleshing out of Popper's statement: "To give a *causal explanation* of an event means to deduce a statement which describes it, using as premises of the deduction one or more *universal laws,* together with certain singular statements, the *initial conditions.*"[8] It was this particular view of scientific explanation that encouraged Popper to replace an inductivist model of scientific method with his appeal to falsification: even if Hume's problem of induction could be solved, induction could not produce the universal laws necessary for scientific explanation.[9] Since a scientific law must be strictly universal, a single falsification instance will be sufficient to show its inadequacy, as "there is an S such that S is not-P" is logically equivalent to the denial of "all S are P."[10]

With the realization that it is easier to falsify than to verify, Popper's early "conclusive falsificationism" was born. For it to work, though, two stipulations for scientific explanations had to be made: (1) all scientific explanation must involve subsumption under laws, that is, it must be *nomological*; (2) the laws involved must be strictly universal; they must not contain any individual concepts.[11] In order to be strictly universal, they must be expressed in the form of *nonexistence* statements ("there is not *x*" or "*x* does not obtain") such that the discovery of *x* would conclusively falsify them.

Though Popper eschewed the "metaphysical" thesis that every event can be deductively predicted, he did propose the methodological rule (call it "Popper's Rule") that "we are not to abandon the search for universal laws and for a coherent theoretical system, nor ever give up our attempts to explain causally [i.e., to place within a deductive inference] any kind of event we can describe."[12] In short, the only scientific explanation that we can really be satisfied with is one where the explanandum follows deductively from the lawlike portion of the explanans. This model thus came to be called *deductive-nomological* explanation.

The goal of science, according to Popper's Rule, is inherently reductionist: "In pure science . . . explanation is always the logical reduction of hypotheses to others which are of a higher level of universality."[13] In other words, a phenomenon is explained if and only if it can be shown to follow as a logical consequence from a corroborated theory, given certain initial conditions; and a law is explained only if it follows deductively from a set of one or more corroborated theories. This reduction of the singular to an instance of a universal law constitutes for Popper the structure of explanation, prediction and testing alike.[14] Regardless of which of these three is in view, all "theoretical or generalizing sciences" make use of the same method: they consist in "offering deductive causal explanations, and in testing them (by way of predictions)" (131). As long as this structure is followed, contextual considerations are irrelevant; it does not matter from what source the scientist has obtained her theory—a dream, luck, divine revelation. Further, it does not matter that scientific explanations are not "ultimate explanations"; they are in no way dependent upon metaphysical or theological assumptions.[15]

Note that Popper's Rule consists of two conceptually separable requirements, the systematic and the nomological. Popper is correct in holding up the search for universal laws and for a "coherent theoretical system" as the ideals for natural science. When universal laws can be applied without problems in a particular scientific discipline, we are justified in seeking deductive-nomological explanations from that discipline. However, pace Popper, the quest for coherent theoretical systems is surely separable in principle from the deductive requirement of nomological explanation. Explanations can be parts of coherent but nonnomological theories in sciences that lack universal laws, either at an early stage of their development or inherently, that is, because of the nature of their subject matter. For

instance, there is good reason to think that the interpretive social sciences
are inherently nonnomological.

Moreover, Popper's Rule faces difficulties even in nomological sciences.
For the Popperian scientist to test a theory or putative law he must be able
actually to obtain singular statements sufficiently certain, or known, to
falsify the theory in question. But we will see that the observation statements that were to provide the bedrock of Popper's methodology in *Logic*
are theory-laden in a way that cuts to the heart of conclusive falsificationism. It appears unlikely that the search for generally agreed upon basic
statements can be carried out without a more explicit consideration of the
influence of contextual factors on this agreement.

Whatever the problems with Popper's actual position, it remains paradigmatic for the way in which one's theory of explanation shades over
without break into a theory of rationality. In resisting *essentialism*—ultimate explanations in terms of essences—Popper stipulates as mandatory
for science (and as basic to epistemology in general) that "there can be no
explanation which is not in need of a further explanation."[16] No theory is
ever absolutely certain; any given theory can become problematic, can
itself be explained or falsified, since it is through falsification "that we
actually get in touch with 'reality'" (360). Rationality is therefore constituted by (1) a rational testing procedure and (2) the refusal to end this
process with any (necessarily arbitrary) stopping point: "In other words
every *rational* theory, no matter whether scientific or philosophical, is
rational in so far as it tries to *solve certain problems*. A theory is comprehensible and reasonable only in its relation to a given *problem-situation*, and it can be rationally discussed only by discussing this relation."[17]

Hans Albert, working to systematize and generalize Popper's approach,
has developed these stipulations into a comprehensive epistemological
position that he labels *critical rationalism*. Understood as a philosophical
extrapolation from scientific practice—hence freed from the restrictiveness of basic statements, universal laws, and conclusive falsifiability—
Albert's restatement has much to commend it. Natural scientific method,
he argues, which "correctly understood has little to do with the specialized
object-areas of the natural sciences,"[18] is the model for a critical rationality
lying between complete neutrality and total commitment. Any nondogma-
tic quest for knowledge proceeds in the same way: suggesting solutions to
specified problem situations, seeking to falsify them, and revising the solutions. This *pancritical rationalism*[19] or fallibilism is, Albert asserts, the
only way to avoid the "Münchhausen Trilemma," which maintains that
rational assessment inevitably falls into either an infinite regress, a logical
circle, or the breaking off of criticism at some arbitrary point, that is, a
"justification by *recourse to a dogma*."[20]

Albert replaces Popper's earlier prohibition of any "conventionalist stratagem or twist" with the castigation of "immunization strategies," or attempts to hold some part of one's theorizing above all criticism. Forbidding immunization strategies of all types is meant to prevent "the dogmatizing of theoretical viewpoints and thereby their transformation into towers of metaphysical doctrine immune from all critique" (69). The outcome of this stricture is a broad theory of rationality, the fruit of the Popperian approach:

If one replaces foundationalism with the *idea of critical examination,* the critical discussion of all assertions that have been questioned with the help of rational arguments, then one may have to dispense with self-produced certainties. On the other hand, one then has the prospect, through trial and error—through the tentative construction of testable theories and their critical discussion in the light of all relevant points of view —to come closer to the truth, though without ever reaching certainty.[21]

Albert is certain that critical rationalism will destroy any claim to rationality in the sphere of religion. In opposition to Albert's allegations about religion, I maintain that, once his program is modified to take account of the social sciences, it will represent not a critique of all religious belief but a positive guideline for constructing and testing religious explanations.

Although Popper also believed his fallibilist epistemology could be generalized, he has never given up his methodology of strict falsificationism.[22] Consequently, three beliefs about explanation remain essential components of the Popperian philosophy of science: (1) The context of justification can be separated from the context of discovery. It does not matter how the scientist came up with her explanation; the question of rationality only addresses the formal structure of the finished theory. (2) Explanation proceeds in terms of universal laws and initial "boundary" conditions that can be specified in advance. (3) Related to the second belief, it is possible to formulate "singular existential statements," Popper's "basic statements" of the 1930s, that must be "testable, inter-subjectively, by 'observations'." These three beliefs form the common tenets of what I have labeled the formalist approach to explanation.[23]

Although the formalist analysis of explanation had its roots in logical empiricism, especially the work of Carnap and Popper, it finds classic expression in the writings of Hempel and Nagel. Perhaps the earliest book in this tradition devoted explicitly to the explanation question was Braithwaite's *Scientific Explanation* (in substance his Tanner Lectures of 1946). Meant as an introduction to the function of theory, probability, and law in science, his book simply assumed most of what the later tradition disputed—namely, that "it is almost a platitude to say that every science proceeds, more or less explicitly, by thinking of general hypotheses . . . from which particular consequences are deduced which can be tested by observation and experiment."[24] Braithwaite did build his introduction to the philosophy of science around what became the classical loci for formalist discussions of scientific explanation: the status of theoretical terms, the role of models, the requirements of the hypothetical-deductive method, and the differences between deductive, statistical and teleological explanation. With these distinctions the stage was set for Hempel's systematic outworking of the formalist approach.

Carl Hempel

The formalist school found its manifesto two years later in Hempel and Oppenheim's "Studies in the Logic of Explanation."[25] Not that their work was unprecedented: citing antecedents for their deductive-nomological model in Popper (and others), Hempel and Oppenheim admitted that their account was "by no means novel" (251n7). According to their formal analysis of scientific explanation it can be analyzed into the following schema (249):

$$
\begin{array}{ll}
C_1, C_2, \ldots, C_k & \text{Statements of antecedent} \\
 & \text{conditions} \qquad\qquad\qquad \textit{Explanans} \\
L_1, L_2, \ldots, L_r & \text{General Laws}
\end{array}
$$

Logical
Deduction
$$\overline{\qquad\qquad\qquad\qquad\qquad\qquad}$$

$$
\begin{array}{ll}
\qquad E & \text{Description of the} \\
 & \qquad\qquad\qquad\qquad\qquad \textit{Explanandum} \\
 & \text{empirical phenomenon}
\end{array}
$$

The deductive-nomological ideal for explanation involves four necessary conditions: (1) the explanandum must be a logical consequence of the explanans; (2) the explanans must contain general laws and (3) it must have empirical content; (4) the sentences constituting the explanans must be true (247–49).

One would certainly expect that such an analysis would be limited only to explanations in the natural sciences: seldom are social scientific explanations convertible into predictions, and there is reason to doubt that uniformities in human social behavior can properly be called laws at all.[26] But Hempel and Oppenheim, claiming in essence that their formal analysis represents the necessary condition for all empirical science whatsoever, explicitly maintain that their account adequately represents all "motivational and teleological" explanations as well.[27] Human subjects may "have a peculiar uniqueness," but their behaviors still conform to general causal laws. Conversely, the behavior of physical entities, no less than human behavior, depends on an individual history; this is as true for magnetic hysteresis or elastic fatigue as it is for human psychoses. Human goals and motives for Hempel may therefore be treated analogously to antecedent conditions in physical science: "The term 'teleological' may be viewed . . . as referring to causal explanations in which some of the antecedent conditions are motives of the agent whose actions are to be explained" (255). Even at first glance, this holdover from the unity of science movement appears patently inadequate to the human sciences. Indeed, I argue below that human goals and motives cannot be accounted for using Hempel's formalist approach to explanation.

Although Hempel and Oppenheim weaken the requirements for lawlike sentences slightly in comparison to Popper, who required that laws not be limited to a finite domain and contain only purely universal predicates, their treatment is in essential continuity with both his and Braithwaite's positions.[28] We are thus justified in viewing Popper, Braithwaite, Nagel and Hempel as belonging to a single school. Despite the criticisms that I raise below, I believe that the work of these formalists has made an essential contribution to our understanding of scientific explanation. It represents a formal ideal for the construction of natural scientific theories, yielding a picture of what a strong explanation in the context of a fully developed theory might look like. As one opponent notes, Hempel's analyses "have uniformly exhibited the kind of clarity, depth, incisiveness, and fairness that ideally suit them to provide a solid basis for understanding the fundamental philosophical issues."[29] I suggest, then, that we can still view the formalist program as offering a picture of ideal explanation in a "completed" science—if a justified theory provided Hempelian explanations, there would be no further formal demands to make of it. (Of course, whether there are further contextual and pragmatic components to the explanatory task is another question).

Nevertheless, Hempel's careful definitions of law and explanation for a model language are in the final analysis inadequate. Since the difficulties are not idiosyncratic to Hempel's approach but represent shortcomings of most formalist analyses, and since the debate between formalism and contextualism is still raging today, we must examine them at some length. I consider six major difficulties with the formalist program, ranging from limitations in scope and partial breakdowns to fundamental flaws.[30] This admittedly technical exercise is necessary if we are to be fully aware of the inherent difficulties with the formalist program, difficulties which necessitate the shift to the coherence theory of explanation upon which this book is based.

The problem of scope. Deductive-nomological explanation requires that the explanans use lawlike sentences, which Hempel defined as *fundamental* sentences (viz., universal conditionals containing no "individual constants") or their logical consequences or derivatives (272). He later conceded the inadequacy of this definition to Nagel, who had demonstrated that Hempel's specification was "far too restrictive" since it would rule out, for example, the Keplerian laws (both before and after Newtonian theory) because of their essential use of individual constants.[31] Criticizing in turn Nagel's proposal of the "unrestricted universality" of laws, Hempel admitted that the formalists had yet to find a "satisfactory version of the scope condition."[32]

Formal languages. At the end of his analysis of explanation, Hempel points out that his analysis has been limited to formal languages. He admits that a "significant application of either theory [of systematic power] in epistemology or the methodology of science requires the solution of certain fundamental problems which concern the logical structure of the language of science and the interpretation of its concepts" (288). Unfortunately, the task of specifying the relations between formal languages and the realities of actual linguistic practices in science turned out to be more intractable than Hempel and others had anticipated. As a result, Hempel's admitted need to clarify the "conditions for a sound application" of his models (ibid.) appears insoluble without a major reworking of the basic premises of his formalist program.

Self-explanation. It is not possible for Hempel to rule out "partial self-explanation," namely, cases where an explanandum E is partially derived from a singular sentence in the explanans which has E as a consequence.[33] Now Hempel is surely correct in maintaining that the phenomenon of partial self-explanation does not amount to a total circularity in scientific explanation, since the explanans still goes beyond the content of the specific explanandum (276n36). But can he avoid admitting a partial circularity in this phenomenon, that is, that the explanans is partially dependent on the explanandum? And given that the observation language with which we express the antecedent conditions must also be constructed (sometimes simultaneously with the theoretical language), is this not what the contextualists mean by the effect of theory on observation language? The later notion of theory-laden data is arguably no more than a radicalization of the self-reflective quality of explanations seen here by Hempel.

Explanation sketches. In many cases a theory cannot provide full deductive-nomological explanations and must be content with "explanation sketches" (423f). These sketches provide a sort of outline of the full explanation that will eventually be formulated, without yet making the grade as adequate Hempelian explanations. Yet it seems that much more of scientific practice proceeds at this level than Hempel would want to admit; at least the social sciences are characterized, whether necessarily or contingently, more by sketches than by "the real thing." Even more, when we turn to philosophy and religion, explanatory sketches or meaning-sketches play a crucial role in efforts at explanation.

Coherence. Explanations aim at bringing coherence into our experience of the world: in asserting this, Hempel anticipated to some degree the later claim that decisions about observation statements, boundary conditions, and explanatory adequacy depend in part on systemic factors. Hempel notes that laws and theories attempt to "establish systematic connections among the data of our experience" (278). Although he never acknowledged the significant role of coherence considerations in deductive-nomological explanation, in his major article on explanation he admits the "epistemic relativity" of probabilistic or "inductive-statistical" explanation, namely, that we can only speak of inductive explanations "relative to some class K of statements representing a particular knowledge situation."[34] Moreover, in psychological explanation the "many complex interdependencies among the psychological concepts in question" allow for "quasi-theoretical connections" at best (474). The way in which Hempel's shift toward coherence here relativizes his own deductive-nomological program and prefigures later theories of explanation has often been overlooked. The more recent debate in the philosophy of science tends to maintain this coherentialist goal—of seeking a "systematic understanding of empirical phenomena by showing that they fit into a nomic nexus" (488)—while denying that these "data of our experience" (278) are ever directly (pretheoretically) accessible in themselves.

Observation sentences. Hempel's early use of a sharp theory/observation distinction, largely taken over from Carnap and the Vienna Circle, raises insuperable problems for his theory of explanation.[35] This issue, perhaps more than any other, has driven home the relativizing effects of context in science. As Hempel later summarized his position, he had sought to explicate the ways "in which theoretical terms are assigned specific 'meanings' with the help of an observational vocabulary."[36] Clearly, for the falsificationist model of rationality as well as for Carnap's inductivist approach, a given theory must be testable (falsifiable or verifiable respectively) on the basis of observation statements that have not been "corrupted" by the theory in question. To the extent that Hempel and Nagel retained the verificationist criterion in some form (viz., only empirically verifiable sentences are meaningful at all), they will have to rely on the theory/observation distinction to settle questions of cognitive significance as well. If I can show that the theoretical and semantic adequacy of these formalist approaches rests essentially on a clear separation of theory and observation, then any threat to that distinction is a threat to the formalist project as well.

Admittedly, the doctrine of meaning underlying the major formalist approaches to scientific explanation is ambiguous in the extreme, making criticisms based on this area somewhat precarious. Frederick Suppe lumps Carnap and Hempel together as requiring an observation-based seman- tics[37]; but this combination need indicate no more than the artificiality of locutions such as "*the* received view." Consider the relationship between deductive-nomological explanation and a verificationist criterion of mean- ing in Hempel's publications alone. Hempel dismissed the quest for crite- ria of cognitive significance as early as 1950.[38] In 1969 he completely re- jected his earlier attempts at a theory/observation distinction in one paper,[39] while still defending nomological explanation in all the sciences in another.[40] Recantations notwithstanding, Hempel not infrequently slips back into verificationist language, as when he asserts that untestable moti- vational explanations lose their cognitive significance, or that when terms of functionalist analysis are used in a nonempirical manner "the sentences containing them have no clear empirical meaning."[41] Note the contrast with Popper's approach, which had required theory-free, basic observation sentences as potential falsifiers of theories; unlike Hempel, however, Pop- per never made this requirement into a criterion of cognitive significance, using it only to demarcate science from metaphysics. Although Hempel explicitly rules out falsifiability as either a criterion of cognitive significance or of demarcation (121f), he rightly maintained in his earlier work that the deductive-nomological model requires a division in principle of the vocab- ulary of empirical science into observational and theoretical terms.[42] The same seems to be true of Nagel as well.[43]

Hempel admits that he once held an observational vocabulary to be the only means for specifying the meaning of theoretical terms.[44] But Putnam's devastating 1960 critique of the theory/observation dichotomy (and of Car- nap and Hempel's "partial interpretation" of theoretical terms by observa- tional terms) left little hope for the attempt "to formalize the process of introducing technical terms."[45] There now seems to be no hope of intro- ducing observation terms that are not to some extent theory-laden. Hempel's inability to solve this task at best severely circumscribes the scope of deductive-nomological explanation and, at worst, amounts to a refutation of the formalist program. More specifically, Hempel's admission of defeat on the theory/observation question foreshadowed the greater role that hermeneutical considerations would come to play in the philosophy of science. For, as Hempel now admits, "the internal principles and bridge principles of a theory, apart from systematically characterizing its content, no doubt offer the learner the most important access to an 'understanding' of its expressions, including terms as well as sentences."[46]

What is the upshot of these various criticisms of Hempel's program? As I hinted above, I prefer to speak of its circumscription rather than refutation in the context of natural science. The difficulties with the formalist approach cannot be said to have invalidated the quest for formal desiderata for explanation in the way that, for instance, the criticisms of conclusive falsificationism have conclusively falsified it. Hempel is within his epistemic rights when he refers to areas of the formal analysis of explanation that require additional work as' tasks for further reflection.[47] Still, certain provisos must be attached in light of the criticisms raised here: the Hempelian stipulations can demand allegiance only in fields (a) where there is agreement on the exact explanandum and the factors relevant to the explanans, (b) where the context is clearly nomological, and (c) where the subject matter requires causal rather than intentional explanations (see chap. 3). The second and third provisos circumscribe Hempel's brand of formalism to the natural sciences, whereas the first gives it a limited or "ideal case" role even here.

The Fate of Formalism after Hempel

The range of application of deductive-nomological explanation is thus more limited than Hempel thought; indeed, this is arguably the clearest conclusion that can be drawn from the last twenty years of debate about explanation. Postponing for the moment consideration of the pragmatics of explanation, four stages in the formalist discussion might be adduced, providing a sort of rational reconstruction of its history and fate. (1) In 1948 Hempel and Oppenheim, building on Popper, Carnap, Braithwaite and others, first gave full expression to the deductive-nomological model of explanation. (2) In fleshing out the formal structure of inductive-statistical explanations over the following two decades, Hempel found greater divergencies from deductive-nomological explanations than he had anticipated.[48] After granting the greater role of context and coherence, and the merely probabilistic derivation of the explanandum from the explanans (which in induction contains statistical, though still general, laws), Hempel had finally to admit the *epistemic relativity* of statistical explanation. That is, this type of explanation "is essentially relative to a given knowledge situation as represented by a class K of accepted statements."[49] The startling consequence is that one can speak of true deductive-nomological explanations but *not* of true inductive-statistical explanations; the latter must be relativized to a given class of accepted statements (403).

(3) Picking up on these admissions by Hempel, Wesley Salmon and others sought to develop an alternate *statistical-relevance* model of explanation.[50] The model derived certain general conditions for statistical relevance from probability theory, which were meant to be sufficient conditions for adequate scientific explanation: "According to [the statistical-relevance model] . . . , an explanation consists not in an argument but in an assemblage of relevant considerations. On the model, high probability is not the desideratum; rather, the amount of relevant information is what counts. . . . The goodness, or epistemic value, of such an explanation is measured by the gain in information provided by the probability distribution over the partition."[51] It is perhaps not necessary to dwell at length on the details of the proposal, since Salmon now grants the criticisms of Stegmüller, Humphreys, Rogers and especially Peter Achinstein that the statistical-relevance model is not an adequate characterization of scientific explanation: statistical analyses "fall short of providing genuine scientific understanding."[52]

(4) Salmon's most recent attempt is to present an ontic rather than epistemic or modal conception of explanation (e.g., 16ff, 276). He adds a new necessary condition: "To give a scientific explanation is to show how events and statistical regularities fit into the causal network of the world."[53] He now treats explanation within the confines of the "honorable" tradition of "mechanistic philosophy" (thus excluding from consideration quantum physics[54]) and devotes the heart of his book to attempting an adequate analysis of causality (chaps. 5–7).

There are obvious limitations to an ontic approach to explanation. First, it maximizes rather than minimizes dependence on metaphysical assumptions, making it painfully unattractive to nonrealists. Second, its scope is narrower than Hempel's, since it identifies scientific explanations with the explanations of classical physics.[55] Still, such limitations do not in and of themselves invalidate Salmon's work. For instance, linking theories of explanation to particular fields of inquiry seems justified when we consider differences between the explanatory task in the natural and social sciences. Likewise, there is something refreshingly honest about Salmon's out-front metaphysic. He is able to formulate and defend his ontological commitments in a way that is not possible for those who admit to metaphysical assumptions only under cross-examination by their critics.

Several important conclusions can be drawn from our examination of these formalist efforts; taken together, I believe they require a radical shift in our approach to the explanation question. To mention just three: (1) *A plurality of models* of explanation is necessary, even within the natural sciences. As Mary Hesse notes, "It would [be] strange if every occurrence of 'explains' in the language could be captured by the same formal explication."[56] Even Hempel conceded that deductive-nomological and inductive-statistical explanations are only analogous, for example, in that both employ covering laws; and we have seen how tenuous the analogy becomes when pressed. (2) For both the inductive-statistical and statistical-relevance models, essential *reference must be made to a particular context* in assessing explanatory adequacy. Given "a class K of accepted statements" and certain a priori (initial) probability relations, we can speak of a justified explanation. In fact, a wide array of additional pragmatic factors must be taken into account in judging explanatory adequacy. Clearly this is a far cry from a single, universal model of scientific explanation.

(3) Parallel with the second conclusion, it appears that *various possibly explanatory factors could have explanatory relevance*; making the decision between them is a crucial part of assessing the rational merit of explanations. Appraising explanations is organically linked to assessing the weight of various viable factors. Salmon still holds that explanations can be appraised according to some general statistical technique; indeed, it is his advocacy of a general model developed apart from situational factors that justifies his inclusion in this section despite his significant divergences from Hempel. But assessments of relevance also depend upon subjective and nonepistemic factors, with the result that contemporary theories of explanation must delve into the social sciences as well as logic. It might be the case—although I resist this conclusion—that the sociology of knowledge will invalidate *any* concern with the formal aspects of scientific explanations, as claimed by the so-called strong programme in the philosophy of science of Barnes and Bloor. It is possible that pragmatic considerations render any formal methodological analysis obsolete; this is the pivotal question raised, for example, by Jürgen Habermas's recent theory of communicative action. Clearly, the formalist project of Hempel and others has left us with a Pandora's box of broader questions that cannot be answered using the resources of that approach alone.

Nonetheless, we have not discovered any reason within the formalist project itself, despite its internal difficulties, that requires us to abandon all attempts at formal analyses of scientific explanation. To bring home this point we might return full circle to a recent comment of Popper's, almost fifty years after the first publication of *The Logic of Scientific Discovery*. In his final reaction to the falsification debate, the 1982 introduction to his *Realism and the Aim of Science*, Popper underscores a distinction he had made as early as 1934. I quote in full:

We must distinguish two meanings of the expressions "falsifiable" and "falsifiability": (1) "Falsifiable" as a logical-technical term, in the sense of the demarcation criterion of falsifiability. This purely logical con-

cept—falsifiable in principle, one might say—rests on a logical relation between the theory in question and the class of basic statements
(or the potential falsifiers described by them). (2) "Falsifiable" in the
sense that the theory in question can *definitively* or *conclusively* or
demonstrably be falsified ("demonstrably falsifiable"). I have always
stressed that even a theory which is obviously falsifiable in the first
sense is never falsifiable in this second sense.[57]

A descriptive history of science may find that scientists have never proceeded in a purely rational manner and that Feyerabend's "anything goes"
is the most accurate descriptive account of the history of science that we can
muster. Nonetheless, it may still be possible to do normative philosophy of
science or to offer a normative theory of rationality. If we are working with a
mechanistic model (as in most macrophysical natural scientific explanations), subsumption under covering laws and an isomorphism between
explanation and prediction *does* still appear to be a goal worth pursuing—
whether or not these ideals are applicable in quantum mechanics or psychology and however bad our track record so far. Again, all other things
being equal—that is, as long as the explanans is not trivial or irrelevant to
the explanandum—a statistical explanation that explains why it was much
more probable for a given event to occur rather than not to occur seems
preferable over one that does not attain this goal. That this is not the whole
story on explanation is not ground for dismissing it *tout court*. On the
contrary, the criticisms we have considered suggest only that formal analyses must be used in conjunction with an adequate pragmatics. Indeed, as
mentioned, Hempel saw this already in 1948 and Popper as early as 1933,[58]
however much they may be faulted for underemphasizing pragmatics in
their published works. I thus take it as a desideratum that our final view of
science as an explanatory project should, after due consideration of the
contextualist shift, still contain reference to the formal structure of ideal
explanations—even if only as a regulative principle or guideline in the
midst of a practice that falls far short of this (or any) ideal.[59]

The Contextualist Shift in Philosophy of Science

From Formalism to Hermeneutics

There is some irony in the fact that history has credited Kuhn with
single-handedly bringing to an end the formalist approach to philosophy of
science. In fact, the die was cast much earlier, in (among other things) the
fall of logical positivism and the rise of the later Wittgenstein. It was
inevitable that philosophers of science would begin to examine carefully
the actual processes of scientific discovery, the details of human percep-

tion, and the formation and determinants of human language. Since what emerged was a radically different, pragmatic view of scientific rationality, we must trace the contours of this shift in order to assess its implications for a theory of explanation, scientific or otherwise.[60]

It is hard to specify exactly when (or for what reasons) the pendulum began to swing away from formal analyses. Did it begin with reactions against the more extreme tenets of logical positivism, as represented by the unity of science movement and Ayer's *Language, Truth and Logic?*, with monographs in the history of science that challenged the descriptive adequacy of the major formal models?[61] or (to include appropriately nonrational factors) with an onslaught of articles by philosophers of science trained in the social sciences and anxious to break with dissertation advisors who were too authoritarian in their control of their graduate students? It is clear, however, that the shift did not burst full-blown on the scene in 1962 with Kuhn's *Structure of Scientific Revolutions.*[62] In order to comprehend the radically different way that the question of explanation was now to be posed, we must examine the growing reasons for a change in the accepted picture of the scientific process itself.

A good place to start is with Stephen Toulmin's early introduction to science,[63] which did not show the major influence of Wittgenstein in the way his later works would. Toulmin still speaks of the "logical character" of laws as a formalist might (77), and he discusses scientific explanation in terms of the discovery of laws that enable prediction (chap. 3). Yet he correctly resists an explication of science in terms of "deductive connexions" (41). In the most general sense science is a process of understanding that addresses the question, How can a class of phenomena "be accounted for" in terms of some principles? (43) This task in turn leads to Toulmin's treatment of science in terms of models and maps. Models determine our "method of representation," linking phenomena and the symbolism that will account for them (30), and physical theories are most like maps, with the function of representing the world in a way that will guide us (chap. 4). In these phrases the first glimmers of Wittgenstein's influence on the philosophy of science can perhaps be detected. Note, however, how different the realist implications of Toulmin's mapping idea are from the "many rationalities, many worlds" positions that came from Wittgenstein's later work.

The work of N. R. Hanson also helped to make the case for this alternative conception of science. Like Toulmin, he stressed the process of discovery. The formalists had made the mistake of concentrating on classical disciplines such as planetary mechanics, optics, and classical thermodynamics. But these disciplines do not adequately represent modern science—nor even these sciences as they really were at the time: "In a growing research discipline, inquiry is directed not to rearranging old facts and explanations into more elegant formal patterns, but rather to the discovery of new patterns of explanation."[64] To understand the process of inquiry, we need to examine scientists at work, beginning with their most basic activities such as observation (chap. 1). In a presentation heavily laden with quotes from Wittgenstein—indeed, even Hanson's writing style is a mimicry of the *Philosophical Investigations*[65]—Hanson argues that seeing is a "theory-laden undertaking." His plea is for a concentration on the *use* of language and notation in science in order to put to rest the specters of phenomenalism and positivism: "Physical science is not just a systematic exposure of the senses to the world; it is also a way of thinking about the world, a way of forming conceptions [a language game?]. The paradigm observer is not the man who sees and reports what all normal observers see and report, but the man who sees in familiar objects what no one else has seen before" (30).

But I believe it was Toulmin's Mahlon Powell lectures of 1960 that gave the clarion call for this new approach. It is fascinating to observe the radically different manner in which Toulmin addresses precisely the same questions as Hempel. He proposes to "stand back, and for once [!] ask the wider questions: What is explanation?"[66] But Toulmin has learned from Wittgenstein in general to distrust all generalizations; hence he sets out from the methodological precept that "there is no universal recipe for all science and all scientists" (15; cf. 21). He comes to this precept from studies in the history of science (or is it the other way around?), which reveal an amazing multiplicity of scientific methods. Indeed, asking about "what scientific explanations involve in practice" (16) leads Toulmin to the conclusion—several years before Kuhn's *Structure*—that there are certain "ideals of natural order" or "explanatory paradigms," somewhat like Collingwood's "absolute presuppositions," which play a key role in human intellectual history and make science possible:

> Science progresses, not by recognizing the truth of new observations alone, but by *making sense* of them. To *this task of interpretation* we bring principles of regularity, conceptions of natural order, paradigms, ideals, or what-you-will: intellectual patterns which define the range of things we can accept (in Copernicus' phrase) as "sufficiently absolute and pleasing to the mind." An explanation, to be acceptable, must demonstrate that the happenings under investigation are special cases or complex combinations of our fundamental intelligible types. (81, emphasis mine)

Note the criterion for explanatory adequacy implied in the last sentence: no formal feature of explanations—in fact, nothing intrinsic to them at all—

makes them acceptable; only their effectiveness in making sense of the world can recommend explanations to us. Here the task of explanation is clearly subordinate to the quest for understanding; this fact, I believe, must be determinative for any theory of explanation.

What we are seeing in the early writings of Toulmin and Hanson is a new approach to explanation that addresses precisely the issues that Hempel's program had ignored: the centrality in science of making sense of the world; the interpretive and pragmatic elements in actual scientific inquiry; and the role of *explanatory paradigms*. The importance of this last concept requires a quick look at the sources that have influenced its current usage. A direct line of influence can be traced back at least as far as Georg Christoph Lichtenberg (1742–1799).[67] Lichtenberg held that natural processes could be "declined" according to *paradigmata* or patterns. Although he was highly critical of hypotheses, he thought we needed pictures of events to facilitate the application of mathematics to nature. Lichtenberg believed discovery by means of paradigms to be the most fruitful of all the heuristic devices of science. The truth of these assumptions or pictures is linked only to their explanatory power and to their relative simplicity: "The door to truth is through simplicity."

The crucial role of pictures reemerges in the *Principles of Mechanics* of Heinrich Hertz. In drawing scientific inferences, Hertz argues, we form "images or symbols" of external objects; we are successful when the consequents of the "images in thought" are themselves "the images of the necessary consequents in nature of the things pictured."[68] When we seem to have achieved some conformity between nature and our images, we can use them to develop, "as by means of models," further predictions about the world that go beyond our present experience. Hertz is significant for the paradigm story in that he admitted that various images of the same objects are possible and that "one image may be more suitable for one purpose, another for another" (2–3)—though Hertz still believed there were general criteria for deciding between them, at least in the field of mechanics.

Wittgenstein's use of the paradigm notion reflects both influences. He apparently knew Lichtenberg's work well and was attracted to it; moreover, he appeals explicitly to Hertz's picture theory of propositions in the *Tractatus*.[69] The term *paradigm* does not actually appear in the *Tractatus*; still, the notion of propositions (*Sätze*) as pictures could be said to anticipate Wittgenstein's later view of language as a gestalt that we employ in describing the world.[70] For example, his treatment of Newtonian mechanics as a grid (6.32–361) can be viewed as an important precursor to Kuhn's philosophy of science. However, contextualists such as Kuhn freely employ Wittgenstein's notion of the picturing function of language without accepting the notion of *the* world to which the pictures refer. Also, Wittgenstein's insistence on the many kinds of picturing or modeling relations (*abbildende Beziehungen*)—"the gramophone record, the musical thought, the score, the waves of sound" (4.014)—draws attention to the inherent plurality of representations and to the role of persons in creatively formulating their pictures.

The *Investigations*, though, *are* paradigmatic for the use of the term in contemporary philosophy of science. In this work we find a clear emphasis on the constructive activity of language users, as well as on the wide variety of (nonpropositional) things that we do with (in, through) language, both of which are nicely illustrated by the paradigm concept. A Wittgensteinian paradigm is a picture or model "with which comparison is made,"[71] which sets the use of a word. We teach the use of signs in a language game "by pointing to paradigms" (par. 51); we judge language uses as incorrect in comparison with "a particular paradigm of our grammar" (par. 20); a paradigm is "an instrument of our language" (par. 57) that enables us to use certain words. If we lose a particular paradigm, such as the meter bar or the paradigm of a particular color, we could no longer use the word. Indeed, at one point Wittgenstein uses the term in precisely the same sense that philosophers of science later would: a given paradigm ("calculating in the head") may "los[e] its purpose" if "the phenomena gravitate towards another paradigm" (par. 385), in which case we may wish to employ a different paradigm that better accounts for the recalcitrant phenomena. It is this aspect of Wittgenstein's usage that is most explicitly reflected in Kuhn's later use of the term *paradigm*.[72]

The implications of the shift toward Wittgenstein in the theory of scientific rationality have been far-ranging. The new focus on language use is simultaneously a focus on the activity of the scientific community as it observes, forms concepts, and revises them when confronted with new data. When we look more closely at the actual practice of science, we immediately discover that communal conventions influence many aspects of theory choice and usage, that the language of science and its pragmatic or historical context are closely linked. Moreover, the decision about extending a given paradigm to cover a new range of data is not a cut-and-dried process à la Popper's logical-technical construal of falsifications. Wittgenstein plays with some of the options in the *Investigations*: the new data can become a limit case of the paradigm; the paradigm, no longer applicable, may cease to function as a grammatical guide for a language game; or we are unsure what to do. Clearly, some amount of arbitrariness is involved: we have at best certain intuitions about the adequacy of a paradigm for new cases; hence a certain subjectivity is interpolated into the process of adopting a given paradigm or language game. In facing the alternative of which game to play, Wittgenstein and his followers would maintain, there can be no appeal to general criteria: criteria function only *within* a particular game.

Seen in light of the contextualist shift, then, *explanation is relativized and becomes an element within the broader hermeneutical task that is science.* Philosophers of science cannot elucidate an abstract and authoritative structure, encapsulating the essence of adequate explanation in all its instances. At best they can lead their readers into a given scientific discipline, seeking to convey what its models are, how it proceeds, how it puts its world together.[73] The hermeneutical approach will dismiss attempts at general definitions as either tautological or arbitrarily restrictive; its goal is to "see what 'explaining' involves in practice" (22). Any equation of explanation with prediction can be dismissed, for instance, through a consideration of Babylonian astronomy and Kepler's Laws, both of which predicted planetary motions without explaining them; other theories explain without predicting. Prediction is thus neither a necessary nor a sufficient condition of science.[74] Instead, for Toulmin an explanation is adequate if and only if it contributes to our understanding of a phenomenon, whether or not it results in predictions. Like Newton's theory, it must "make sense" of what is observed (34). In the end, making sense of the world may be the *only* criterion that some contextualists are willing to require of explanations.

When the hermeneutical moment is acknowledged, as now seems necessary, more than just the theory of explanation is altered; an entirely different conception of the nature of scientific rationality results. The scientist begins with an "ideal of natural order" that "stands to reason" or is self-explanatory for her. The major scientific effort, then, focuses on demonstrating the correctness of these "principles of regularity and explanatory paradigms" (chaps. 3–4). The issue of evaluation is complicated by the fact that varying paradigms lead to different "forms of theory" (chap. 5) and different "styles" of science (96ff). Note however that, unlike later paradigm theorists, Toulmin is not led by this insight toward skepticism about the possibility of *any* evaluation or toward controversial claims of incommensurability: "The crucial issue is, rather, what types of happening a particular form of theory will help us to understand and where its use will be unhelpful or misleading" (84).

The hermeneutical approach to science (as opposed to the formal-explanatory) makes it difficult, though not necessarily impossible, to specify any general evaluative techniques or criteria. However, the influence of preconceptions on data and theory form does not make science nonempirical. Some standards remain. Toulmin speaks correctly of the fruitfulness of a given ideal or paradigm over a long period of time. Yet the guiding metaphor is no longer the static image of a map, but rather evolution: a theory has better survival value in science if in the process of variation and selection it is better adapted than its predecessors. With this notion we have in a sense already jumped beyond Kuhn to the work of Imre Lakatos and his distinction between progressive and degenerating research programs.

There is no reason to deny all objectivity in science: "when it comes to interrogating Nature . . . we must leave her to answer for herself—and answer without any prompting" (101). Yet the interrogation is always colored by preconceptions, or what the hermeneutical tradition has called the hermeneutical circle: when we come to Nature "it is always *we* who frame the questions" (ibid.). Theory construction is not a linear process, since both theory and data are affected by pretheoretical ideals and paradigms, which only later (at the step of theory testing, and after sufficient time has elapsed) will be judged fruitful or not. A formal analysis of the theory/data relationship lacks the scope to take such factors and such a circle into account. A broader viewpoint is demanded: "We can never make less than a three-fold demand of science: its explanatory techniques must be not only (in Copernicus' words) 'consistent with the numerical records'; they must also be acceptable—for the time being, at any rate—as 'absolute' and 'pleasing to the mind'" (115).

The Ascendence of the Kuhnian Paradigm

Kuhn's first monograph[75] examined the precursors and subsequent influence of the notions central to the Copernican revolution, though perhaps without the insight into their methodological implications found in Toulmin's book. Indeed, given the work of earlier historians of science such as Koyré (cited above), one is surprised at Kuhn's belief that "the combination of science and intellectual history is an unusual one" (viii). The central thesis and "novelty" of Kuhn's first book lies in its demonstration of the plural structure of the Copernican revolution. His effort to show the astronomical, physical, philosophical, and theological influences on this paradigmatic revolution helped bring the genre of history of ideas treatments of scientific developments to the attention of methodologists of science, a genre that should already have been familiar through the work of writers such as Burtt, Whitehead, and Lovejoy.[76]

Nonetheless, in one important respect Kuhn here anticipated his more famous *Structure of Scientific Revolutions*. In his treatment of the assimilation of Copernican astronomy (chap. 6) Kuhn demonstrates how deep-seated a conceptual scheme can be. After the Copernican switch, there was an initial period in which a loss of "conceptual coherence" (226) occurred in other fields, particularly due to conflicts with Aristotelian cosmology; only later was an integration into "the complete and coherent universe envisaged by the seventeenth century" attained with the aid of the Newtonian world picture. At the beginning any new conception will be an ad hoc, probably paradoxical device for "economically describing the known." Only later, when the passage of time and the gradual revision of common sense in the affected disciplines have overcome the initial sense of incoherence, does a new conception become "a basic tool for explaining and exploring nature" (230). Kuhn here—for the first time since the contextualist shift in philosophy of science—begins to link the new perspective on explanation with the concept of coherence.[77] His concluding attempt to show how the concept of a planetary earth "came at last to make coherent sense" (chap. 7) is one example of the crucial interplay between explanation and the broader quest for conceptual coherence—coherence within theories, among theories, and between theories and other nonscientific areas of experience.

For Kuhn also, then, the necessary condition for explanatory adequacy is precisely this making sense of a domain of experience for the purposes of a given discipline. He and Toulmin correctly employ the term *coherence* to indicate the hermeneutical (rather than purely formal) nature of this project. Although the notion of coherence is too vague to pass as a sufficient criterion for explanations within natural science—it needs to be supplemented by more specific criteria such as empirical fruitfulness and mathematical simplicity—its inclusion as a necessary condition has important implications. As Kuhn has seen, stressing the coherence criterion eliminates that artificial isolation of philosophy of science from other academic disciplines that typified positivistic approaches. It links the study of science to more general historical efforts, especially in the history of ideas. In fact the sociologists of science would argue that the link is broader than intellectual history. Since we now incorporate the whole scientist into our treatment of the discovery and evaluation of scientific explanations, we must include her psychological, social, and economic setting as well. If they are right, the shift leads as appropriately to, for example, institutional or hermeneutic analyses of scientific theories as it does to the work of a Kuhn or a Blumenberg. Indeed, if natural science is hermeneutical to the extent that the contextualists allege, the gap between it and the social sciences cannot be as wide as many have imagined.

We have reached the perspective on the explanation question in response to which *The Structure of Scientific Revolutions* was written. As has become clear, the conceptual foundations for the shift had already been laid; a short, programmatic tractatus was now needed to center discussion around the new proposals. Somewhat despite himself, Kuhn ended up writing just the required piece.[78] The work built on the bases already recounted, though in greater detail, adding its own generalized sociological account of the acceptance, employment, challenge to, and rejection of these explanatory ideals or paradigms.[79] The word *structure* in the title indicates Kuhn's optimism that a single picture of science could be developed. But, whereas formalists such as Hempel had addressed the general structure of theories or explanations, Kuhn here seems to have in mind a *social scientific* structure, for he utilizes the techniques and terminology of the social sciences in his analysis. Instead of analyzing the formal structure of explanations, he insists that we address their *pragmatic setting* and *communal functions*.

The details of Kuhn's thesis in *Structure* are well enough known that no time need be lost in their exposition.[80] Schematically, Kuhn's critique of the Received View centered around four points:

1. "Normal science" is dominated by paradigms, or shared basic beliefs about the world. At a given time, scientists will not question the dominant paradigm; it will structure the direction of their research by providing the presuppositions for their work.
2. There is no gradual transition between paradigms. All the criteria for arbitrating disputes or choosing between paradigms are themselves paradigm-dependent. When enough difficulties have accrued to one paradigm, a "scientific revolution" occurs and a new paradigm replaces the old one. Students of religion were not slow to notice Kuhn's frequent use of the term *conversion* in this context.
3. Following from this paradigmatic structure of science, Kuhn holds that all data are theory-laden. There are no neutral observation statements; a given paradigm helps decide what may and may not count as data.
4. Theories are not verified or falsified. What constitutes a so-called crucial experiment varies with the theoretical context. Popper's schematization is inaccurately simplistic; the history of explanation does not show discordant data falsifying theories conclusively. Instead, implicit theoretical assumptions in the data can be challenged, and a recurrent discrepancy can be set aside as an unexplained anomaly or integrated by means of an auxiliary hypothesis.

Kuhn's extreme theses have not gone undiscussed or unchallenged: each of the above points has met with stiff resistance during the last quarter century.[81] As the essays in *Paradigms and Revolutions* show, many natural and social scientists have maintained that the influence of paradigms on theory is minimal in their disciplines. Other thinkers have pointed to equivocations in the notion of paradigm, with Margaret Masterman going so far as to find twenty-one different uses of the term in *Structure*.[82] Toulmin in 1965, and others since him, have argued decisively that normal and revolutionary science cannot be so neatly separated.[83] The incommensurability of paradigms and the irrationality of paradigm choice have likewise come under attack, often in major or monograph-length treatments of crucial examples such as the Copernican revolution and its influence on Galileo, or Einstein's special and general theories.[84]

In three major articles, written as early as 1965 but all published in 1970, Kuhn modified (or at least clarified) the claims of *Structure*. He now admits that the 1962 treatment "made a paradigm seem a quasi-mystical entity or property which, like charisma, transforms those infected by it."[85] To eliminate the most significant ambiguity in *Structure*, Kuhn now speaks of "disciplinary matrices" or "shared group commitments" that tie together a community of no more than a hundred scientists,[86] and of "exemplars" or "concrete problem solutions" passed on from teacher to student within a given scientific community. The term *matrix* serves to avoid the term *theory* as used by formalists such as Popper and Hempel. Kuhn eschews talk of theories in order to emphasize that scientific explanations occur only in interpreted form (viz., within a community). Models and textbook examples are as important as theories, for a matrix "consists, among other things, of verbal and symbolic generalizations *together with* examples of their function in use" (501). The idea is to oppose Popper's notion that "canons of rationality . . . derive exclusively from those of logical and linguistic syntax."[87] Kuhn's appeal to social psychology is not new—he thinks Popper, Watkins, et al., make it as well (233). Indeed, he is essentially repeating the claim that Toulmin had made earlier by denying that "the problem of theory-choice can be resolved by techniques which are semantically neutral" (ibid.).

Despite his unfortunate penchant for over-neat schematizations of the structure of the scientific community in times of peace and war (or normal and revolutionary science), Kuhn has made a contribution toward our understanding of scientific practice. Though asserting that one cannot prove or compel assent to a new theory, he does not hold that theory choice is an irrational leap of faith. Much of scientific activity is puzzle solving, and the exact criteria often vary with the puzzle; yet the scientific community can often agree whether a given program of research is progressing or degenerating. And he appears to allow for some general standards that characterize the broader scientific community: "accuracy, simplicity, fruitfulness and the like."[88]

If Kuhn has contributed to our understanding of science, why work to supplement his position with that of Imre Lakatos in the following section? There is reason to worry that Kuhn is too extreme in his contextualizing. Rather than stopping with the role of context and interpretive considerations in evaluating individual explanations (as, say, Toulmin did), Kuhn *reduces* explanations to their context. Different scientific explanations are incommensurable: there can be no direct comparison between them. But strict incommensurability seems as foreign to scientific practice and the history of science as strict falsifiability. If the languages of two matrices are really worlds apart, why think that even the vague sorts of general observations that he allows—this matrix has solved twenty-one puzzles; that one offers new possibilities—can be made? If incommensurability, why not Feyerabend's "anything goes"?

A sign of the malaise is Kuhn's treatment of scientific standards merely as values rather than as epistemological standards. Kuhn has incorporated the subjectivity of the scientist and the scientific community into the standards for explanatory adequacy to such an extent that no distinction between epistemic and axiological factors remains. Without doubt, the once popular quest for purely *objective* criteria must now be replaced by the attempt to formulate standards sufficient for establishing *intersubjective* agreement on justification or validity. But this shift away from what we might call (in lieu of the term *positivism*) *objectivism* still leaves us with important standards for comparing (however poorly) competing knowledge claims. There is no reason not to include criteria like Kuhn's simplicity alongside better-credentialed criteria such as freedom from contradiction.[89]

Explanation and the Context Principle

Instead of remaining with Kuhn, it is instructive to view the complex of issues raised by *Structure* (and its later emendations) on its own terms. Three foci of the discussion deserve mention.

(1) *Problem solving.* As we saw above, Popper had already placed problem solving at the center of his theory of rationality: "Every rational theory . . . is rational in so far as it tries to solve certain problems," and it is reasonable only in regard to "a given problem situation."[90] Although in *Structure* Kuhn spoke of "puzzle solving" in normal science (the paradigm allegedly gives rise to "textbook problems" for normal scientists), Musgrave has shown that for the later Kuhn the puzzles have again become problems that, unsolved, can hasten the end of a paradigm.[91] Larry Laudan more recently constructed an entire philosophy of science around the definition of science as the striving for "problem solving effectiveness."[92] Predictably, if our search is for "acceptable answers to interesting questions," we will only need criteria for adequate problem solutions, not standards for "'true', 'corroborated' or otherwise justifiable" theories (13–14). Specific problems, rather than general formal requirements, provide a "context of inquiry" and, over a period of time, give rise to a "research

tradition" (chap. 3; def. p. 81). The evaluation of explanations is therefore relative to contemporary competitors and doctrines of theory assessment as well as to previous theories within the tradition. Consequently, "determinations of truth and falsity are *irrelevant* to the acceptability or the pursuitability [*sic*] of theories and research traditions" (120).

I argue in later chapters that the notion of problem-solving rationality is also applicable (with suitable modifications) as a model for evaluating explanations in philosophy and theology. In anticipation of that discussion, we should note that reliance on the context of inquiry as established by specific problem situations raises the criterion of coherence to a position of paramount importance. In this model of rationality, the adequacy of a proposed explanation is virtually equated with the ability of the explanans to fit the explanandum into an accepted framework (in this case, the framework implied in the formulation of the problem situation). The flip side of this centrality of context for assessing explanations, however, is the apparent divorce of adequate explanation and truth, a consequence stressed by Laudan and others. This divorce has prima facie devastating consequences for theological explanation—unless, of course, the truth-indicativeness of the coherence criterion can be somehow reinstated.

(2) *Epistemological anarchism.* Feyerabend has done more than any other thinker to bring home the more radical implications of Kuhn's position. In Feyerabend's hands, the situational variance of *contextualism* reduces to the complete relativism of *conventionalism*. Given Kuhn's incommensurability, "what remains are aesthetic judgments, judgments of taste, and our own subjective wishes."[93] In Kuhn's science, according to Feyerabend, there is no longer any distinction between science and art (228n2); we might as well abolish the honorific connotations attached to the word *science*. Science becomes "an attractive and yielding courtesan" (229) and should be acknowledged and treated as such. More specifically, Feyerabend calls for "epistemological anarchism" in science, the position that "anything goes."[94] Proclaiming himself a Dadaist, Feyerabend points out the consequences of abolishing the science/nonscience distinction: we should view the Bible as an alternate cosmology (47n1); voodoo can enrich our physiology (50); acupuncture may be preferable to modern medicine (51); we should break our methodological rules whenever possible, as Galileo did (app. 2); and finding a satisfactory theory depends, for instance, on having a satisfactory sex life (174).

Whatever its truth value, Feyerabend's philosophy of science has added some color to the recent debate. In addition to its color, *Against Method* drives home the point that actual science is rather high-handed with methodological prescriptions. Feyerabend has helped bring about a closer examination of science as an institution, as in the work of Gerald Holton.[95]

His writings have challenged the sharp separation between science and metaphysics both in theory and practice, arguing for instance that only by including myth and religion in science can we correct for theory prejudices in observation.[96] I suppose that theologians might view Feyerabend's work as progress: religious assertions are no longer meaningless (Ayer) or sharply demarcated from scientific assertions (Popper). But this is at best a type of *tu quoque* argument: religion may be in bad shape on the rationality question, but science is just as bad. It should hardly be a comfort to the theologian to find someone lowering science to the level of "religion, prostitution and so on" (28). Moreover, as we will see, many of the religious traditions are *less* anarchistic than Feyerabend's science. A good case can be made for significant criteria of method and justification in theology (see chap. 6).

(3) *The pragmatics of explanation.* If Kuhn's use of social scientific analyses typified the contextualist shift, Bas van Fraassen has brought home its implications for explanation. Like Kuhn, he describes the coloring of appraisal by contextual factors and broadens the list of evaluative criteria to include not only mathematical elegance and simplicity, but also our "specifically human concerns, . . . our interests and pleasures," such as whether "it matters more to us to have one sort of question answered rather than another."[97] In the course of a survey critique of earlier theories of explanation, van Fraassen demonstrates that what I have called the formalist tradition had concentrated on the syntactics of explanation, on its logical form alone, disregarding the pragmatics.[98] Causal accounts of explanation such as Wesley Salmon's are inadequate for the same reason: the vast disagreements about the "real cause" of an event stem from the fact that (as Hanson wrote) "there are as many causes of x as there are explanations of x."[99]

Kuhn's analysis of social factors must therefore be supplemented by linguistic pragmatics, the consideration of language in use. Van Fraassen himself wishes to draw rather radical consequences from the shift: "there are no explanations in science," for explanation must consist in an exhibition of (independently or communally chosen) "salient factors" in the "causal net."[100] But features are salient to a given person because of "his orientation, his interests, and various other peculiarities in the way he approaches or comes to know the problem—contextual factors."[101] Pragmatic factors even influence our analysis of the basic why-question of explanation (contra Hempel): "Why did Adam eat the apple?" may ask at least three different questions: Why Adam? Why eat? Why the (an) apple? (126–29). In any given case, we ask "Why P?" in contrast to other members Q of a given set X of options, though the set X of alternatives is often left tacit.[102]

The introduction of pragmatics into the theory of explanation has, I believe, devastating implications for exclusively formalist approaches. As Passmore wrote much earlier, "There can be no purely formal definition of an explanation. . . . How [the formal] schema is used will depend on what we know and what we want to know; and these are not formal considerations. . . . *Explaining, in short, is a particular way of using a form of argument; it has no logical form particular to it.*"[103] The variability of the "particular ways" challenges not only the hegemony of the deductive-nomological model of explanation, with its insistence that individual cases be subsumed under general laws, but also any purely formal theory of natural scientific rationality.

We commit a non sequitur, however, if we maintain that the new awareness of the pragmatics of explanation invalidates the importance of formal *explanatory ideals* in science. That many explanations of a phenomenon are possible depending on pragmatic context does not exclude the role of standard cases in science, standard why-questions that are raised, and standard causal networks in which scientists in a given discipline are interested. One could easily construct a spectrum of variability, moving from purely formal considerations, which are highly impervious to context, to more and more theory-specific (and thus context-relative) factors. At the one extreme, for science, or rational discourse, to be possible at all, we must assume that a scientific proposition means what it asserts and not the opposite. Still highly resistant to change, but not immutable, are the basic patterns of inference fundamental to the various disciplines. Relativistic assumptions in physics, like mechanistic assumptions before them, will only be discarded if a (not yet conceivable) theoretical framework is produced that revolutionizes our current understanding of the physical world. Other present explanatory parameters could be more easily abandoned, for example, those imposed by a particular theory of electron interference. (Of course, one can still demand that any new theory be able to model the sort of phenomena currently explained by the present theories.) The point is clear: only when one gets to rather specific explanatory questions does the context-relativity of explanations begin to play a noticeable role. It is important that one takes one's relativism in small doses, and only when needed.

The pragmatic focus of van Fraassen and others, then, reveals again how significant the contextualist shift is for our theory of explanation. Indeed, contextual considerations have emerged as so central that we could summarize the results of this section under the heading of a *context principle of rationality*. To put it negatively, explanatory claims cannot be evaluated apart from their context, for example, in the natural sciences apart from the empirical problem or situation that they intend to explain. Explanation requires reference to the framework one uses in interpreting a given situation, in formulating a research problem, or even in specifying the data to be explained.

Positively, I propose that *coherence* has now emerged as a central component of the theory of explanation. As an umbrella criterion for explanatory adequacy, coherence requires the systematic interdependence or "fit" of the various components of an explanatory account, both internally (call it the consistency criterion) and externally—with the situation (pragmatic criteria), with the data implied and expressed by the explanandum (the correspondence criterion), and with the broader context of experience (the comprehensiveness criterion). Without belittling the role of empirical fruitfulness or mathematical simplicity, the context principle thus makes "goodness of fit" a necessary component of rational explanations.[104]

It follows that formalist treatments represent at best a sort of limiting case: all other things being equal—or, within the framework of a specified interpretation—natural scientists should seek to formulate and employ general laws in order to provide a full explanation of a state of affairs. But formalist treatments have in the past been a major component in the case for demarcating the natural sciences from the social sciences and nonscientific disciplines. If formalist requirements can be dropped and a coherence-based theory of rationality put forward in their place, we may perhaps have the groundwork for a general theory of rational explanation that is broad enough to handle both the sciences and theology.

One sharp contrast between the two areas is immediately evident: in religion we may have little more than context (system-internal coherence) to go on, whereas in the sciences we can appeal also to criteria such as empirical fruitfulness. The difference is important. Still, the theory-ladenness of empirical data has now reduced the distinction to something less than absolute. Instead, we can now more accurately speak of a variety of types of coherence, as the term *umbrella criterion* suggests. For example, what used to be called theoretical consistency can better be expressed as a coherence relation between various theory components. Pragmatism is the stress on the coherence or fit between theories and practical contexts, and the appeal to consensus may be taken as the appeal to the coherence of sets of beliefs held by various theorists.

Perhaps most importantly, a theory's "relation to the world" now comes out roughly as the coherence of a set of theoretical predictions with a given set of observation statements.[105] If a theory's correspondence to empirical reality can in fact be determined only in terms of the mutual fit of sets of statements, one is no longer justified in positing a fundamental difference in kind between empirical and nonempirical disciplines.

Formalism and Contextualism Mediated: Imre Lakatos

Formalist and contextualist thinkers have not gone their separate ways in pristine isolation. There have been important confrontations of the competing methodological positions, often fought by Popper and his followers on the one side, Kuhn and his on the other. Feyerabend's position raised the stakes: if the Popperian school could not respond adequately to Kuhn's *Structure*, all talk of the rationality of science would be cast into question. In the ensuing discussion the concerns represented by the contextualist shift—though not necessarily Kuhn's particular interpretation of its implications—have received widespread acknowledgment. By contrast, what has been noticeably missing is a *coup de main* by Popper, the presentation of a more adequate form of falsificationism.

Popper does appear at points to have softened his position. For example, basic statements have played a smaller and smaller role as the years have passed,[106] and reservations have been added to potential falsificationism: "To this problem, my answer is positive: Yes the *assumption* of the truth of test statements *sometimes* allows us to justify the claim that an explanatory universal theory is false."[107] Here, "assumption" connotes the reliance of the test statement on another theory or set of statements, and "sometimes" alludes to the nonautomatic character of the falsification process. Popper continues to demand a mandatory empirical basis for falsification; but his has become a complicated, even convoluted empiricism. In his article, "Epicyclic Popperism," Errol Harris notes: "In these circumstances, would it not be advisable to scrap the epicycles and transfer the centre of the theory from the 'empirical basis' to the consilience of hypotheses? Let us have done, once and for all, with Empiricism and all its remnants: 'basic' statements, novel facts, and unexplained processes of corroboration."[108] In fact, this shift away from the acceptance of empirical facts as unproblematic, and toward a model of rationality as the consilience or coherence of hypotheses, is precisely the development that makes a comparative study like the present one possible.

Popper was not able to play an important mediating role in the formalist-contextualist debate. One of the reasons was certainly age: Popper was sixty when Kuhn's *Structure* was published. Indeed, he has not actually retracted any of his views in the ensuing debate.[109] Instead, the role of mediator in the Popper/Kuhn controversy was played most effectively by Imre Lakatos. It was his 106-page contribution to *Criticism and the Growth of Knowledge* that first sketched the outlines of a viable synthesis between the Popperian and Kuhnian schools. Incidentally, one observes a similar synthesis of positions in the 1969 symposium on the structure of science at Urbana, Illinois, albeit somewhat less clearly, due to the absence of contributions from Popper or Lakatos.[110] In general, Lakatos's work provides the means for avoiding the inflexibility of Popper's falsificationism and the irrationalist leanings of Kuhn's sociohistorical relativism. With the help of Lakatos's revisions, it is much easier to ascertain the enduring insight of Popper's opus: not falsification, but the conjecture-refutation schema that it exemplifies; in short: *the replacement of a justificatory (inductive) by a fallibilist epistemology.* To be rational does not mean to add up empirical data in favor of one's position, but rather to put forward theories or hypotheses in a context in which they can be criticized.

Lakatos's modifications thus help to broaden Popper's philosophy of science into a theory of rationality of more general applicability. Essentially, I argue that the view of rationality that is most fruitful in linking the various academic disciplines (including those concerned with religion) is one no longer bound to the foundationalist project of defending knowledge claims through inductive or verificationist means. Instead, the methodology that I wish to abstract from the philosophy of science discussion has three major requirements: the isolation of a problem-situation or why-question; the formulation of some hypothetical answer (e.g., to explain a chosen body of data); and a specified process or set of criteria by which the explanatory hypotheses can be intersubjectively criticized. In addition to contributing to this generalization of Popper's fallibilist approach, Lakatos' modifications correct what I would call the nonhermeneutical structure of Popper's philosophy of science. His occasional asseverations to the contrary notwithstanding, Popper portrays science as a unidirectional process. By contrast, when basic statements are replaced by theory-laden data, Popper's problem-situation methodology gives rise to a theory of scientific rationality in which contextual considerations are seen to constitute question and answer reciprocally—without, however, invalidating all talk of formal structures or general standards in science. Popper did see correctly that scientific explanations and their evaluation are based on a careful analysis of a given problem-situation, together with its assumptions and the various possibilities for resolving it.[111] But he was never willing to supplement his "logic of discovery" with a "psychology [or sociology] of research."[112]

What then is this mediating position advanced by Lakatos?[113] As Lakatos formulates it, "The main difference from Popper's original version [of falsificationism] is, I think, that in my conception criticism does not—and must not—kill as fast as Popper imagined" (92). Where Popper posited a succession of bold theories and their dramatic overthrows, Lakatos proposes a methodology of scientific *research programs.* A research program consists of a *negative heuristic,* that is, a "hard core" of beliefs that are either unconscious, assumed without question, or treated by its proponents as if they were irrefutable. It also contains a *positive heuristic* or long-term research policy. The negative heuristic may not be falsifiable, but the positive heuristic will in the course of research inevitably give rise to a "protective belt" of auxiliary hypotheses (e.g., scientific models and answers to possible refutations) which are falsifiable.[114] As a given part of the protective belt is challenged, the positive heuristic will suggest ever more complex models to deal with the "ocean of anomalies" (50), and to (try to) "turn them victoriously into examples" of the research program (111).

In his model Lakatos has been able to incorporate the advances gained by the contextualist shift without giving up completely the formalist program. Many of the terms of Popper's and Hempel's work recur, but always with a Kuhnian weighting. Hence there can be "crucial counter-evidence"; but it is recognized "only with hindsight." There is falsification; but it is dependent on the emergence of better theories that anticipate new facts (34–36). And there is an objective test of theories, though it lies in the fit or coherence of an interpretive theory about putative facts with an explanatory theory or tentative explanation: "It is not that we propose a theory and Nature may shout NO; rather, we propose a maze of theories, and Nature may shout INCONSISTENT" (45). He later put it: "Nature may shout *no*, but human ingenuity . . . may always be able to shout louder" (111).

Lakatos has correctly located explanations inescapably within the grip of research programs; only in this context can they be meaningfully formulated, analyzed, and evaluated. Nevertheless, programs of research can over a long period of time prove fruitful or unfruitful, giving rise to Lakatos's distinction between "progressive" and "degenerating problemshifts." In the former, "each new theory has some excess empirical content over its predecessor, that is, . . . it predicts some novel, hitherto unexpected fact" that is in turn corroborated (33). For degenerating problem shifts, Lakatos thinks paradigmatically of global theories like Marxism.[115] Here is a theory that, he feels, has continually used its hard core to revise its protective belt as new conflicts with its predictions occurred, yet without ever predicting any facts that were later discovered to be true (87–89).

Lakatos and the Rational Assessment of Explanations

Rational Assessment in Science

As with the contextualists Toulmin, Hanson, and Kuhn, we have not been able to abstract from Lakatos's compromise any theory of explanation that is independent of the question of the rationality or irrationality of science. Time and time again, we have found our quest for such a theory being channeled back toward the rationality debate. At best we have been able to salvage the role of formal criteria as providing a sort of general explanatory ideal, as representing an idealized or limiting case in which one has abstracted from all pragmatic and contextual factors. If the contextualists are right, there is little point in continuing further with formal analyses of explanation. In fact, we will be doing well to preserve a few broad intersubjective (transparadigmatic) standards, a few shared epistemic values accepted by most of the scientific community. Behind the contextualists' skepticism one can hear the voice of the later Wittgenstein: "Don't ask what explanation *is* in and of itself; ask how explanations are *used* by the scientific community."

The voice should be heeded. In the end we can derive a complete picture of scientific explanation only by including a look at how explanations are conceived (the psychology of discovery), how they are institutionally influenced (the sociology of research), and how they are evaluated by the scientific community. In this book I concentrate primarily on the third of these tasks, the question of rational assessment in science, using a modified form of Lakatos's proposal as a red thread. The question to bring to Lakatos's position must be formulated in terms of the definition of and requirements for intersubjective explanation sketched in chapter 1. If we find the scientific process to be irrational by its own lights, talk of intersubjective evaluation to be a mere chimera, we will hardly expect to discover *more* "objectivity" in the religious arena.[116] However, should we be able to make sense of intersubjective assessment of theories or explanations in science, perhaps the process, suitably adapted, could serve as a model for intersubjective evaluation of explanatory claims in religion.

For Lakatos a theory is "born refuted" and never overcomes all the objections to it. But as long as progressive problemshifts in the protective belt can be made "in the spirit of the heuristic," one is rationally justified in continuing to pursue a given research program and in holding to its explanations as rationally justified.[117] If decisions cannot actually be made between progressive and degenerating problemshifts, then Lakatos, who has already conceded much ground to contextualist philosophers of science, will find his position reducing to the incommensurability doctrine of Kuhn and Feyerabend. And if rational choice between research programs is impossible, rational assessment of explanations is equally so.

A number of counterexamples to Lakatos's definition of a progressive problemshift have been produced, leading Lakatos to modify his understanding of them. For instance, Zahar's articles on Einstein's research program (cited above) convinced Lakatos to loosen the requirements for "novel facts." In one of his last articles, Lakatos granted that a novel fact is *any* fact explained by a theory but not originally intended by that theory (1:185). Hence, we can speak of the empirical progress of a research program in the sense that it explains facts previously outside its purview, as well as with regard to its new predictions.

The most serious challenge to Lakatos, however, has come from his friend Paul Feyerabend. In a series of articles,[118] and in the book *Against*

Method to which Lakatos was to have written a response, Feyerabend has portrayed Lakatos as an irrationalist at heart. Feyerabend's Lakatos occasionally let slip that he was an irrationalist, or at least embraced epistemological anarchism at crucial junctures in his methodology, or, at the very least, could be convinced that his notion of research programs was in effect anarchistic whether he wished it to be or not. Thus Feyerabend writes, "Scientific method, as softened up by Lakatos, is but an ornament which makes us forget that a position of 'anything goes' has in fact been adopted."[119] At any rate, this Lakatos would stand much closer to Mill's "openness" than to Popper's restrictive approach.[120]

It is hard to know how Lakatos would have responded to Feyerabend's anarchistic urgings had he lived to read them. Though the question is unresolvable, I suspect he would have resisted them firmly, as he did until his death in February 1974. His major articles were inevitably concerned with defending and enabling talk of scientific progress, and he explicitly denied the carte blanche interpretation of his theory.[121] More important is the question, In advocating a rationality based on scientific research programs, is one *forced* into epistemological anarchy? I see no reason to concur with Feyerabend here. The theory of research programs may allow significant latitude, for it neither demands of scientific theories a certain formal standard, nor legislates for scientists when to accept or reject a theory as falsificationism does. However, it remains a normative theory, setting standards and demanding "that some of the scientists' 'basic value judgments' can and should be overthrown, especially when a tradition degenerates or a new bad tradition is founded" (180).

Lakatos's theory is incorrectly read as a set of prescriptions for daily scientific activity, for the same reasons that we found Popper's theory to be mistaken in focusing on this level. Lakatos's theory, rather, is a framework for viewing the long-term rationality of the scientific enterprise. As a framework, it can be "filled in" for a number of disciplines.[122] The theory does ascribe a major role to contextual and instrumentalist elements within science. Nonetheless, critics such as Feyerabend have not yet shown that an ounce of contextualism is equivalent to a pound of epistemological anarchism. Criticism may not "kill as fast as Popper imagined," and it does not function in isolation from the subjectivity of the individual scientist or scientific community; nonetheless, it continues to exercise some control over this subjectivity. At least in natural science, the goal of intersubjectivity (in the sense of pansubjectivity) is not an entirely vacuous one.

Lakatos's work has provided an important new orientation for the methodology debate in science. Rather than searching for criteria to demarcate science from nonscience, as Popper had, he stressed instead the question of "the appraisal of those theories which lay claim to 'scientific' status," which is "the primary problem of the philosophy of science" (2:224–25). We have seen that Popper's model was too restrictive to serve as a methodological guideline, since it laid strictures on every rationally held theory in science. As a result, it ran into direct conflict with science as practiced, consigning much of what scientists normally do to the twin hells of ad hoc hypotheses and immunization strategies. In a 1981 study, for instance, a group of scientists were interviewed about Popper's requirements; their responses underscore the conflict between Popperian theory and scientific practice.[123] In general, the scientists interviewed held that Popper's requirements for theories and practice were inapplicable in their work, and that he assumed objective appraisal of what were in fact "matter[s] of personal judgment."

Conversely, conventionalist approaches do not forbid *any* behavior and allow no (nonrelative) distinction between good and bad science. Though I am aware of no empirical study of scientists' reactions to conventionalism, my initial attempts to teach Feyerabend to physicists and chemists suggest that they will generally reject this alternative as equally foreign to their practice. As Lakatos notes, "Conventionalist historiography cannot offer a *rational* explanation of why certain facts were selected in the first instance or of why certain particular pigeonhole systems were tried rather than others at a stage when their relative merits were yet unclear" (1:107). That is, to the extent that science is normed behavior and there is some continuity in the norms (ideals, criteria for adequacy) over time, a purely conventionalist interpretation must be descriptively inadequate.

Interpreted along the lines here suggested, then, Lakatos's schema provides several important building blocks for a theory of the rational assessment of explanations in the natural sciences—and perhaps in other disciplines as well. According to this view, explanations are integrally tied into a broader context or ongoing research program. Such programs of organized inquiry are evaluated only over a long period of time; not freedom from falsification, but fruitfulness in leading to intellectual progress determines their epistemic merit. Progress thereby becomes a multifaceted notion, encompassing empirical, theoretical, and heuristic elements. Not only accounting for—making sense of—corroborated *facts*, past and future, but also establishing *theoretical connections* marks a successful research program. The third element, heuristic progress, refers to the increasing scope of the basic agenda or hard core of a research program. I suggest that heuristic progress be interpreted as a measure of the program's coherence, indicating the manner in which the protective belt of working hypotheses actually stems from or instantiates the basic tenets of the research program.

Even so, heuristic or coherential progress is only one of the means of assessing empirical research programs, since the world still provides them with an (at least partially accessible) standard, namely, empirical fruitfulness (and, correlatively in most cases, theoretical adequacy).[124] Since this sort of empirical testability diminishes as one moves through the social sciences toward philosophy and theology, these disciplines are forced to rely ever more heavily on the coherence or incoherence of a program of study.

Are Theories of Rationality Rational?

One important issue remains to be discussed before moving on to the social sciences: can positions about the methodology or rationality of science *themselves* be criticized, and if so, by what standards? If competing methodologies cannot be evaluated relative to one another, there is not much hope of progress in this field; one must then ask whether the whole discussion of theories of rationality is itself rational at all. Conversely, if we can elucidate a way of evaluating the various theories about scientific rationality, it may suggest a direction for work on a theory of rationality that is not limited to scientific contexts. Again here, Lakatos has contributed a helpful framework for approaching the question, oriented around reconstructions of the history of science.[125] Without reviewing more than the merest sketch of his position (and that in my terms rather than his), we should pause to note the significance of his theory for the present discussion.

Let us distinguish three levels of discourse, labeling them L_1, L_2, and L_3. At a first level (L_1) one finds scientists employing various methods in doing science. This is the actual practice of science as it has varied through history. Proposals concerning the correct methodology of science, and reconstructions of what constitutes the history of genuine science, occur on a separate level (L_2), which we might call the historiography of science. One here takes the historical facts and makes a normative judgment as to which activities are rational. In doing so, one splits L_1 into an internal history—science in its normative or honorific sense—and merely external history, to be explained by social psychologists, Marxists, and so forth.

Of course, one of the ways that proposals in L_2 can be evaluated is to see how much of L_1 they are forced to label external: obviously, an L_2 theory that could explain virtually none of the accepted history of science would not win many adherents. But Lakatos has proposed an additional method. If L_2 represents a methodology (or "normative historiography") of science, let L_3 stand for a *metamethodology*, a theory of the historiography of science. Lakatos then suggests that "all methodologies [can] function as historiographical (or meta-historical) theories (or research programmes) and can be criticized [on a level L_3] by criticizing the rational historical reconstructions to which they lead" (1:122).

To carry out this proposal, Lakatos reconstrues four major L_2 options—inductivism, conventionalism, naive falsificationism, and his own methodology of scientific research programs—as theories *about* theories of science (i.e., as level L_3 theories). He assumes correctly that we can find instances of actual scientific practice that conflict with each major theory of science. Taking the L_2 proposals as theories, then, and the history of science as the data they are trying to explain, he asks what L_3 account can best explain the difficulties that these theories of science all face. The test, in other words, is self-referential: how well can each methodology do in explaining its own shortcomings?[126]

What is the result? Lakatos concludes that we could not derive an inductivist theory of science inductively from the actual behavior of scientists. Nor can a conventionalist metamethodology account for the discrepancies between scientific practice and conventionalist construals of science. According to the falsificationist standard, now applied on L_3, each (L_2) theory of science is falsified—including falsificationism itself! By contrast, theories of science *can* be constructively criticized and compared (on L_3) using a research program approach. A given theory of science may be more or less fruitful in guiding our inquiry into the history of science, in giving rise to new hypotheses about science, and so on. It is therefore to be preferred over its rivals as a theory about science.

I will not review the difficulties that do arise in Lakatos's argument; it is possible, for instance, that a weaker form of inductivism could work reasonably well on L_3. However, his strategy *is* effective for demonstrating the difficulties with, but also the possibility of, attempting to present the outlines of a general theory of rationality. The dangers of circularity in any such attempt have long been recognized: how can one argue for a theory of argumentation without begging the question? For Lakatos, the problem emerged as the conflict between our rational reconstructions of science and the history of science itself.[127] But we might generalize his conflict, and his solution, to the broader question of theories about the rationality of academic disciplines.[128]

The various academic disciplines are attempts to analyze some body of data rationally. They might be either (L_1) bodies of inquiry that are directly about the world (L_0?), or (L_2) disciplines such as the sociology of science that are about other (L_1) disciplines. In either case, theories of rationality, like Lakatos's metamethodologies, clearly belong in L_3; their task is "to try to organize basic [epistemic] value judgments in universal, coherent frameworks" (1:132). Note that if such frameworks fall squarely within philosophy, they cannot be encompassed within any higher level of abstraction: to talk about philosophy is still to do philosophy. No separate perspective exists from which to criticize theories of rationality. Can Lakatos's strategy for evaluating methodologies of science be modified to do justice to this difficulty?

Once again, we might use the terms *internal* and *external* to refer to the verdict passed by a theory of rationality: if it finds most choices made within a discipline to be in conformity with its pronouncements about rationality, then most of that discipline's practice is internal to it. If a theory of rationality must label decisions between theories in a discipline as irrational, they are external to it. As we saw, a falsificationist theory of rationality must write off most scientific decision making as external or irrationally chosen; only those decisions made on the basis of conclusive falsifications qualify as internal or rational. But conventionalist theories of rationality are equally in trouble. For only decisions made on subjective or purely conventional grounds are actually internal to this account; ironically, all instances that are better accounted for in terms of rational persuasion and reason-giving are external to it and remain unexplained by it. I will not pause to debate inductivist theories of rationality; they do better than falsification and conventionalism, although the strategy of inductive justification faces serious problems of its own. But certainly the research program theory of rationality, as I have reconstructed it—the emphasis on problem situations, tentative hypotheses, and pervasive criticizability—allows us to judge the procedures used in most academic disciplines as rational. There are thus good grounds for viewing it as the best available guideline for a general theory of rationality for the explanatory disciplines.

Of course, if Lakatos's approach is to be employed for addressing the problems of rational explanation, it must be freed from any intrinsic dependence on the context of natural science. Much can stay. We can still talk of a belt of auxiliary theories surrounding the hard core of a position. [129] Empirical progress is clearly inapplicable outside of empirical contexts; nonetheless, we will be able to adapt the notions of theoretical and heuristic progress (as defined above) in the following chapters. Admittedly, the concept of a research program carried a heavily natural scientific connotation in Lakatos's actual work as an historian of science. Basically, in Lakatos's usage *research program* meant the program and interests which a group of scientists brought to their study of the empirical world. As we analyze disciplines further removed from the empirical world, problem situations will tend to replace research programs—or better, research programs will gradually be modified to fit the requirements of nonempirical disciplines.

What will not change is the context-relatedness of explanations. We have examined the formal structure of explanation as analyzed by philosophers of science from Popper to Salmon. Though the formalist approach has been heavily criticized, it remains relevant as an ideal standard for the structure of explanations, at least in most of the natural sciences. Nevertheless, as we have seen, explanations ultimately have to be analyzed together with the particular discipline to which they belong and the problem situation they address. General commonalities in the process of rational evaluation are won not by disregarding the uniqueness of the various disciplines but by discovering features and standards that they in fact share as explanatory endeavors.

CHAPTER THREE

Explanation with Understanding
The Problem of Rationality
in the Social Sciences

We have explored the tensions between the formal structure of explanation
and the contextual factors that influence the actual formulation and evaluation of explanations in the natural scientific disciplines. There the link
between the rationality and explanation questions could be relatively direct, since few thinkers dispute that a central goal of natural scientific
theories is to explain the empirical world. The situation is different in the
social sciences. Here a long and learned tradition has downplayed the
significance of explanation in this field, either because of its inappropriateness to the value-laden character of human existence, or its inability to
grasp the inner reality of meaning questions (Dilthey), or because of its
exclusively nomological nature (Windelband). Many have argued that the
study of human society should be aimed instead at overcoming cultural
barriers, or increasing our self-understanding, or at "changing the world"
(Marx)—not at some abstract, objectivizing goal such as explanation.

Consequently, our task here is twofold. We must not only specify the
nature of explanation in the social sciences but also defend these disciplines
as primarily explanatory disciplines. Among the goals other than explanation that have been advocated, none has a longer history or better credentials than *Verstehen* or empathetic understanding. We *explain* why the
tides rise and fall but, it is argued, we must try in the first place to *understand* the behaviors of an individual, a social group, or a society. The major
positions in this debate fall roughly along a spectrum: some essentially
reduce explanation to understanding; others preserve a role for explanation

but subordinate the explanatory goal to the quest for understanding; and some dismiss understanding completely, treating social theories in effect as identical with natural scientific explanations.

I attempt an account of social science that does not paint explanation and understanding as incompatibles, such that social inquiry is reduced to one of the two alone. Admittedly, some writers today see no need to mediate between the two, being satisfied instead with positions that interpret the so-called sciences of man without one or the other element. I doubt that one can establish that social science must seek a synthesis that encompasses both description or understanding and explanation. Thinkers are free to define the term *social science* in their own preferred sense (though they may run the risk of equivocating on the term *science*). However, I believe that it *is* possible to formulate a strong response to those theorists who dispense with any role whatsoever for explanation in the social sciences in favor of pure understanding or description. We can make the counterargument successfully only if we address the explanation/understanding issue with an eye to the more general question of the rationality of the social sciences; conversely, the rationality question cannot be resolved without passing through the muddy waters of the explanation/understanding debate. Hence the treatment here will acknowledge and utilize the interdependence of the explanation and rationality questions and will move frequently from the one level of discussion to the other.

As a prelude to assessing the strengths and weaknesses of the major contemporary options, I survey the difficulties that formalists such as Hempel face in the social sciences, contrasting their attempts with approaches indigenous to the social sciences. I then present as a case study the recent work on social scientific rationality by Jürgen Habermas, whose position nicely highlights the complex of issues that a theory of explanation must face in this field. While his recent theory of communicative action draws attention to the complexity of the social world that we seek to explain, it does not ultimately give explanation the central role that it should have (and usually does have) in the social sciences. Specifically, Habermas's communicative concerns will need to be subordinated to criteria for evaluating the *theoretical* adequacy of social scientific explanations. In a final section, therefore, I explore the implications of the debates regarding understanding and hermeneutics for the broader question of social scientific rationality.

It is essential to differentiate the two semantic levels of our question. The social scientist attempts to make sense of and to explain her objects of study. But these objects are also agents who impose their own structures of meaning on their experience, creating and interpreting "meaninged" or semantic worlds (I will use the two terms as synonyms). Whereas in the natural sciences we discovered one framework of interpretation (the scientist's), here then are *two* levels on which projects of explanation are being carried out, those of the social actor *and* the social scientist.

Any exploration of the relationships between these two levels inevitably sets certain parameters for the treatment of religious explanations. On the one hand, religious believers are social agents; their religious project of constructing a coherent, meaningful world therefore evidences significant parallels with the semantic quest in other areas of human experience. Consequently, the discussion of human meaning construction below directly prepares the stage for the discussion of explanation and religious belief in chapter 5. On the other hand, many believers are also involved in the project of specifying the nature of and justification for religious explanations. Certainly western theology has been deeply concerned with these issues, often in direct confrontation with the sciences. As a result, some of the standards for explanatory disciplines may also be relevant to explanations advanced in the study of religion and theology. Of course, the significance of references in religion to transcendent beings and a dimension of experience not normally the focus of social science will have to be weighed. But before any such parallels can be drawn, the synthesis of formal and contextual factors defended above must be extended to cover the formalist-antipositivist debate, the communicative construal of social science, and the consideration of human meaning contexts.

Formalist and Antipositivist Approaches to Explanation

The Formalists' Proposal for Social Scientific Methodology

The formalists have worked in detail on problems and examples arising in the natural sciences.[1] Comparatively speaking, they have done very little with the social sciences; what one does find generally fails to incorporate distinctively social scientific issues and conclusions. It will be sufficient to examine briefly the attempts by Popper, Hempel, and Nagel to apply their theory of explanation as a model for social scientific methodology.

One should note that Popper never had much interest in the social sciences. In his intellectual autobiography he writes, "Yet the social sciences never had for me the same attraction as the theoretical natural sciences. In fact, the only theoretical social science which appealed to me was economics."[2] What one does find in Popper's social scientific work is a virtually unmodified application of his approach to natural science. For instance, his *Poverty of Historicism* is an attempt to refute historicism, which he takes to be a sort of blend of historical determinism, holism, and utopianism.[3] From *The Open Society and Its Enemies* we may assume

Popper still has Marxism in mind as the object of his attack. With questionable justification, he views Marxism as originally a scientific theory that claimed to predict the future course of history, concluding that it has now either been falsified or died the death of a thousand qualifications. The implied moral is the need to avoid all global theories of this type in social scientific theorizing.

In the *Poverty of Historicism* Popper's only constructive proposal for the methodology of social science appears under the rubric "piecemeal social engineering" and is somewhat incidental to the goal of the work as a whole. The task of the social engineer is "to design social institutions, and to reconstruct and run those already in existence" (64–65). The choice of ends is, of course, beyond technology. Viewing institutions "as machines rather than as organisms," the engineer will approach them from a functional or instrumental point of view, making "small adjustments and re-adjustments" (66) to improve their functioning. Only this sort of approach to social contexts is testable and hence scientific. By contrast, if a utopian social theory aims at the "transformation of man," its failure could always be blamed on the persons involved rather than on any weakness in the theory. "But without the possibility of tests, any claim that a 'scientific' method is being employed evaporates" (70).

According to Popper's much-discussed contribution to the debate with Theodor Adorno, one should proceed in the search for social scientific explanations using the same process of conjectures and refutations that he had developed for the natural sciences. Popper castigates as "totally mistaken" the belief "that objectivity is far more difficult to obtain in the social sciences . . . than in the natural sciences."[4] In Popper's favor it must be said that he explicitly eschews any naturalism or scientism that would force on the social sciences the same empirical and mathematical constraints used in most natural sciences. By defining social science as the set of problems and attempted solutions that occupy social scientists, he avoids precisely that reduction of social science to a quasi-physical discipline that typifies, for example, the more extreme methodologists of behavioral psychology. And by insisting that the objectivity of scientific method in no way presupposes the pure objectivity of the scientist, he counters a criticism that has unnecessarily separated the sciences of nature and of humankind.[5]

Popper, however, has not modified his insistence on a single, formal account of scientific method.[6] He assumes without question the possibility of a separation between "the interests that do not belong to the search for truth" and "the purely scientific interest in truth."[7] All science, he insists, operates with deductive systems and a single type of explanation: "A completely explicit explanation always consists of the logical deduction (or deducibility) of the explicandum from the theory, together with the initial

conditions" (117). Popper consequently speaks of a "purely objective method" in social science, a "situational logic" that uses "objective Verstehen" to
show that given actions are or are not situationally appropriate (120–22).
Ackermann's gloss nicely captures the implications of Popper's position:

> One major theme in Popperian social theory is that the methodologi-
> cal account provided by his philosophy of science should apply *with-
> out alteration* to the theories of the social sciences. . . . Popper re-
> fuses to see *any distinction* in the relative unpredictability involved in
> the social sciences. . . . Any need to posit a separate methodology for
> the social sciences can be circumvented, in Popper's view, by devel-
> oping a correct nonpositivistic and indeterministic methodology for
> the physical sciences.[8]

Here we have the most controversial claim of the deductive-nomological
model of explanation regarding the social sciences. Can it actually provide a
single, purely objective method that is able to bring methodological unity
to natural and social sciences alike? Or will this claim prove to be untenable
in light of the radically different "objects" dealt with in the fields of human
study?

We have already examined Hempel's views on natural scientific explanation, noting his insistence that explanation in the social sciences proceed
in the same manner. Hempel mentions a number of alternative models of
explanation (though usually without recounting the causes that impel social
scientists to advance them), trying to show in each case that they are mere
variants of his own "covering-law model" of explanation. For instance,
"genetic explanation" explains phenomena by describing the successive
stages of the sequence of events which led to their occurrence. But, whether or not historians are consciously aware of it, such explanations must
assume some "general principles" that make the occurrence of any given
step "at least reasonably probable" given the preceding step.[9] Hempel
admits that historiography requires a large amount of straight description
of historical facts and stages of development; yet one must assume that
certain sub-laws are in effect at each stage of the event if genetic explanation is to qualify as explanation at all.

According to a second influential model, "explanation-by-concept,"[10]
historians explain historical events by categorizing them, for example, "it
was a social revolution." Yet, as Hempel rightly notes, not every category is
applicable, but only those in which "the particular cases fit into, or conform
to, some general pattern that is characteristic" of them.[11] Though even
Hempel grants that adequate historical explanations are so specific that
they can be called nomological only in a rather empty sense, he still maintains that they are in every case composed of a number of specific (proba-

bilistic) laws that are actually of greater generality. Finally, Hempel argues, explanation of human behavior in terms of dispositions is exactly parallel to the (lawlike) dispositions of objects to react in a certain way, for instance for windows to break when struck with a sharp object (457–63).

Even explanations of human behavior in terms of complex psychological reasons, often held to necessitate a distinctively psychological mode of explanation, become grist for Hempel's covering-law mill. Here the variables are the multitude of (subjectively perceived and differentiated) situations and the variety of possible responses by the agent. After an excursus into the theory of means-ends rationality, Hempel advances his formal model for all such explanations (471):

> A was in a situation of type C
> A was a rational agent
> In a situation of type C, any rational agent will do x
>
> ---
>
> Therefore, A did x

Placed into this "descriptive-psychological" form,[12] explanation by reasons becomes for Hempel a subset of dispositional explanations, which he has already shown to be compatible with the covering-law model. Any objectives and beliefs that social scientists might wish to ascribe to an agent are allowable (testable, meaningful?) only when expressed in terms of that agent's disposition to behave in a certain way, which we can in turn ascertain only from her actual behavior (as opposed, e.g., to her attitudes and intentions).

In general, Hempel treats social scientific explanation on the basis of the model of a consciously rational agent. He is thereby able to avoid becoming enmeshed in considerations of individual motivations and perceptions of the world, as well as the sorts of cultural factors that would require the social scientist to introduce methods not utilized in the natural sciences. Instead, only behavioral manifestations are significant for these explanations. Unfortunately, as Hempel realizes, his stipulations on the model entail that it is only applicable "where the decision problem the agent seeks to solve is clearly structured and permits of a relatively simple solution, where the agent is sufficiently intelligent to find the solution, and where circumstances permit careful deliberation free from disturbing influences" (482). But such requirements are better suited to an examination-hall setting than to most actual social situations. Their inadequacy in the face of actual human dispositions and (nonnomological) intentions lends prima facie credibility to the demands of the antipositivists for a radically different approach to social scientific rationality than that proposed by the covering-law theorists.

Of the thinkers I have called formalists, Ernst Nagel has shown the greatest understanding of the methodological peculiarities of the social sciences. Many of the problems covered in his *Structure of Science*[13] are drawn directly from the philosophy of social science and will be treated below. He is aware from the outset of the diversity within the social sciences and of their dissimilarities to the natural sciences: "Even a cursory inspection of generalizations and explanations in the social sciences reveals many differences between the formal characteristics as well as between the substantive content of the various concepts employed by these disciplines" (535). Nagel even considers the claims of interpretive sociologists (Weber, Winch) that social scientific explanation must involve reference both to individual subjective states not intersubjectively accessible and to value orientations beyond the scope of the allegedly objective natural sciences. His greater familiarily with the *Verstehen* tradition allows him to bring the tensions between the two schools of thought into somewhat clearer focus.

On the other hand, his fuller awareness of methodological difficulties notwithstanding, Nagel in the end shares Popper's and Hempel's confidence in the adequacy of nomological explanation for the social sciences. None of the allegedly distinctive features of this field, he believes, need refute the claim that we can establish for it "general laws which can serve as instruments for systematic explanation and dependable prediction" (450). Controlled experiments may be difficult or impossible, but this is also the case in astronomy or astrophysics; moreover, at least "controlled empirical inquiry" remains possible (453). There may be great variety between cultures; nonetheless, he posits invariant "relational structures" of which the different cultures are specializations (462). However the human object of study differs from the natural, he argues (475–502), it need not invalidate a liberal behaviorism (477). The social scientist can explain the varieties of human behavior ranging from fear reactions to the Protestant work ethic within the parameters of the nomological approach, without employing any unique methods or a formally different model of explanation.

Without delving further into the details of formalist proposals for social scientific methodology, let us turn to the *Verstehen* theorists, the defenders of a radically different understanding of social science. Does their characterization of the social sphere provide sufficient reason for rejecting the formalists' unitary model of science? If the criticisms and concerns of the antipositivists, including Habermas's recent contributions, are insufficient to burst the methodological parameters of nomological social science as here outlined, we may treat explanation in the field according to a formalist methodology of social science laid out along Popperian or Nagelian lines. If, however, we discover in the *Verstehen* tradition valid necessary conditions for an adequate science of the human world, then the discussion of social scientific rationality, and thus also of explanation, will have to proceed beyond the parameters set by the advocates of a unitary methodology in science.

Dilthey and the Birth of the Human Sciences

We have covered the attacks on the formalist approach by philosophers of natural science such as Toulmin and Kuhn, whom I labeled contextualists. Although their criticisms are equally relevant here, let us now consider a school of criticism stemming from within the human sciences themselves.[14] The thinkers in question challenge the belief in the methodological unity of science, arguing that the social or psychological world as an object of study requires a distinct set of methods for its comprehension. To this school the most insidious foes are *positivists*, or those who seek to foist the reign of natural scientific methods onto the territory of the human sciences. I thus refer to them collectively as the *antipositivists*.[15]

By choosing separate labels for the disputants in this debate (formalists versus antipositivists rather than, say, positivists versus antipositivists), I intend to imply that separate issues and complexes of concerns motivate the combatants. The proposal of a general methodology of social science does not stand in direct contradiction to the hermeneutical concern with meaning and multiple knowledge interests. Hence there is hope that the attempt to mediate between the two is not purely quixotic. However, the work of some general theorists is more opposed to the project of interpretation than that of others. Any mediating position must allow for general standards of social scientific explanation while at the same time fostering the study of contexts of meaning. This makes the position that we are seeking *formalist* in the sense of advocating general standards, though not (as with the formalists in the natural sciences) by requiring a single formal model as the necessary and sufficient condition for a theory of explanation. I therefore designate the goal toward which we are progressing a *formal-semantic* theory of social scientific explanation and will argue that Lakatos's methodology of research programs holds particular potential for this task.

Among the antipositivists, Wilhelm Dilthey has had perhaps the most profound influence on the subsequent discussion. Several of his insights are particularly significant for the contemporary discussion of theories of meaning and social scientific rationality. Since his work has been underappreciated in the American discussion, and insofar as it forms an (often unfootnoted) backdrop for much of the remainder of this book, I treat it in some detail here.

As a thinker who reacted to the radical exclusiveness of Comtean positivism with an equally radical formulation of the uniqueness of the human sciences (*Geisteswissenschaften*), Dilthey serves as an informative ideal type of subsequent, understanding-based epistemologists. In "The Demarcation of the Human Sciences,"[16] he maintains that the sciences outside the natural sciences have in common a reference to humans, to their relations with one another and with external nature. They thereby share a common foundation, all being "founded in human experiencing (*Erleben*), in the expressions (*Ausdrücken*) of experiences and in the understanding (*Verstehen*) of these experiences" (7:70–71). These central factors characterize the human sciences because of the special relationship "in which the unique, the singular, and the individual stand to general formal similarities (*Gleichförmigkeiten*) within this group [of sciences]" (7:71). It is important to note that Dilthey is not adverse to formal specifications of common features in the human sciences. Rather, he disputes that the general relationships that one does ascertain here can be viewed as lawlike in the natural scientific sense.

The methods of the natural sciences are limited to the empirical, to observation. To Dilthey they seemed "to garble the historical reality" (1:xvii), since they are limited to a "knowledge from outside" (5:169–70). Our experience, however, has its "original context . . . in the conditions of our consciousness, . . . in our nature as a whole" (1:xvii). Observation provides access to reality-as-it-appears, but we have a more direct route available: "We possess reality as it really is only through the facts of consciousness given in internal experience" (1:xviii). The central means to this knowledge is immediate experiencing (*Erleben*), or the "making internal (*Innenwerden*) of reality" (7:218).

The task of a theory of the human sciences, then, is to detail the unique features of epistemic processes in the psyche. Any adequate theory will have two parts, an internal and an external. One must always begin with internal "lived experiences" (*Erlebnisse*), the total, nonmediated reaction of the whole self to life-situations, complete with its cognitive, affective, and conative elements. This is the crucial starting point missed by the unity of science theorists. But the phenomenon of human life also involves the manifestation of these immediate reactions in "expressions" (*Ausdrücke* [7:217–18]) or life-expressions (*Lebensäusserungen*), a process whereby the inner and immediate becomes external and given to the senses. What is immediately present to us in experiencing "is, in the expression of this experiencing, as it were retrieved ['pulled out'] out of the depths of the psychical life" (7:328). Three general types of these life-expressions can be identified in Dilthey: mental facts (7:205), human acts (cf. 7:320), and "vital expressions" (*Erlebnisausdrücke*). Of the three, the theory of human acts influenced Max Weber, Alfred Schütz, and Jürgen Habermas, whose "rationality of action" (*Handlungsrationalität*) theories made human action the primary sociological category. Vital expressions, on the other hand, served as the inspiration for the psychologistic reading of human productions in terms of the life-experiences of the participants, as in the psychic and imaginative expressions on which Collingwood's theory of history concentrated. [17]

The study of the past (historiography) is for Dilthey an especially clear example of the uniqueness of the human sciences. Human history, as the expression of human spirit (*Geist*), consists of a vast number of life-expressions; historiography therefore requires a method appropriate to its content. As is well known, Dilthey proposed the method of *Verstehen*: the historian must reexperience (*nacherleben*) or reproduce (*nachbilden*) for herself these earlier expressions. Explanation (*Erklären*) alone is manifestly inferior and inadequate for the task: "We explain by means of purely intellectual processes, but we understand by the working together of all our mental powers in comprehension" (5:172). *Verstehen* is "a finding again of the I in the You" (7:191). More than logic, it involves a direct vision; it is not an inferential process, but has its own life and meaning in itself. Through *Verstehen*, through a "carrying over of the individual self" into the Other, we imaginatively reconstruct or relive the Other's experiences (5:277). Dilthey justifies this possibility of a "placing oneself inside" (*Sichhineinversetzen* [7:214]) through a tacitly metaphysical appeal to the principle of life shared by all humans. [18]

Dilthey's thought is divided roughly into an early and a later period, based on a shift in his thinking sometime after 1883. [19] I believe the two perspectives are complementary and both are useful: the early period defends the independence of the human sciences from natural scientific hegemony; the later, the inevitable transition from philosophy of social science to broader philosophical (or theological) questions. Because Dilthey's starting point had been the concept of psychic structure, psychology had at first provided the framework for interpreting the process of understanding. Later, as his thought focused more on the need for considering the *whole* of which psychological phenomena are a part ("trans-personal contexts" or the "totality of the psychic life"), he began to employ a metapsychological framework. Life as process and self-developing unity, and hermeneutics as the science of conceptualizing life's manifestations in history, became central instead. This preoccupation with the larger wholes of social life would later become the battle cry of thinkers like Adorno, Habermas, and Gadamer in opposition to the empirical social research of the formalists.

In the later Dilthey, then, the human sciences are characterized by their concern with the categories of *Sinn* (sense, meaning) and *Bedeutung*. *Be-*

deutung (significance, or "signification" [Hodges]), in contrast to Frege's frequent use of *Bedeutung* as reference, is "the category for the un-dissected life-context" (7:237). The term indicates a relation: "*Bedeutung* characterizes the relationship of the parts of life to the whole which is grounded in the essence of life" (7:233). The significance of a social phenomenon cannot be understood in isolation; it exists and is known only in a reciprocal relation with *Sinn*. Dilthey's famous example of this circle of hermeneutical understanding is the sentence: it is composed of words, of "indeterminately determined components," each of which contributes to the meaning of the whole while receiving its significance from the whole (7:220). The individual life must be understood in precisely the same manner, with each moment of life receiving its "significance through its connection (*Zusammenhang*) with the whole" (7:233). The same obtains also for humankind as a whole: "one would have first to await the end of history in order to possess the complete material for determining its significance" (7:233).

A surprising number of the more recent declarations of independence by social scientists stem from one of Dilthey's several arguments for the uniqueness of the human sciences.[20] For Dilthey the natural sciences deal with "abstract contexts," the human sciences with life's own categories, with the epistemological reciprocity that is internal to it (7:235–36). Of these two very different methodologies, only *Verstehen* can grasp the inner connection between part and whole. The science of *Verstehen*, hermeneutics, unlike the natural sciences, is able to view a text or an action within the context of an individual's life, a social world, or a moment in history. By contrast, the objectifying methods of the natural sciences neglect the social wholes upon which meaning depends and disregard the integral link of the inquirer with the object of inquiry, namely, that "the one who researches history is the same one who himself makes history" (7:278).

The Critique of Positivism

I will not pause here to criticize or apply each of these themes from Dilthey's work. Nonetheless, it is clear that this broad complex of concerns has fueled the social scientific critique of positivism in the last few decades. Stemming from the (not overly successful) debate between Theodor Adorno and Popper in 1961, a number of articles have lashed out at the sort of social science proposed by the formalist authors covered above.[21] By examining what the various authors understand the onerous term *positivism* to connote, what they dislike about it, one quickly discovers the special concerns and factors that typify the antipositivist philosophy of social science.

Adorno, for instance, insists upon the primacy of the object of inquiry over the method of inquiry: "Science should mean becoming conscious of the truth and untruth of that which the phenomenon under observation wants to be in and of itself."[22] Yet ironically, his resistance to any general scientific methodology hardens into an equally general ideal for science drawn from German idealism and phenomenology. "Methods do not [i.e., should not] depend on some methodological ideal," Adorno cautions correctly, "but rather on the thing itself" (130). One cannot help but wonder, however, how much help this emphasis on the self-revealing *Sache*, reminiscent of Husserlian phenomenology, will help in selecting research strategies and arbitrating disputes in social scientific work.

At any rate, positivistic sociology, with its "pluralism of ways of proceeding" and "diversity of methods," forgets that "society [the object of sociology] is one."[23] The formalists' proposal for social research is fragmented, occupied with trivial questions, unaware of the (usually untestable) essentials. By contrast, the object of social inquiry can only really be understood when viewed as a totality (in the Hegelian sense); it must consequently be grasped "from above" and by means of intuition. Hence only a methodology incorporating "the speculative moment" (134) can attain to the "postulation of insight into the essence of modern society" (83), something which Adorno maintains is beyond the reach of any empirical, positivistic methodology such as Popper's. But, I suggest, whatever the merits of speculative philosophy, its full-blown incorporation into social science in this manner is not the answer to the methodology dispute. We are much more likely to achieve theoretical progress and agreement if we begin "from below," with the actual practice of social science, and move *toward* the more speculative (e.g., Hegelian) construal of social science.

In a similar vein, the early Jürgen Habermas accuses positivism of the "replacement of epistemology by the philosophy of science," the key sign (and sufficient condition?) of which is that "the knowing subject no longer provides the system of reference."[24] Positivism is philosophical only long enough to immunize itself against philosophy (67). In so doing, it ignores the "synthetic accomplishments of the knowing subject" and the "problematic of the constitution of the world" and thereby makes itself irrational (68). Similarly, it presupposes the validity of logic and mathematics without reflecting on their foundation in the meaning of knowledge itself. Habermas consequently rejects a universal scientific method and the objectivism that its program implies.[25]

His contributions to the *Positivist Dispute* are hardly less acerbic. Habermas there accuses analytic philosophy of science of resulting in "adulteration" and "irrelevence" when applied to the "world that is the product of human activity" (157). He fires off a barrage of criticisms, castigating the positivists for an overly limited concept of experience, for leaning on a notion of system that they themselves cannot explicate, for forgetting that social research is part of the object that it is under investigation (i.e., society), and for inadequate awareness of the role of historical, dialectical, axiological, and praxis-oriented concepts in the human sciences (159–70). Any universal scientific methodology is "objectivistic" and ignores the fact that "meaning" is the "foundational concept" of sociology.[26]

Most of Habermas's criticisms can be subsumed under the rubric of the inappropriateness of method to object. Certainly his basic concern is justified: sociology does have to do with questions of meaning, with a "perceiving and judging subject."[27] The imposition of a natural scientific methodology, unmodified, on the human sphere *should* arouse our suspicion. Habermas thinks that the danger of neglecting the human dimension is great enough in general methodological discussions that we must simply treat the human sciences as sui generis. But to voice fears such as these is not the same as demonstrating an intrinsic incompatibility.

Adorno and Habermas are still usually considered social scientists, even if they wish to expand the discipline to include such topics as the interpretation of meaning, the critique of ideologies, and political philosophy. The problems burdening a discussion of methodology in the human sciences would become even more daunting, however, if we were to broaden our horizon to include the field of hermeneutics proper. Although I cannot do justice to that project in the present survey, it is necessary to mention the work of Hans-Georg Gadamer and Paul Ricoeur in passing, if only to note their particular opposition to the positivists.

Gadamer, for instance, accuses any allegedly "presuppositionless science" of blindness toward the traditions within which it actually functions, and of falsely dichotomizing between "history and knowledge."[28] He considers positivism—or the "naive methodologism" that is its outworking in the human sciences (463)—to represent an extreme position that lacks historical sensitivity and cannot attain to a knowledge of the individual (467). Still, it is by no means clear that every methodological inquiry will have to commit the egregious crimes of which Gadamer accuses the positivists.

Ultimately, Gadamer is dissatisfied with the abstracting ("present-at-hand") approach of *all* attempts at knowing, scientific or otherwise, and wishes to subordinate them to his Heideggerian hermeneutical perspective. Modern science's concept of method has "its limited justification" (466) for purposes of controlling the world, but is in the end merely a type of "knowledge for domination" (409). Gadamer accuses science of "existential relativity," since it can speak of entities only insofar as they are given in space and time as objects of experience (410). Science is guilty of an untenable objectivism, for in fact object and subject cannot be separated but "belong to the same historical movement" (479). Since the "historicity of Dasein" rules out any talk of eternal truths, a deeper sort of category is required than any science can provide. Under the influence of Heidegger and his demand that human existence be studied in a manner distinct from the Being of other beings, Gadamer turns away from any sort of concern with method and toward a hermeneutics in which the categories of historicity and Being are central.

Paul Ricoeur has likewise criticized the efforts of Popper and Hempel, albeit in somewhat closer dialogue with the philosophy of science. In "The Model of the Text: Meaningful Action Considered as a Text,"[29] he shows that if actions are considered as texts to be interpreted, Popper's method of "objective Verstehen" must reduce to a Hirschian hermeneutics.[30] According to Hirsch, the reader should employ historical-critical methods to reconstruct objectively what an author's originally intended meaning must have been. By contrast, Ricoeur denies that ascertaining what the actors meant by their actions is all we aim for in trying to understand them. And this is certainly right: although understanding intended meanings is part of interpretation of texts and actions (as Ricoeur admits elsewhere), it is not the whole story. Explanations in social science need not be tied to the self-understandings of the agents involved, though I take it as a desideratum that they account for them in some way.

Against Hempel, Ricoeur argues in "The Narrative Function" (274–96) that the nomological approach to historiography will necessarily exclude that "narrative specificity of history" that is central to the historical phenomena. Moreover, historical explanation performs a variety of different functions; these can only be grasped by one "who does not approach the historical text with a unique, monolithic model of explanation in mind" (276). One must distinguish between a physical event, which simply occurs, and historical events, which come to us in chronicles, legendary stories, and memories. Social reality is inherently ideological; it "always has a symbolic constitution and incorporates an interpretation, in images and representations, of the social bond itself" (231). Consequently, Ricoeur takes as his goal the achievement of a "strict complementarity and reciprocity" between explanation and interpretation or understanding.[31]

Ricoeur's thought serves as an important reminder that discussions of the nature of historical explanation cannot be settled apart from the broader debate about explanation in the human sciences. The question of explanation in historiography and its relation to the natural sciences has often been addressed without adequate reference to the general methodological discussion in the philosophy of social science.[32] By contrast, Ricoeur effectively treats the problem of historical understanding (as his book's title indicates) from the perspective of hermeneutics and the human sciences.

That it is now possible, even necessary, to include the problem of history within the philosophy of the human sciences reflects again, I believe, the contextualist shift in the philosophy of science. When the hermeneutical and contextual nature of all scientific inquiry is acknowledged, many of the characteristics formerly taken to be unique to historiography are seen as merely particular cases of general issues in interpreting human action. The problems of the individual and of shifting historical contexts merely re-capitulate in the temporal dimension the interpretive problems that social scientists face in the present. In fact, sociological theorists have dealt with both of these problems in discussing the relative weighting of longitudinal and latitudinal studies. The success of Ricoeur's subsumption of the histor-ical within the hermeneutical problematic, which I take to be one of the central theses of his book, justifies the methodologist in concentrating first on problems of social meaning and explanation, and then treating the issues surrounding historical explanation as outworkings of his general theory.

How can the formalists' proposals be reconciled with the sorts of crit-icisms raised by the antipositivists? In the philosophy of natural science we saw that the opposing positions of the formalists and contextualists could arguably be accommodated by a mediating position along the lines of Lakatos's theory of scientific rationality. However, to attempt a reconcilia-tion of the parties in *this* feud at this point in time would imply that there is significant agreement in the philosophy of social science, at least regarding the key issues and problems. But this is emphatically not the case. John Kekes speaks of "the prevailing confusion about rationality in the social sciences,"[33] and Anthony Giddens writes of the malaise or "state of disarray" characterizing the social sciences today that has resulted from the disin-tegration of the "orthodox consensus" of the postwar period.[34] Even the first steps toward a general theory of explanation and understanding in this field must therefore be made rather tenuously and with specific reference to the material characteristics of the social realm.

It should already be clear from my presentation of the main positions in this debate that I do not hold either the formalist or the antipositivist approach alone to be adequate. Dilthey's account represents significant insight into the process of comprehending human action; contra Nagel, I believe it does mandate the employment in the human sciences of methods not applicable in natural science. However, the formalists have provided a clear account of what a standard explanation would look like in an ideal (or "completed") social science; contra Adorno, I do not think that we neces-sarily corrupt the object to be explained in seeking general methodological principles to guide the explanatory project. Of course, it is all too easy to say that one aspires to a mediating position, much more difficult to advance a detailed, coherent proposal. If we grant that the object of social scientific research (viz., humans) requires modifications in natural scientific methodology, we must describe this object and detail the manner of inquiry appropriate to it. If we wish to maintain the indispensability of both explanation and understanding, we must specify their relationship much more precisely. To accomplish either of these tasks it will be necessary to paint a general picture of the distinctive rationality of social scientific thought. For only from that perspective can one make any but arbitrary pronouncements on the place of the explanatory effort in social theory.

In his more recent work, and above all in his 1981 *Theory of Communicative Action* (*TCA*), Jürgen Habermas has drawn closer to such a mediating position. Without discarding his earlier hermeneutic orientation and insistence on the uniqueness of the human object, Habermas now maintains the necessity of a general theory of rationality in the social sciences in an informed dialogue with philosophers of science of the analytic tradition. There is thus ample justification for a detailed analysis of Habermas's proposal, which is already being labeled a classic of social theory.[35] Though it is not possible to accept Habermas's proposal as a full answer to the problems of rationality in the human sciences, it can at least warn us of the difficulties that an adequate proposal must face in the contemporary discussion.

A Case Study in Social Scientific Rationality: The Communicative Rationality of Jürgen Habermas

Few social scientific thinkers have devoted as much attention and perhaps none as many pages to the question of rationality in their field. Though we can only scratch the surface of the virtually endless literature by and about Habermas, an exposition of his work on social scientific methodology will draw attention to many of the essential facets of the explanation question. Specifically, I wish to concentrate on the notion of "communicative rationality" in *TCA*[36] in order to highlight some of the desiderata for a theory of social scientific rationality. If Habermas is correct in subordinating theoretical requirements to the communicative process, my attempt to separate the levels of participant and theory becomes untenable. A detailed critique of Habermas's conception will therefore be required to set the stage for any further comments on explanation and understanding.

The Theory of Communicative Rationality

It is difficult, or at least arbitrary, to say which aspect of Habermas's thought provides *the* entrance into his theory of communicative rationality.

In the finished form of *TCA*, virtually *every* philosophical and sociological question serves as grist for the communicative mill. Nonetheless, I suggest as a first approximation that his opposition to positivism led Habermas first to turn to the pragmatics branch of linguistic philosophy and then to his theory of communicative rationality as a sociologically fruitful, pragmatic foundation for social theory.

In support of the contention that this *negative* motivation plays a fundamental role in Habermas's view, note the brief summary of twentieth-century philosophy which begins chapter 3 of *TCA*. Habermas develops his argument for the primacy of communication in the philosophy of language in three steps. First, the reaction against Carnap's semantics by Wittgenstein, Davidson, and Dummett led to the realization that "the meaning of sentences . . . cannot be separated from language's inherent relation to the validity of statements" (276; cf. 10). Habermas's second move criticizes a second abstraction: the theory of meaning cannot be developed apart from actual validity claims, and validity claims cannot be limited to assertoric sentences. Again, Wittgenstein plays the key role,[37] for it was his later philosophy which Austin and Searle developed into a full theory of "speech acts," in which the semantics of sentences "was no longer limited to the representational function of language but is open to an unbiased analysis of the multiplicity of illocutionary forces" (277). Still, a third limitation remained: Searle's approach dealt only with a truth-conditional semantics, so that his pragmatics could not account for the appellative and expressive functions of language. Only when Habermas generalized the concept of validity beyond the truth question within the framework of his universal pragmatics,[38] he alleges, could a theory of language broad enough to serve as the foundation for a general theory of communicative action be produced.

Habermas therefore takes communicative theory to be the only adequate basis for a philosophy of language, and he turns to the implications of his position. A suitably expanded theory of language, he realizes, implies an equally expanded theory of rationality. It turns out that each of the "limited" views of language dismissed in the preceding paragraph can be correlated with its own equally limited notion of rationality. The first abstract rationality mentioned was Carnap's formal inductive notion, or that of Popper's falsificationism; the second (that of Austin and Searle) identified the nonrational (performative) aspects of actual language use without sufficiently freeing itself from the earlier positivist concept of rationality, namely, one committed to the primacy of a truth-conditional semantics. Only Habermas's final move to a rationality of "redeemable validity claims" (*einlösbare Geltungsansprüche*) of *all* types, he feels, overcomes the limitations inherent in earlier theories of rationality. That is, he holds his

approach finally to counter the hegemony of the truth claim, supplementing it with the equally fundamental validity claims of *rightness* and
sincerity.

Habermas tells us that he is seeking a notion of rationality that is not
brought to sociology from the outside (*TCA*, xl), but one that does full
justice to the various claims humans actually make in their communication.
Indeed, he claims to merit the allegiance of social scientists precisely on the
basis of his reprioritizing of social theory in terms of human communication
rather than in the broader philosophical terms often found in the history of
social theory. Nonetheless, we must raise the further question: is his theory of rationality also sufficient for making sense of sociology as an explanatory science? Does the fact (if it is a fact) that his three types of validity
claims are equally basic in the context of human action imply that they will
also be so within the context of science?

The strength of Habermas's approach lies in the latitude in his theory for
examining discourse as actually used in all its forms. He appears to be the
descriptive linguist par excellence, a phenomenologist of language who is
not constrained by some strict theoretical structure as were earlier thinkers. This is perhaps most apparent in the early pages of the book (e.g., 10–
22), in which various language uses are catalogued. But the nonnormative
appearance does not last long, for Habermas, despite his love of broadly
inclusive taxonomies, quickly shaves down the five forms of argumentation
that he discovers to three basic types of action—teleological, normatively
regulated, and dramaturgical (76; cf. 84ff)—and the objective, social, and
subjective worlds to which they correspond (e.g., 309). Moreover, in defending the preferability of his notion of communicative action to any of the
other three options, he is forced to argue that the empirical phenomena can
be adequately conceptualized only as communication—that is, only in
terms of these three parameters and only when all three are used together.[39] Only then do we reach the "complexity of speech acts that *simultaneously* express a propositional content, the offer of an interpersonal
relationship, and the intention of the speaker" (96, emph. mine).

Habermas continuously paints his own position as the position of the
middle. This time-worn philosophical strategy portrays the writer as the
sane moderate among extremists; yet it also brings with it its own difficulties. Habermas's theory of rationality attempts to mediate in two different
(though obviously related) debates, each of which introduces a separate set
of problems. First, he wishes to avoid the exclusiveness of, say, Popper's
theory of rationality without falling into a purely conventionalist approach
such as that of Wolfgang Klein (26–31). Klein has completely dispensed
with any logic of argumentation in favor of a logic of acceptance, in which
validity and acceptability can no longer be distinguished. Against Klein,

Habermas wants to retain the notion of "objective validity," a validity "transcending spatio-temporal and social limitations" (31). Surely we must condone his goal: the notion of a social science implies that we at least strive for theories that are valid in a sense stronger than the fact that we happen to accept them now.

But can Habermas in the end successfully distinguish his own position from that of Klein's? Since he bases the normative weight of his proposal on communicative practice alone, rather than on any formal requirements for validity, he can ground the claim to objectivity only through the fulfillment of his ideal preconditions for communication. Yet it is not clear that such ideal preconditions themselves can be noncircularly derived. If they are based on the communicative practice that we happen to accept, they are fully as conventional as Klein's position. Yet if they have some other grounding (say, a transcendental argument for the necessary conditions of all communication *überhaupt*), it is not clear why the same strategy should not also provide certain formal requirements. Moreover, even if we could specify an ideal speech situation, its ideal character would presumably severely limit its usefulness for epistemic judgments.

Second, Habermas attempts to mediate between descriptive and transcendental theories of validity claims. Merely descriptive approaches are not able to grasp or make sense of the "rationally motivated binding force" (*Bindungskraft* [278]) of validity claims in the context of human action. However, Habermas strongly dissociates himself from the foundationalism of classical transcendental philosophy (xli). Eschewing both options, he wishes to argue from the existing forms of reason as they have been historically embodied (however imperfectly). To this end he ascribes a "quasi-transcendental" status to his rational reconstructions. For instance, in studying the historical development of western science and philosophy, we must seek "a formal analysis of meaning constellations that makes it possible to reconstruct the empirical succession of worldviews as a series of steps in learning that can be insightfully recapitulated from the perspective of a participant and can be submitted to intersubjective tests" (67). But it is difficult to see what the status of a quasi-empirical, quasi-transcendental rational reconstruction would be. Is it necessary or contingent? How would it be criticized? Habermas's actual approach does attempt to do justice both to the actual historical facts and to the necessary moment of abstraction. What is questionable is his attributing an experience-transcending status to his reconstructions or explanations that seems to immunize them from possible future refutation.

Habermas explicitly affirms that his quasi-transcendental method should in no way be confused with the positing of a hypothesis in empirical science, acknowledging that his approach is "unusual for an empirical sociologist" (220). Finally, I suggest, his rational reconstructions have a transcendental structure: they consist not of empirical generalizations but of necessary conditions for some area of phenomena. Moreover, they can involve a counterfactual element (220, 240) that could not be derived from empirical social research alone. One *assumes* that "modern structures of consciousness condense to the three complexes of rationality indicated," and then reconstructs the history of the West in such a manner that it allegedly leads necessarily to this (theoretically constructed) result. Habermas hopes that "this (rather risky) model" will allow him to speak of the "necessary conditions for a nonselective pattern of rationalization" (240).

Unfortunately, one year after the publication of the German original, the *Habermas: Critical Debates* volume was published with its hard-hitting criticisms of Habermas's earlier transcendental approach by, inter alia, McCarthy and Lukes.[40] The debate about the status of Habermas's theory of universal pragmatics raises a note of caution for theorists of social science in their reconstructions of scientific practice. If Habermas is making a transcendental claim about social science, it is hard to see how it could be falsified. If it is an empirical claim, then there is evidence that he is wrong, as in the studies of Asian cognitive development that Lukes cites. Much of Habermas's method of rational reconstructions, as well as his reading of the rationalization of modern society, can still be utilized. Yet his work is strengthened if we interpret his claims about scientific method not as quasi-transcendental but as empirical hypotheses in need of testing by further research and by their fit or coherence with other portions of social theory. This notion of empirically grounded rational reconstructions plays a central role in the concluding discussion of this chapter.

Speech Acts and the Primacy of Communication

Many aspects of Habermas's comprehensive project are worthy of further attention. Dieter Misgeld has focused his critical attention on Habermas's use of the life-world concept that, he argues, conflicts with the very possibility of objective argumentation that Habermas wishes to maintain.[41] Habermas's dependence on the hermeneutics of thinkers like Talcott Parsons, Giddens, and Gadamer on the one hand, and his reliance on thinkers of the Wittgensteinian tradition such as Peter Winch on the other, lends prima facie credence to this suggestion. However, let us turn instead to a second crucial dimension: Habermas's selection of speech act theory as the centerpiece of his theory of communicative rationality. In an earlier article, Habermas had tried to develop a consensus theory of truth that would enable him to treat truth, rightness, and sincerity as equiprimordial.[42] In *TCA* he no longer makes direct appeal to the consensus theory. Can the theory of speech acts in his recent work justify him in treating theoretical, regulative, and expressive contexts as equiprimordial in language as actually used? If so, does it follow that the three contexts should also be equally foundational for a theory of the rationality of social science itself?

Habermas's tripartite construal of rationality in the study of the social sphere is an important move beyond monothematic construals, for example, those focused exclusively on the objectively rational. Obviously, much actual social behavior lies outside the model of the ideal rational agent. Yet even irrational behavior, for instance, that associated with clinically defined psychoses like autism and schizophrenia, may evidence an inherent pattern or logic that the human sciences must analyze nonreductionistically. Habermas's theory provides the conceptual means for carrying out this sort of project.

Similarly, Habermas's three categories (theoretical, regulative, and expressive) could also serve as a useful basis for understanding religious behavior. Under the influence of Wittgenstein and Austin, students of religion since the 1950s have underscored the noncognitive uses of religious language, separating the illocutionary force of a sentence from its propositional content. We might even develop a sort of Habermasian analysis of religious sentences using the operators E, R, and T for his expressive, regulative, and theoretical contexts and p for propositional content. "I feel that it is wrong for Hindus to eat meat" could be represented "$E(R(p))$" and "It is right (blessed?) to believe in the one true God" as "$R(T(p))$."[43] The conscious application of Habermas's position in the study of religion would help to supplement theoretical with expressive and regulative analyses of religious language, without however eliminating the theoretical or propositional component completely.

In the study of both social and religious contexts, then, Habermas's suggestions assist social scientists in recognizing and overcoming constricted notions of rationality. Yet, whatever its usefulness in this respect, when we focus upon the *explanatory* goal of social scientific theories, a different evaluation is called for. In this case, I will argue, priority must be given to theoretical or *constative* rationality over Habermas's communicative rationality if the notion of explanation is not to be vacuous. I defend this thesis beginning with his treatment of speech acts.

Habermas's speech act theory draws directly from Austin in differentiating three components of speech acts: locutionary, illocutionary, and perlocutionary acts. *Locutionary* refers to the content of propositional sentences; in locutionary acts, which Habermas presents once and then strangely neglects, the speaker "expresses states of affairs; he says something" (*TCA*, 288). The ensuing discussion establishes that Austin, who "fixated on the model of institutionally bound speech acts" (295), did not adequately separate illocutionary and perlocutionary acts. Perlocutionary acts, in which the speaker produces an effect on the hearer, fall under the category of strategic interaction; illocutionary acts, in which the speaker "performs an action in saying something" (289), count as communicative action. Clearly, Habermas would judge any analysis of language or rationality that stressed locutionary acts (i.e., the assertoric function of language) to be hopelessly one-sided unless it placed equal emphasis on the illocution involved, namely on how the speaker performed an action in making the assertion.

For the German sociologist, the priority in any theory of rationality must finally go to the actual *process* of redeeming validity claims. By validity claim redemption he means to indicate that with every validity claim the speaker implicitly accepts the responsibility to substantiate or defend her claim through a process of social communication. In every case this process takes precedence over the product, that is, the actual content of the communication.[44] Of course, it is not the case that Habermas completely eliminates the propositional component in communicative action. Indeed, in rejecting congeniality as sufficient for communicative action, he insists that a communicatively achieved agreement must be "propositionally differentiated" (287). His thought thus preserves some place for propositional content alongside illocutionary force; elsewhere he speaks of the "standard case" as involving the validity of a sentence with propositional content (316).

Nonetheless, I suggest that Habermas does not acknowledge a certain priority that pertains to propositional content. For him, approaching the rationality question from the standpoint of communication theory as he does, the pragmatic elements in language (the pragmatic context and illocutionary force of a sentence) are prior to bare assertions of states of affairs taken by themselves. Habermas might agree that, from the point of view of a formal-semantic analysis of language—an analysis centering on contexts of meaning but including the study of general (nonpragmatic) features of assertions and arguments—propositional content would be prior. For he does admit that all communicative action must be propositionally differentiated, that is, must implicitly or explicitly imply some propositional content. But he continues to move immediately from the analysis of meaning pursued in semantics to a pragmatic analysis of the *use* of such propositions in communication. Hence Habermas's complaint about analytic philosophy: it "neglects those actor-world relations that are essential to social interaction" (274).

Surely Habermas is correct in attempting to expand upon purely abstract analyses of language. There could be no dispute with communicative theory as a *supplement* to theoretical or formal treatments of language, one that attends also to the rationality of regulative and expressive uses of language—if that were Habermas's intention. But communicative theory does not merely supplement theoretical approaches. Chapters 1 and 3 of *TCA* (arguably, the entire book), and Habermas's more recent book *The Philosophical Discourse of Modernity*, present his argument for the actual priority of communicative rationality.[45] He argues that all utterances— whether their content is theoretical, regulative, or expressive—are instances of language use (i.e., speech acts) and that therefore the rules governing linguistic usage must govern, determine, and explain them. Asserting that a given state of affairs obtains is only *one* of the many things we do when we utter an assertion; further, regulative and expressive utterances involve their own validity claims concerning what is the case, ones very different from the validity claims of assertions. Habermas believes that only an understanding of rationality based on communicative theory is able to do justice to these various distinct types of validity claims.

In order to grasp what is at stake, it is essential that we consider Habermas's treatment of assertions. His account of the assertoric element in language is especially relevant for a methodology of social science, since social scientific explanations are framed in terms of assertions rather than "I like" or "one should" statements. Habermas claims that the rationality of assertions reduces to the question of the validity of individual assertoric speech acts. As a result, he doubts "whether the concept of the validity of a sentence can be explicated independently of the concept of [pragmatically] redeeming the validity claim raised through the utterance of the sentence" (*TCA*, 316). Before we turn to criticism of this claim, note its resemblance to the "pragmatics of explanation" of van Fraassen and other contextualists in the philosophy of science. Indeed, it is surprising that the contextualists have not made greater use of Habermas' treatment, since it provides a much more systematic and detailed pragmatic theory than the vague accounts that philosophers of natural science have given.

I characterized the goal of this chapter above as the quest for a formal-semantic theory of social scientific explanation, where *formal* is understood without the nomological connotations of the natural scientific formalists. Habermas rejects any formal semantics, that is, any theory of meaning that is not ultimately pragmatic. In substantiating his negative judgment concerning formal criteria for scientific explanations, he makes appeal to the truth-conditional semantics of Michael Dummett. Dummett has denied that we should look for the truth conditions of sentences in anything but pragmatic terms: "It is not necessary that we should have any means of deciding the truth or falsity of the statement, only that we be capable of recognizing when its truth has been established."[46] Dummett's epistemological orientation necessitates replacing theoretical talk of truth conditions by familiarity with the "internal relations of a universe of language that can be explored only in and through argumentation," that is, through the practical knowledge of how actually to redeem a given truth claim (*TCA*, 318). It is interesting to note again the later Wittgenstein's influence: Dummett's skepticism concerning truth conditions is an outworking of the position that meaning can *only* be understood as the use to which we put particular statements.

At the outset of his discussion, Habermas had stipulated that "rationality" should refer to the "various forms of argumentation *as possibilities of continuing communicative action* with reflective means" (10, emph. mine). Though he there considered the move, popularized through the writings of the Popper school, of "basing the rationality of an expression on its being susceptible of criticism and grounding" (9), he rejected it as too abstract and narrow. The ensuing discussion of various forms of discourse and critique then led to the blanket definition: "Rationality is understood to be a disposition of speaking and acting subjects that is expressed in modes of behavior for which there are good reasons or grounds" (22). In many ways this is an excellent behavioral definition of rationality in the social realm: rationality is a dispositional trait predicated of human agents as actors. Moreover, Habermas's definition does allow for the appeal to reasons, albeit within the parameters of a theory of action. But does a dispositional account provide an adequate framework for handling human perceptions of meaning? That is, does it best capture what it is for human interaction to be meaningful, and hence understandable? Specifically, does Habermas's definition adequately encompass the rationality of that subset of human behavior that is the scientific, explanatory endeavor? Or must not the appeal to "good reasons or grounds" within the pragmatic context of communicative action be supplemented by a formal-semantic specification of what makes "good reasons" good if it is to account for the nature of rationality in social science?

Explanation and Social Scientific Rationality

Certainly human action involves a variety of categories of speech acts, each of which may be rational in a different manner. But is Habermas correct in urging the priority of the concept of communication for the *rationality of social scientific research*? I believe the communicative turn is revealed as inadequate when one attempts to specify what social scientific explanation actually is and in what sort of discourse it functions. In the context of explaining scientifically a set of behaviors, the regulative and expressive functions of language are necessarily subordinated. There is a switch of levels: one abstracts from a given context of action and attempts on a theoretical—though as we have seen not purely objective—level to formulate and defend valid statements about the subject matter in question.

In a discussion of the rationality operative on the explanatory level (that is, in a methodological discussion), theoretical rationality must consequently be granted priority over regulative and expressive rationalities. Using Habermas's terms, I would argue that constative rationality, which he discusses in *TCA* as a subcategory of communicative rationality without granting its full significance, typifies the second-order discourse of the social scientist. Although the social sciences have as their object human subjects in communicative contexts, social scientific rationality remains the rationality of theories. John Kekes has developed the distinction concisely in his methodological work:

> The primary question concerns the rationality of theories, for the rationality of persons depends on the rationality of their actions and beliefs, and the rationality of actions, in all but the most primitive situations, depends upon the rationality of the beliefs upon which they are based. But beliefs do not occur in isolation; they are part of a system.[47]

Unfortunately, Habermas fails to separate the levels; his thought lacks the transition from speech-act rationality (as validity-claim redeemability) to the rationality of theories. Of course, social scientific discourse is human discourse as well and can be analyzed as merely another instance of communicative interaction. Yet to do so is to neglect the very factor that characterizes it as an explanatory science. Social scientific explanations *refer* to the world of human interaction and attempt to formulate true and criticizable assertions about it.

The same point can be made with reference to the normative component in Habermas's earlier appeals to consensus and universal pragmatics. In his consensus theory, not just any de facto consensus is truth-indicative, but only a universal consensus that is based on the normative concept of an "ideal speech situation."[48] But Habermas has failed to give any formal specifications of the theoretical qualities implied by this ideal, offering only a communicative description (freedom from constraint, equal opportunity to participate, etc.). Universal pragmatics, based as it is on a not-yet-realized ideal speech situation, offers no criterion for the rationality of a given theory or proposal. Given the absence of ideal speech situations in the present, only some specification of the formal requirements or desiderata for social scientific explanations, above and beyond pragmatic preconditions for communicative discourse, can guide decision making and separate allowable from unallowable moves in argumentation. We need to know what constitutes the force of the better argument in terms of argument forms themselves, above and beyond the pragmatic description of the (counterfactual) ideal speech situation in which they are supposed to arise.

In fact, Habermas himself is not able consistently to hold the theoretical, regulative, and expressive contexts on the same level. There are hints of an implicit primacy of theoretical discourse within *TCA*, despite the disclaimers. In his section "'Rationality'—A Preliminary Specification," Habermas seems on closer inspection tacitly to derive his "cognitivistic" position regarding ethics from theoretical discourse. The fact that he begins with an analysis of the discourse of theories is not, I think, coincidental. At least three signs of the de facto primacy of theoretical discourse in social science can be discovered. First, in concluding his opening discussion of theoretical rationality, Habermas links it with the other types of rationality with the statement: "To sum up, we can say that actions regulated by norms, expressive self-presentations, and also evaluative expressions, *supplement* constative speech acts in constituting a communicative practice" (17, emphasis mine). Second, only after his detailed presentation of the preconditions of *theoretical* discourse can Habermas make his transition to the next type of rationality; and he does so with the assertion, "The situation is similar in the moral-practical sphere" (19). Finally, the criticism of truth claims provides the model: "the validity claims connected with norms of action, can, analogously to truth claims, be redeemed discursively" (ibid.).

Of course, Habermas would not wish to admit that the rationality of truth claims has any priority over that of therapeutic or self-expressive claims. But one receives the distinct impression in his presentation that he has developed the concept of communicative discourse from the constative model of truth-claim discussion, then generalized it into ethical and regulative contexts. How else is one to understand the stipulation that norms—whose validity claim is not truth but rightness—be discussed "under conditions that neutralize all motives except that of the cooperative pursuit of truth" (19)?

If I am correct in thinking that Habermas's analysis of other speech acts is derived from that of constative speech acts, then his claim for the priority of communicative rationality in social science is seriously weakened. Further, if constative rationality can be taken as foundational for the other types of discourse, especially in the analysis of second-order disciplines such as the social sciences, are we not justified in proceeding with an internal investigation of the *structure* of arguments and explanations in this field? For Habermas's defense of an exclusively pragmatic (as opposed to formal-semantic) analysis was based on the priority of communicative discourse, and we have found reason to question this priority both in principle and in the actual outworking of his system. One may therefore conclude that there is some place for a formal analysis of social scientific explanations in the philosophy of social science—if only to explicate the regulative ideals that guide theory formation in the discipline. Recall our conclusion that the ideals of the formalists in the natural sciences remain even after the contextualist shift. Against the unity-of-science school, we have found no reason to think that the *same* ideals will apply to social scientific explanations; but, contra Habermas, this is not adequate reason for concluding that therefore all consideration of formal requirements on theories is inappropriate.

It is now possible to draw together explicitly the lines of argument that have emerged in the discussion to this point.

The emphasis on pragmatics, on the *use* of signs or language for communication between subjects, is a necessary corrective to the exclusive concern with semantics and syntactics. The analysis that Habermas has presented of the knowledge process as the intersubjective redemption of validity claims draws attention to the importance of situational and pragmatic considerations in social scientific work. Of course, the stress on pragmatics does not stem from Habermas; the Marxist tradition and the Frankfurt School in social theory, and the work on pragmatics by thinkers like Austin and Morris in analytic philosophy, had already made their impact. Still, Habermas has been able to synthesize large segments of the earlier discussion into a more-or-less unified communicative theory.

By the same measure, Habermas is correct in highlighting multiple subregions of rationality. More is contained in a speech act than the mere assertion of a state of affairs. An analysis of communication and its rationality along Habermasian lines is an integral component of social scientific discussions of social phenomena. As I suggested, one could also analyse religious statements in terms of their theoretical, normative, and expressive components.

However, the communicative turn in social scientific theory is not the last word on the nature of social scientific explanation. In any second-order explanatory effort, theoretical discourse and constative rationality should be granted precedence. We must therefore supplement the description of how explanatory claims are discursively redeemed with an analysis of the standards regulating the evaluation of their content. The complete treatment of social science involves both external (pragmatic) and internal (formal-semantic) factors.

The same requirement arises as well with regard to the question of the *truth* of theories. Mary Hesse, in her 1982 article "Science and Objectivity," presents Habermas's view that scientific truth is not just instrumental, and she suggests that Habermas might defend the need for truth-claiming theories "on the grounds of technical efficiency." But even for this link of truth with theories, "it seems that we would need a closer relation between correspondence truth and the truth of theories than Habermas permits."[49] The point is that an adequate theoretical conception of rationality must consider the nature of the world (as the sum total of "that which is") as well as the nature of communicative action about the world.

It can even be argued that Habermas's communicative rationality, as an explication of social scientific rationality based on the (communicative) notion of an ideal speech situation, reduces of its own accord to a primarily theoretical (propositional, semantic) endeavor.[50] If an argument—which for Habermas has both propositional and speech-act components—is to be a good argument, it must occur in an ideal speech situation in which the interests, prejudices, and culture-boundedness of the participating subjects play no role. But one is then speaking of ideal subjects without making any references to "concrete (contingent) subjects and times of utterances of the sentences (personal pronouns and indexicals)." Puntel has labeled this "the disappearance theory of the communicative dimension," since all that plays a role in ideal communication—except for the somewhat vacuous assertion that *some* subject must assert the sentences—is the propositional content involved.

Finally, there is ample reason to question the realizability of Habermas's situational ideal. Indeed, it is more than a little ironic that David Frisby's criticism of Popper fits Habermas's conception as well: "It appears as if Popper has no more powerful corrective to ideology than intersubjectivity within organized science. . . . Scientific objectivity is made to rest upon the old liberal model of disinterested men assembled round a table to reach a consensus."[51] Perhaps Habermas's ideals represent a good ideal characterization of explanation in the theoretical realm when understood in the sense of Puntel's disappearance theory of communicative rationality. For precisely this reason, however, they leave us with the need to specify the parameters of social scientific explanation apart from reference to pragmatic discourse. I have defended the importance of a theoretical discourse, abstracted from the regulative and expressive components of the everyday social world, in which explanations about social actions and attitudes can be constructed and criticized. Here formal-semantic as well as pragmatic standards apply. It remains to specify more exactly how the content of these explanations is to be conceptualized, and what dependence, if any, they have on intuitive understanding.

Toward a Theory of Social Scientific Explanation

We have now advanced far enough in our discussion that we can begin to sketch out a theory of explanation in the social sciences. Given the guidelines that have emerged out of our treatment of the various positions, how might we specify the distinctive nature of social scientific explanation? How are explanation and understanding linked in this field? In what ways can the more general discussion of social scientific rationality contribute to resolving these questions?

It may be helpful to recap the framework so far developed. The subject matter of the social sciences is of course different from that of the natural sciences. But it is inaccurate to claim that one group of sciences is objective, the other subjective. Few today would deny the role of subjective factors in the formulation and evaluation of natural as well as social scientific explanations. Theoretical concerns have varied greatly over the course of science's history; what we observe reflects to some measure what we believe about an object or person; researchers are often passionately desirous of proving or disproving a particular hypothesis. This diversity of theoretical contexts and types of questions has brought the subjectivity of human interpreting and judging into the heart of the explanatory task.

It therefore seems clear that we must speak of *both* natural and social science as hermeneutical, in the sense that in each human researchers are seeking to *interpret* a given domain of phenomena in a way that will make it comprehensible. The scientific project is, in this crucial sense, a quest for understanding. Awareness of this fact has led in recent years to a general rejection of the older dichotomies between natural and human sciences. For Paul Feyerabend, for instance, there is no reason not to equate natural and social science, since both are anarchistic. Somewhat more cautiously, Mary Hesse has argued that the alleged discrepancies between the fields disappear one by one under the newer views of science. She concludes:

> My thesis is that there is not so much a parallelism as a linear continuity between the empirical and the hermeneutic. . . . *At each stage of the continuum*, appropriate interpretive conditions enter the process of theorizing—the formal and material regulative principles at all stages from physics onwards, then interpretations in terms of forms and deviances, stabilities and instabilities in biology, and finally evaluations incorporated in world views in the sciences of man and in history.[52]

Hesse's work, which makes extensive use of the thought of Jürgen Habermas, effectively demonstrates the continuities that the hermeneutical or contextualist turn has brought to light in recent years. Indeed, one might ask, if we cannot quite *equate* the methodologies of the natural and social sciences, can we not at least locate them as two stages on a single, unbroken continuum?

Yet this conclusion is unwarranted. Talk of a gradual continuum neglects a distinctive feature of the human sciences that continues to separate the study of the human sphere from (even hermeneutically conceived) natural science. For in addition to the interpretive framework imposed by every researcher, the *object* of research here is itself already symbolically structured. If all science is hermeneutical, in the human sciences we encounter what Giddens has called a "double hermeneutic." The social scientist faces "a pre-interpreted world where the creation and reproduction of meaning-frames is a very condition of that which it seeks to analyze."[53] A variety of special interpretive problems must therefore be solved if we are to gain access to these symbolic worlds or to make progress in explaining their genesis and composition. In this context, methods based on *Verstehen* or understanding suggest themselves as essential to the explanatory task in the social sciences. But how is this *Verstehen* to be construed, and in what manner is it related to the explanatory task of the social scientific disciplines?

In the first place, note that talk of *Verstehen* does not immediately throw one into the waiting arms of hermeneuticists like Gadamer or Ricoeur. The alternative to the formalists' neglect of meaning-construction is not necessarily the complete reduction of explanation in social science to "empathetic understanding" of human "meaning-frames" (Giddens). Nor must we buy into the psychologistic theory of *Verstehen* supported by Collingwood and the early Dilthey. Psychologism makes introspection of one's psychological states the final criterion for knowledge in the various academic disciplines, the ultimate arbiter for (and meaning of?) all truth claims. But there is no obvious reason why the use of *Verstehen* methods must automatically preempt all other epistemic considerations.

Nonetheless, that the notion of *Verstehen* subordinates the explanatory task in social science has recently been suggested by several thinkers, mostly notably Peter Winch.[54] Winch's position seems to fuse Dilthey's early approach to *Verstehen* with Wittgensteinian language-game theory. He holds that one can only explain a tribal culture, for instance, when one has understood it, which requires becoming a native, internalizing the "universe of discourse" and the unique criteria of intelligibility operative in it. But here we must side with Alasdair MacIntyre, who correctly accuses Winch of overly circumscribing the methodology of the social sciences.[55] Without doubt, to understand in a participatory sense is a goal in social scientific research. But one can acknowledge the centrality of understanding without condoning Winch's particular construal of the process and its preemption of explanation. There are certainly cases, especially in the study of tribal peoples, where the subjects being studied would not understand any explanatory account of their behavior—if only because the very concept of "giving a scientific account" is foreign to them. If there are any nonconscious components to action whatsoever, as in Marxist or Freudian analyses, the participant cannot be the last court of appeal. As MacIntyre argues, "sometimes to understand a concept involves not sharing it."[56]

The role of empathetic understanding is therefore crucial but not all-encompassing. The abiding contribution of Dilthey's work in the human sciences does not lie in his defense of *Verstehen* as the essence of social science, but rather in his awareness of its role as a heuristic principle or necessary condition for proceeding in the social scientific disciplines. But if *Verstehen* is to play this heuristic role, it cannot be reduced merely to an affect, such as the feeling of empathy or concern for those whom one studies. How then should we understand understanding?

I suggest that we begin with the model of understanding as an immediate grasping of patterns of meaning. This allows us to link it less to the affect of empathy than to the intuitive comprehension of a complex event or state of affairs. According to this position, the goal of social scientific understanding is insight into the connectedness of a given social context, into the way it fits together. One seeks to comprehend the interrelationships of the various actors in their social setting, the relations of meaning that bind them together into one social world. Obviously, viewing understanding in this manner entails a theory of meaning that is not purely subjective ("I now know what it feels like to be an Azande"), but which instead makes the relationship of fit or coherence intrinsic to meaning itself.

How are we then to connect this sort of understanding with social scientific explanations? We might begin with what I take to be an obvious point: social scientific explanation need not (and cannot) give up its primarily propositional form in order to be adequate to its object. Scientific explanations are instantiated in sentences. This leads to a corollary: explanation is only possible where a switch in the form of representation occurs, from the use of words or the occurrence of actions to the formulation of statements about them. I would like to speak of this as a switch of levels, without implying any sort of value judgment between the levels.

There is a reason why the explanation/understanding distinction did not play much of a role in the natural sciences. We saw in chapter 2 that nomological explanation could be defended as a general ideal in many of the physical sciences, at least in the case of standard why-questions and within the context of a specified theoretical project. Explanations in this field generally rely on a set of general statements (an explanans) that ideally offers necessary or sufficient conditions for the occurrence of an event (explanandum). In most cases all that is required for understanding the explanandum is to describe it using theoretical and observation terms (remembering that this distinction may be theory-relative). Typically, we then explain it by subsuming it under a general law (Hempel) or within an interpreted theoretical system (van Fraassen).

But the meaning-pervadedness of the human subject (Dilthey's *Sinnhaftigkeit*) requires a more explicit emphasis on understanding in the human sciences. Here one understands an action or situation by grasping (intuiting, seeing) what it means or signifies; one must place it within the process of individual or communal world-construction. To say that we merely describe the social explanandum (as in natural science) overlooks the process by which we first construe it as meaningful. However, explanation of social events must still be formulated in theoretical terms. Consequently, any adequate theory of explanation in the social sciences must maintain a sharp distinction between two separate levels, that is, between the actions that we aim to understand and the explanations that we formulate concerning those actions.

One might object that explanation in social science bears no resemblance to explanations anywhere else; it may not be an answer to a why-question or even propositional at all. Yet if one insists *too* strongly on its uniqueness, the use of the term *explanation* becomes equivocal and one might just as well dispense with it completely, as Dilthey did in his original dichotomy between *Erklärung* and *Verstehen* (and as others have done since him). It may be that explanation—in the sense of a theory or group of statements that have intersubjective validity as an answer to a why-question—is impossible in the human sphere; at least the possibility cannot be ruled out a priori. However, *if* one still wishes to employ the term here, as most social scientists today would, then it needs to be specified in a manner at least analogous to its use in other fields.

We must now attempt to specify the nature of this second-order explanatory discourse about human interactions. To guide the discussion, I propose that explanation in social science be taken to mean *a rational reconstruction in a primarily theoretical context of particular human actions and structures of meaning*. After describing the phenomenon in question, one attempts to reconstruct a network of subjective or social factors in the second-level terms of the relevant discipline. The result is a theoretical framework that represents the world of the subject(s) involved together with the interconnections, beliefs, and valuations that make it a more or less consistent or meaningful subjective whole.

By stipulating that it be a *rational* reconstruction, we draw attention to the requirement that publicly accessible reasons be given for the superiority of one's own theories over other existing or conceivable options. Rational here means intersubjectively criticizable. This requirement in turn gives rise to two different types of standards. On the one hand, the explanatory effort in social science faces certain general guidelines for rational discourse. Habermas's attempt to spell out the various parameters of an ideal speech situation remains extremely helpful in this regard. On the other, some formal specification of the nature of a good argument or adequate explanation for a specified discipline or research program is also required. Such specifications vary widely between, say, psychology and economics—and within psychology, between, for example, cognitive and social psychology. Nonetheless, we may still discover some general features shared by most social scientific explanations as we continue.

What of the term *reconstructions?* Its connotation of rebuilding underscores the fact that the world of individual actions and self-understandings cannot simply be transported, unmodified, into the arena of explanation. However, actually experienced complexes of meaning are the indispensable elements, the building blocks, for social scientific theories. I have adapted the term for describing the explanatory project in social science (and, later, in theology) from suggestions made by Dilthey, Habermas, and Lakatos. Dilthey defended the reconstruction of life-expressions as the goal of the human sciences. However, he tried to ground the reconstructive process (at least in his later work) on a metaphysical principle, the shared unity of life, rather than (as here) on the methodological requirement of intersubjective criticizability.

Since the 1973 postscript to *Knowledge and Human Interests*, Habermas has also used the notion of rational reconstruction to distance himself somewhat from the transcendental-philosophical approach of Karl-Otto Apel.[57] He has now abandoned the transcendental subject in favor of the "generative character of the rules [of language]," and seeks to reconstruct the "deep structures" beneath actual linguistic performance. This "rational reconstruction of generative rules or cognitive schemata" can then be tested: one can lead the subject by means of so-called maieutic procedures to assert or deny the adequacy of the reconstruction for her own language usage.[58] In contrast to Apel's approach, Habermas's reconstructions are meant to allow for testing and warranted critique. To the extent that he still interprets his reconstructions transcendentally, however, he may be claiming a status for them that remains beyond any possible criticism on the part of other social scientists.

Finally, the parallels with Lakatos are especially significant. Lakatos employs the term *reconstruction* to show that theory-making takes place on a logically distinct level from the phenomena under study. There is no immediate access to the phenomena to be explained for purposes of verifying hypotheses. The explanatory task thus involves a creative positing or constructing of hypotheses rather than a direct intuition or derivation. Yet the process is rational: both Lakatos and Habermas insist rightly that proposed reconstructions are criticizable in principle. Although both thinkers make only limited use of the concept of rational reconstructions, I suggest that it has potentially a much broader utility—indeed, that it provides a suitably general characterization of the nature of explanation itself.

In outlining the general issues raised by social scientific why-questions, we have found no reason to insist upon the nomological or covering law requirement, despite the fact that it remains as a sort of regulative ideal for the natural sciences. In fact, social scientists attempt to draw the most general conclusions that their data will allow, perhaps because explanations limited in scope to a particular time, place, or group are less interesting and less theoretically fruitful. Yet we have found no compelling methodological arguments for holding social science up to a nomological standard. This conclusion is further evidence for the claim that disciplines cannot be fully analyzed without reference to their various objects of inquiry. Since the concept of explanation varies to some extent with the scientific discipline involved, the unity-of-science doctrine of methodological unity across sciences must be rejected. The quest for a single unified science thus remains unfulfilled: we must acknowledge at least some of the methodological discontinuities stressed by Habermas and the other antipositivist thinkers. The actual practice of the social sciences—that is, the *sorts* of explanations they offer and the requirements for their derivation and formulation—reflects the inherently "meaninged" nature of human existence and action. In light of this fact, we can consider in somewhat greater detail the unique forms that social scientific explanations must take.

Explanation and Human Meaning-Contexts

One way of explicating how explanations can take human meaning-contexts into account involves the distinction between causal and teleological explanations. The distinction is not new; two long and largely distinct traditions in science, labeled by von Wright the *galilean* and *aristotelian* traditions,[59] exemplify the alternatives. The galilean tradition, which gained influence with the advance of causal-mechanistic explanation in post-Newtonian science and Comtean positivism, has been characterized by its emphasis on the unity of method, on the mathematical ideal-type of a science, and on the importance of general laws in explanation (4). In modern science, aristotelian explanation has thrived in disciplines employing the notions of function, purpose(fulness), system or organic whole (e.g., cybernetics), and those in which aims and intentions play a significant role. The aristotelian tradition allows in principle for a plurality of explanatory types, while de facto favoring explanations in terms of final causes; by contrast,

galilean explanation has sought to reduce finalistic explanations in biology
and the human sciences to causal explanations.

It is not hard to see why Habermas and the antipositivists have been so
critical of the reduction to causal explanations, for they involve a radically
different explanatory structure. A successful research program in sociology, stemming from Talcott Parsons, has distinguished human action from
mere behavior according to a variety of parameters, based on the intentional (and therefore semantically structured) orientation of the acting subject.[60] In this research program, the unity of an action enduring through
time is constituted by the single intention that gives rise to the action; thus
we usually speak of the "object" of an agent's intention, that is, what he
intends to do.

The so-called practical syllogism, first formulated by Aristotle, is helpful
for drawing attention to this intentional ("in-order-to") structure of action.
Von Wright summarizes a long discussion of the teleological structure of
psychological explanations (chap. 3) with his formulation of the practical
syllogism:

> From now on A intends to bring about p at time t.
> From now on A considers that, unless he does a no later than at time t',
>   he cannot bring about p at time t.
> Therefore, no later than when he thinks time t' has arrived, A sets
>   himself to do a, unless he forgets about the time or is prevented.
>   (107)

It is interesting to compare the connection between this syllogism's premises and conclusion with accounts of explanations in the natural sciences
(e.g., Hempel). The connection in the former case is not causal but conceptual: a reason helps form an intention, which leads to a behavior. The action
is not accounted for by referring to lawlike necessities but in terms of
reasons and motivating factors.

In short, we cannot explain human actions except with reference to
reasons, and hence to the specific contexts of meaning that constitute the
background for the action. Teleological explanations work differently from
their causal counterparts: "The *explanandum* of a teleological explanation is
an action, that of a causal explanation an intentionalistically noninterpreted
item of behavior, that is, some bodily movement or state" (124). The social
scientist does not dispense completely with the nomic (lawlike) connections of the physical world, for human actions can be explained only within
the givenness of nature. Nonetheless, nomic connections remain secondary. The scientist of human action is concerned in the first place with "a set
of singular statements which constitute the premises of practical inferences" (142) and with the connections between them that the practical

syllogism conveys. Since the sorts of connections in the two realms of phenomena (natural and human) differ, so also must the explanations that represent or make sense of these realms.

As the linguist searches for and utilizes the basic units of linguistic meaning, we might try to isolate the most basic or significant explanatory units in natural and social science.[61] For the natural scientist the explanatory unit will generally be a causal system of laws and uniformities of some type—even though, as we saw, the second-order (methodological) analysis of scientific rationality requires reference to changing historical and theoretical contexts. For the social scientist, the basic unit will be some variant of the practical inference, with its stress on the giving of reasons and the construction of semantic contexts or worlds. Whereas the natural scientist could be concerned, as lower-level laws are subsumed under more comprehensive ones, only about the possible loss of specificity (predictive or descriptive adequacy) obtainable through lower-level laws, the same process of generalization will produce a fundamental transformation in most social sciences. Think of the transition from psychological theories of the individual to theories of group behavior. The transition allows additional statistical predictions to be made (purchasing patterns; mob behavior), but statistical laws are no longer of the form of basic practical inferences. When one focuses on sufficiently large groups, the semantic and cognitive factors that were essential for explaining individual acts may become blurred.

Another unique aspect of social scientific explanations has emerged through the discussion of value-ladenness. Although his work on understanding and explanation was published as early as 1904, Max Weber's position still offers an attractive middle way between more extreme views on the role of values in social science.[62] Indeed, the emphasis in the preceding pages on structures of meaning instead of nomic connections already reflects the influence of Weber. And the priority ascribed to the individual's process of meaning-construal reflects Weber's development of Dilthey's *verstehende Soziologie*: "all knowledge of cultural reality . . . is always knowledge from particular points of view."[63] As a result, Weber maintained the centrality of values in the human sciences: "The *significance* of a configuration of cultural phenomena and the basis of this significance cannot . . . be derived and rendered intelligible by a system of analytical laws (*Gesetzesbegriffen*), however perfect it may be, since the significance of cultural events presupposes a *value-orientation* towards these events. The concept of culture is a *value-concept*" (76). This significance means that the social researcher must take the relevant "subjective presuppositions" of his subjects into account (82); as Weber notes, these, as well as the researcher's own interests, may vary with culture and epoch.

The result is a methodological centrality of value questions (a *Wertbezo-*

genheit) not paralleled in the natural sciences.[64] Yet what is remarkable in Weber's work is his advocacy of the compatibility of value-ladenness with the "objective" methods of the social sciences.[65] For Weber the choice of the *ends* of research is nonscientific: according to interest one might ask either how to maintain a societal structure (Popper's "social engineering"), or how to modify it (or its participants) in a revolutionary manner. Nonetheless, given a particular choice of ends, a rational selection of *means* to those ends is possible. One can in principle determine which economic policies are likely to bring about a given end or which research methods will yield reliable answers to a given type of question.

The actual decision between various proposed means, of course, is a material question for sociological or psychological research, and consensus may not immediately be forthcoming. Still, at this general level, the means/ends distinction offers a partial rapprochement between positivist and antipositivist concerns.[66] Habermas wrote *Knowledge and Human Interests*, for instance, to counter the natural scientific tendency to exclude human interests from discussions of methodology; yet he grudgingly acknowledged the correctness of many analyses in the philosophy of science on questions of the methodology of science.[67] There is at least prima facie reason for thinking that agreement can in principle be reached on the best means for achieving a given end. And this is sufficient to justify the role of general methodological discussions in the sciences.

On the other hand, the choice of methods à la Weber has been relativized to a given set of research interests or values. Indeed, the relativization of rational means to given ends is in fact an alternate way of introducing *context considerations* into the methodological dispute. Although now for somewhat different reasons from those discussed in chapter 2, we here find explanation again to be constrained by nonepistemic contexts and value choices in the sense that we can specify methods of evaluation and implementation only within the context of researcher values or knowledge interests. No single invariant structure of explanation can be specified a priori, contra Popper and Hempel. The formal requirements for explanation will reflect the ends of the various disciplines; these in turn are influenced by the diverse natures of their various objects of study. There is no scientific way to arbitrate the choice of ends, though there remains a scientific way to proceed once consensus has been reached concerning them.

If we have found that a given research goal gives birth to a set of possible methods, is this not in essence a reformulation of Lakatos's research program concept, in this case prompted by *values* as motivating knowledge interests in the social scientific sphere? As Lakatos was reticent to legislate between rival research programs until sufficient time had elapsed, we may here be unable to make a scientifically rational choice between two social explanations or prescriptions because of the different ends that they pursue. Nonetheless—and here we return again to von Wright's discussion of the practical inference—it may be possible to say which of two different courses of action aimed at attaining a given end is the more rational. Likewise, where two rival explanations seek to account for a given meaning-complex, we can with sufficient information often determine their relative explanatory adequacy. Where no direct comparison is possible, the coherence of the competing explanations within their relevant context can play a major role in this task.[68] Admittedly, the social scientific literature bears witness to the difficulties of evaluating alternative explanations of actions even within the context of a given end or shared complex of research values. Yet evaluation remains a viable option as a methodological ideal, as well as continuing to be the actual goal of current social scientific research.

But, the critic might ask, is the practical inference with its individualistic slant really relevant for meaning-contexts at the societal level? Since I have started the discussion of meaning with the individual, it is incumbent upon me to discuss the construction of broader units of meaning. Many thinkers in the social sciences advocate starting instead with societal structures, arguing that such structures are the ultimate basis for social thought and that they can be understood without reference to individuals.[69] Rather than criticizing their particular approaches, I will put forward one conceptual framework for accomplishing the transition from individual to societal structures of meaning, drawn from the work of Alfred Schütz. This transition is of central importance to the present study for two reasons. First, my discussion of explanation in the social sciences to this point has assumed the primacy of individual meaning-construction; but this methodological individualism is adequate in the social sciences only if one can give a convincing account of the move to publicly shared structures of meaning. Second, the following chapters on religion likewise begin with the individual appropriation of religious meaning, moving from there to the shared religious traditions. The detailed discussion here of Schütz's work will thus be presupposed in the treatment of religious meaning to follow.

Alfred Schütz's methodology for a sociology of *Verstehen* moves from private, individual meaning-contexts (*Sinnzusammenhänge*) to broader contexts. His *Der sinnhafte Aufbau der sozialen Welt* ("the semantic construction of the social world") claims to combine Weber's insights with the theory of consciousness of Bergson and Husserl in order "to specify the phenomenon of meaning by means of an analysis of its constitution."[70] It is Schütz's thesis that no human action, whether of an individual or a group, can be understood or interpreted without reference to its inherent meaning-content (e.g., 216). This version of *verstehende Soziologie*, in the tradition of Dilthey except for its reduction of meaning to contexts of action, is built upon the existence of an underlying, prescientific world in which meaning and understanding are already constitutive (10). All consequent sociological analyses on the level of the social world are no more than explications of foundational "acts of positing and interpreting meaning" on the part of individuals (8, 10). Though I will later criticize the unidirectionality of Schütz's analysis, his description of the role of the subject provides valuable guidelines for explaining human meaning-contexts.

Schütz's methodology focuses on how meaning-contexts are constructed. From a phenomenological perspective, series of human actions can be viewed as all present, as connected within a single meaning-context. Ultimately, they are part of a "world of experience" that is constructed out of various orders of human meaning-contexts (216). I use the term *semantic worlds* to refer to Schütz's orders of meaning in this and the following chapters. The crux of a *verstehende Soziologie*, then, is the "interpretation of the *subjective* meaning—that is, the meaning meant by the acting person or persons—of social behaviors" (6). The analysis must always begin with the perception of meaning by the individual, only later adding the realm of intersubjectively perceived meaning.[71]

Making essential use of Husserl's work, Schütz analyzes the constitution of meaningful experience for the individual (45–96). He correctly separates the phenomenon of meaningfulness from more basic levels of human experience. Time or "experienced duration" (*Dauer* or *Zeitbewusstsein*), for example, is a basic element of the process of experiencing for an individual, in that specific experiences are labeled as individually mine because they belong to my duration. The category of meaning belongs to a higher level, that of reflection; it is the result of a judgment. With reference to the time example, meaning involves the "attitude of the ego toward its elapsed duration" (69f). In more general terms, meaning stems from a sort of introspective awareness or internal reflection: "The expression, 'one looks toward or reflects on [*hinblicken auf*] an experience,' and the expression, 'an experience is meaningful,' [are] equivalent" (70).

The nature and needs of the individual as an acting being further affect his constitution of the world. His complex of interests determines, for example, what is for him unquestionably accepted and what parts of the world are problematic and in need of explanation. I find this analysis of the variability of interest by Schütz to be significant in descriptions of social phenomena and crucial for the phenomenology of religious explanations (chap. 5). Motives also play an important role; they form a sort of structure, a projected action, upon which the meaning of an act or event is gradually constructed. Schütz also first introduces the notion of the other (*das Du*) in the context of individual motives, as part of the objective meaning-context that the self has built. Gradually, he claims, an authentic understanding of otherness is won as the self learns to see the other's acts as part of a meaning-context foreign to it. On this basis, finally, a theory of communication as the sign-mediated positing and interpreting of meaning is constructed.

Now Schütz's one-way progression from the bracketed world of the self to the other, reminiscent of Husserl's *Cartesian Meditations*, must probably be rejected.[72] Contemporary sociology provides ample evidence for a reciprocal relationship: the most personal and presumably primordial perceptions of the individual already bear the marks of societal influence.[73] Nonetheless, even if we reject the foundational, primordial status ascribed to the individual's world by Husserl, the role of the individual as a locus of meaning-construction (*Sinnstiftung*) remains unscathed. Sociological factor analysis may establish diverse influences on individual perceptions of meaning. Yet the synthetic activity of the individual does give rise to a unique complex of meaning, a semantic whole with its own distinctive, coherent parameters of meaning (Schütz's *Sinntotalität*). Persons do form their own images of the other out of their diverse meaning-contexts, however much social expectations and stereotypes contribute to the process. This fact is central in the religious dimension, as we will see below.

If the synthetic activity of the subject is granted, the next step is the construction of an intersubjective world. In contrast to *Verstehen*, which for Schütz is linked in the first place to individual meaning-contexts, the notion of a semantic or "meaninged" world (*sinnhafte Welt*) refers back to the alter ego. The point is that the self recognizes in the other a *separate* world of meaning, oriented around a different synthesizing or semantic center, and must relate to this agent *as other*; it is not, as Husserl claims, that the other is somehow constructed by the transcendental ego within its reduced experience. Beginning (methodologically) with the individual subject therefore does not close one off from shared complexes of meaning; the framework of semantic worlds does not force one into methodological solipsism.

Schütz stresses the abstracting nature of knowledge of the social world in a manner reminiscent of Heidegger. His methodology begins with relations in the immediate environment or life-world, which is composed of "experiences of the other in his actual Now and Thus" (219). In attempting to gain social scientific knowledge, one moves through a progressive "anonymizing" or "deindividualizing," arriving finally at an abstract framework in which the other becomes a type, a mere "One." Note the similarity between this continuum and Dilthey's dichotomy between experiencing and explaining: both thinkers define objective knowledge as an opposite pole to understanding and grant primacy to the latter pole. Thus Schütz writes, "The more anonymous the partner is, the less he can be experienced and the more he must be thought" (219). The tension ought not to be glossed over: the transition to the theoretical level of rational reconstructions, defended above, *does* involve a loss of experiential immediacy. Reconstructions are paler than the original. Still, it does not follow that social scientific explanations cannot model the life-contexts to which they refer, that they cannot represent in more abstract terms the semantic worlds that we have been discussing.

Schütz's work is of course not without flaws. Beyond the problems already mentioned, there are difficulties with basing a doctrine of meaning solely on contexts of human action.[74] Further, Schütz is mistaken if he thinks that the move from subjective to intersubjective meaning-contexts is a move from the subjective to the objective. Explanations do not suddenly become objective at the intersubjective level; there also interpretive efforts are required.[75] Nevertheless, Schütz has provided an insightful account of the construction of meaning, one which serves as a helpful starting point for discussions of explanation and understanding in the social sciences and religion. The strength of this account of the social world lies in its focus on the various contexts of meaning as the foundation and building blocks of all human understanding. By contrast, if one ignores the semantic construction of the social world—as, for example, in a purely nomological behavioral psychology, or when social categories are divorced from their location in individual experience—the result can only be an inadequate grasp of social reality.[76]

Explanation with Understanding

It has become clear that a theory of explanation appropriate to the social sciences cannot be separated from the disciplinary context of the social sciences, and hence that explanation here cannot be separated from questions of understanding and meaning. The nature of the social phenomenon necessitates that explanations make reference to the semantic synthesizing function of the individual self, as well as to the interplay between individual worlds and shared social worlds. This insight, emphasized by the *Verstehen* school, affects the methods chosen in the social sciences and hence must be incorporated into discussions of social scientific rationality.

Acceptance of human meaning-contexts, however, does not in itself invalidate the distinction of levels between phenomena and theories. Implicit in any discussion of explanation is still the assumption that one can distinguish first-order talk of the phenomena under consideration from second-order discourse involving the comparison and critical evaluation of explanatory theories. Perhaps only minimal claims can be made on behalf of this explanatory discourse. For instance, it would be mistaken, after our acceptance of the influence of context on theory evaluation, to claim context-free objectivity for theoretical discourse. Nor shall I attempt here some sort of general criteriology for assessing the adequacy of specific social scientific theories.[77] Nonetheless, it does not follow that all talk of the adequacy of theories is to be rejected. Indeed, even Richard Bernstein, who has been heavily influenced by Habermas and Gadamer, acknowledges that incommensurability does not eliminate the abstraction of second-order discourse: "Nevertheless, in the course of the evolution of scientific development, we can come to see the force of the better practices and arguments and why certain historical practices and modes of argumentation are abandoned" (68).

Given the validity of the first-order/second-order distinction, it is now possible to summarize the interdependence between understanding and explanation. Explanation involves formulating, in theoretical terms, answers to why-questions. But one must get to this theoretical level without falsifying the subject matter in question. In the social sciences this means that one must first have understood the phenomenon to be explained. Consequently, we can say that *understanding is a necessary precondition for social scientific explanation*. A variety of attempts have been made to think understanding and explanation together into a single concept. These tend, however, either to reduce understanding to a dispensable heuristic tool without material significance or de facto to replace explanation with intuitive understanding and description. The perspective here advanced has the advantage of drawing attention to the differences between participating *in* (and intuitively understanding) a social situation and attempting to frame explanatory statements *about* the situation. In terms of Kekes' distinction (p. 83 above), it does not conflate the rationality of theories with the rationality of persons.

My proposal has another interesting corollary. If one fails to understand a phenomenon in the human sciences, it will not be possible to have (or to know that one has) a correct explanation. This corollary makes more explicit the normative status of the concept of explanations as rational reconstructions: adequate explanation is an ideal that is not always attainable. To the extent that understanding is hampered or incomplete in regard to a given range of phenomena, the probability of explaining those phenomena adequately is reduced. For instance, an anthropologist's explanations of behaviors observed in a newly discovered tribe may be severely flawed if she does not understand (in the sense advanced in this chapter) the semantic world of which they are a part and cannot rely on experience with other tribes who are better understood.

One could almost construct an a priori hierarchy of explainability. We will expect objects of study to be less or more amenable to rational explanation depending on known or foreseeable difficulties in understanding. It also appears to follow from the hierarchy that the social scientist is in general less likely to attain ideal explanations than the natural scientist, since she faces an additional precondition that does not apply to the natural scientist in explaining nature, namely, the need first to understand her object of study. Natural scientists face a single hermeneutical hurdle, that posed by their own subjectivity; the social scientist, a twofold hermeneutical challenge. Moreover, we may already expect that there will be further, unique difficulties in understanding the religious "object," and therefore that the explanatory project will face even more serious hurdles in the field of religion.

The explanation/understanding relationship can now be located within the parameters of a general theory of theoretical rationality informed by our discussions in the last two chapters. With Popper we can still say that "every rational theory . . . is rational in so far as it tries to solve certain problems." With Laudan, we can speak of science as the quest for "problem solving effectiveness."[78] When a state of affairs has been understood, a potential explanation can be formulated in a theoretical context. In practice, of course, the understanding and the first hypothetical formulation of the explanation may be simultaneous; I have only argued that they are conceptually distinguishable and that the former is a procedural precondition for the latter.

Using the term first introduced in the context of Lakatos's philosophy of science, I have argued that an explanation is a form of rational reconstruction of actual human behaviors and attitudes. All the limitations attributed to scientific rationality by Lakatos (as I reconstructed him) are still relevant here: rational discourse is not purely objective; context may greatly influence the theoretical process; a given research program and its explanations can only be partially evaluated at any given time; and the coherence of a research program or broad theoretical conception may provide the best (and probably provides the most general) criterion for evaluating it. But whereas it was the influence of theoretical structures or communal presuppositions on observation statements that had the major biasing role in natural science, here the move from participation in communicative social interaction to the relative abstraction of theoretical discourse contributes an additional prejudicing factor.

After a brief excursus we turn in the remaining chapters to the field of religion. In chapter 5 I attempt a rational reconstruction of the process of religious meaning-construction using the framework here developed.

Does the ideal of rational explanation still have any applicability in this field? Must the explanation/understanding relationship be conceived differently? What biasing factors arise to complicate the explanatory effort? And are there any further preconditions in religious experience that parallel the precondition of understanding in the social sciences?

CHAPTER FOUR

An Extended Excursus
Philosophical Explanations and the Problem
of Philosophical Rationality

The next task is to consider how religious beliefs and experience function as explanations for the believer and for the religious community. As we begin to draw comparisons with our discussions of scientific explanations in the previous chapters, we will discover both significant discontinuities and some interesting parallels. However, to launch immediately into a comparative study would be to neglect a major shift of perspective from the sciences. One may credibly view scientific theories as in the first place attempts to explain the world, since scientists accept or reject them depending on their (perceived) explanatory success. But as we saw in chapter 1, religious beliefs serve other than explanatory functions; they are often vaguely formulated or are held by believers in a completely unreflective manner. When persons do treat religious beliefs as explanations, they rarely proceed according to the highest scientific standards.

Strictly speaking, an individual's religious explanations cannot be equated with explanations in any discipline. Still, they are not sui generis: they too answer why-questions, make appeal to reasons, are formulated in words. If comparisons with any other category of explanations are possible, a number of the characteristics of religious explanations—their greater generality or depth, their nonempirical nature, their emphasis on systematic coherence and meaningfulness, their reflexive quality—suggest the comparison with philosophical explanations. For this reason, it is essential that we delay our treatment of religious explanations until we have considered, by way of transition from the sciences to religion, the general nature of philosophical explanations and the somewhat intractable problem of philosophical rationality. Let it be said at the outset (and it will be said again) that philosophers do many other things than constructing theories and explaining: they describe phenomena, exhort their readers (think of Nietzsche's "live dangerously!"), seek "not merely to interpret the world but also to change it"—and occasionally merely emote. But I take it that there are at least some instances of philosophical explanations as well.

Narrow definitions of explanation in philosophy inevitably run into conflict with the actual practice of some important philosopher or school of philosophy; to avoid this, one is tempted to proceed by means of only the vaguest generalities. It is interesting to see that Nozick, in his wide-ranging book on philosophical explanations, can say of them at the general level only that they represent the attempt to "render [philosophical issues] coherent and better understood."[1] Indeed, any more stringent requirements are no longer true of all credible philosophical explanations: for example, that they must tell how something is or can be possible in the light of "apparent excluders" (10); that they must provide ultimate principles to explain, say, why there is something rather than nothing; or that they must give the transcendental preconditions for some area of experience. How many formal definitions of philosophical explanation are broad enough to include Whitehead's twenty-seven "categories of explanation,"[2] and how many major philosophers do his categories in turn exclude? Despite the perhaps insurmountable difficulties facing any such endeavor, I will defend the centrality of specified problem-situations, hypothetical theories, and a contextual theory of meaning for philosophical rationality.

Minimally, one can stipulate that philosophical explanations, like other explanations, aim to address and answer coherently some specifiable question. I am skeptical whether anyone can delineate precisely what makes a particular question philosophical: without committing a *petitio principii*, one can scarcely justify any requirement more exclusive than that the scope and subject matter of the questions be limited to what can be asked![3] To be consistent with our earlier formulations, we could stipulate that the question to be asked is a why-question, as long as it is admitted that the surface structure of a philosophical explanation may not immediately reflect its connection to a why-question. But when we try to specify what species differentia makes an explanation *philosophical*, a paradox results: philosophical explanations are often specifically philosophical only in their lack of specificity, in their movement beyond the boundaries of disciplines and accepted understandings. As a necessary, though not sufficient, condition, I would suggest that an explanation is philosophical if it is not limited in scope to any particular discipline or aspect of experience. This feature of (in principle) unrestricted reflection, characteristic of the traditional metaphysical project, gives to philosophy its occasional third-order role of re-flection upon other disciplines' reflection upon experience.[4]

The list of other allegedly necessary conditions for philosophical expla-nations is virtually endless; we cannot expect to lay such a tangled dispute to rest in the present excursus. For instance, philosophy has often played an iconoclastic role, casting into question accepted understandings of real-ity or regions thereof. But it is clearly insufficient to reduce philosophy to the process of skeptical questioning alone. Conversely, we might argue that philosophy necessarily involves the construction of new maps of the world, although I doubt that the map image adequately captures the neces-sarily propositional nature of the philosophical endeavor. And the quest for sufficient conditions for philosophical explanations is even more daunting.

Philosophical explanations may be broader or deeper than scientific explanations, but they are not mystical (though they may shade over into mystical realms). They remain reasoned explanations, even where the reasoning involved is nonlinear or dialectical—hence my insistence that these explanations have as their catalyst specifiable questions. First ap-pearances notwithstanding, this condition is not vacuous. With Popper, we might interpret it as the stipulation that the philosopher must always spec-ify the problem-situation that he is addressing.[5] Now admittedly, problem solving is more generally acknowledged to be central in the sciences. As we saw, Lakatos stressed a shared problem-situation as one of the essential elements of a research program. His shift from Popper's preoccupation with the demarcation between the truly scientific and "metaphysics" to a system of progressive or degenerating problemshifts gave explicit acknowl-edgment to the governing role of the problem in science. Larry Laudan then argued for the solution of problems as *the* determining characteristic of scientific growth, making "highest problem-solving adequacy" his sole criterion.[6] Likewise, the organizing function of the problem-situation con-cept has much to recommend it in philosophy as well.

We may agree with Nozick that the initial motivation of philosophy is often "puzzlement, curiosity, a desire to understand."[7] But after question-ing as deeply as it is able, the philosophic impulse begins again to con-struct, using whatever building blocks it has discovered. This element of *organized reconstruction* I hold to be indispensable for an adequate ac-count of philosophical explanation. Perhaps in exceptional cases philosoph-ical reflection stems from a complete disorientation of the form, "I don't know my way about."[8] But, to adapt Wittgenstein's picture, more often a number of landmarks remain (I still know a street from a building), along with certain ingrained habits of thought (regulative principles of reason: "head for lighted areas!"). Even when "the centre cannot hold" (W. B. Yeats) and anomy threatens—and admittedly, philosophical revolutions

are deeper cutting and potentially more devastating than scientific ones—
philosophical reflection can still pursue the task of organizing our remaining intuitions in a rational manner.

Our earlier discussions of the importance of context and coherence
considerations stand in close relationship with the problem-solving approach advocated here, when taken together with the concept of meaning
that emerged in chapter 3. As we saw, a sentence is only meaningful within
the context of paragraph and opus, an action only in the context of a given
social setting, a proposition only against the backdrop of other accepted
propositions. It is meaningless to speak of a theory or explanation if one
cannot specify what the theory accounts for or the explanation explains,
that is, what problem they are meant to deal with. This is especially the
case in philosophy proper (as opposed to the various "philosophies of")
where there is no limited, clearly specifiable range of experience to provide
a point of orientation. As a replacement for physically defined problems,
one discovers in the history of philosophy a variety of traditional problem-
complexes or "tasks for thought": the problem of free will, of Being, of
transcendence, of other minds. Any given philosophical position will stem
from—and therefore only be meaningful in the context of—some given
conceptual problem; as such, it will evidence connections with other longstanding problems in the tradition. Rational discussion in philosophy is
thus impossible if one does not take cognizance of the relevant problem-
situations. If philosophical disputants are to make sense of one another's
suggestions rather than to equivocate madly, they must come to some
consensus on the questions being addressed.

For similar reasons, I would suggest also that posited philosophical
explanations be understood as hypotheses. Of course, this term may not be
taken as equivalent to the common conception of hypotheses in the natural
sciences: philosophical hypotheses are not necessarily objective, empirical
or nomological. Neither does social scientific inquiry alone offer an adequate framework. Still, the term *hypothesis* is not being used in complete
equivocation. By proposing an idealized model of philosophical rationality
as the construction of hypothetical explanations regarding specified problem-situations, I am stressing in the first place that they are meant as
answers to delineated questions, and that their status remains possible or
preliminary. Nozick argues similarly: "The (possible) explanation . . . is
put forward tentatively, subject to withdrawal in the face of difficulties or
alternative, better explanations, perhaps using deeper principles that also
would explain other things" (11).

Of course, this is not to assert that philosophy consists *only* of such
explanations: as I noted, there remains room for philosophical statements
of intuitive or unproblematic philosophical understanding, as well as for

the attempt at pure analysis and clarification through redescription or paraphrase. But philosophical reflection aims in part at explanation. If epistemology done with one eye on the philosophy of science has anything to contribute to philosophy proper, it is this demand that one view one's philosophical proposals as criticizable hypotheses rather than as final solutions. This concern, rather than weaknesses in the deductive method itself, militates most strongly against the axiomatic procedures of high scholastic metaphysics and eighteenth-century rationalist philosophy; again, the concern for criticizability, not some flaw in the very idea of necessary conditions, is the reason we now view the status of transcendental arguments as hypothetical rather than as established.[9]

A number of philosophers have been tempted to draw more explicit links between discussions of scientific methodology, such as those presented in chapters 2 and 3, and philosophical rationality. It has been proposed, for example, that philosophical assertions should strive for lawlike status, or that they should have entailments that are empirically testable. Taking what one might call a Reichenbachian turn, these thinkers claim that complete guidelines and standards for doing philosophy can be imported wholesale from scientific practice.[10] Such efforts belong to the project of *metaphilosophy*, or the proposal of a normative structure and requirements for doing philosophy. However, they often neglect the fact that "a metaphilosophy will be part of a total philosophical view rather than a separate neutral theory above the battle."[11] How would one defend without circularity the normative role of criticizability, or the centrality of the quest for empirical entailments, or even the Law of Non-Contradiction, against opponents who advocated different standards, say, beauty or revolutionary potential, as of first importance?[12] In the light of such a plurality of options in philosophy, one is well advised to import themes and models from the philosophy of science individually (and with suitable modification) rather than wholesale.

The problem we encounter here is, in a sense, the opposite of the methodological problem we ran into in earlier chapters. There the methodologist was in danger of imposing a normative structure external (and thus possibly irrelevant) to the discipline in question. Here we are *unable* to make an external pronouncement: everything said about philosophy is itself also philosophy. Even the statement that the goal of philosophy is the pursuit of truth represents a value that not all would accept without dispute; if we then ask how we are to understand the truth that we should all be pursuing, agreement is well nigh impossible. At this point we again encounter the difficulty alluded to above: philosophy is set apart by the fact that it is a discipline which includes reflection on its own definition, content, and standards as part of its given assignment. If some sort of pancriti-

cal (i.e., self-sustaining) notion of rationality cannot be defended, philosophy faces the trilemma of an infinite regress, circular argumentation, or an
arbitrary breaking off of the process of inquiry. [13]

On the other hand, even given the difficulties to which I have alluded,
we do not need to forsake all discussion of the general characteristics of
rationality. Means/end rationality, albeit not the sole model of rationality
available, characterizes many cognitive, evaluative and practical (action-
oriented) contexts. Moreover, the giving of reasons and the forsaking of
one's own position in the face of better reasons seem indispensable elements of any rational theoretical enterprise. What constitutes better reasons may have to be specified separately for various contexts or subject
matters. But this relativism does not sound the death knell for the rationality of philosophy. Even given such a contextualization, the move from the
specific reasons of specific individuals, influenced as they are by various
idiosyncratic factors, toward the reasons that would be offered by an ideal
subject in an "ideal speech situation" (as described above in connection
with Habermas) does still seem to characterize philosophical rationality in
all its forms. This movement toward canceling out nonrational factors, and
the rise to ever-wider contexts in which deeper or more encompassing
explanations are advanced, bring coherence considerations into the very
center of the rationality discussion.

The concept of coherence is notoriously difficult to pin down and calls for
a much more extensive treatment than I can give here. Margenau understood coherence to involve "multiple connections" among concepts within
the internal structure of a particular theory or with the concepts of other
theories believed to be valid. [14] The German Idealist philosophers explicated it in terms of systems, though their concepts of system were as
diverse as their systems of philosophy. F. H. Bradley made extensive use of
coherence as the systematic interconnectedness and interdependence of
all aspects of reality, a theme later central in the work of Brand Blanshard. [15]
More recently, Nicholas Rescher has presented a partially formalized account of coherence in terms of "maximally consistent subsets" of data. Yet
even his "coherence machinery" turns out to be "a complex composite of
multiple subcriteria," including such diverse factors as comprehensiveness, "systematicity," and simplicity. [16]

When one appeals to coherence as a philosophical criterion, one at least
implies that assertions must be assessed within a context, that is, in comparison with a more comprehensive set of assertions. The coherence of the
set then refers to "the internal coherence and mutual support its various
stages lend to one another." One can also speak of a conceptual interdependence or an "ultimate goodness of fit." [17] My thesis is that such considerations are central to both the meaning and the truth of philosophical expla-

nations (and thus, perhaps, to religious explanations as well). This position is worthy of a book-length treatment of its own (which I hope soon to provide); still, since it plays a role in the following chapters, it can at least be outlined, as a sort of first approximation, at this point.

Linguistic analytic philosophers have distinguished between at least two types of meaning: referential and contextual meaning.[18] One defense of referential meaning stems from Frege's distinction between *Sinn* and *Bedeutung*, often translated as "meaning" and "reference."[19] According to more extreme versions of this position, the meaning of a word stems primarily, or solely, from the object that it picks out in the world. An exclusive emphasis on the referential side of meaning underlies, for instance, those schools of thought such as logical atomism that rely solely on correspondence with states of affairs as the definition or criterion of truth.

I do not believe that such a sharp distinction between the referential and contextual elements of meaning is tenable. Interestingly, Frege is an ally here. It is well known that Frege's notion of *Sinn* required consideration of the context of the sentence as a whole. But in the early *Grundlagen der Arithmetik*, even his concept of *Bedeutung* is closely linked to that of context. "We must ask about the *Bedeutung* [meaning *and* reference?] of words in context, not in their isolation," he writes; and later, "It is enough if the sentence as a whole has a meaning (*Sinn*); from this its parts also receive their content."[20] Nygren develops the context argument: "For not only does the meaning of a particular statement depend on the immediate context of which it is part, but this context itself derives its meaning from the total context of which it too is part."[21] No artificial distinction can ultimately be sustained between the referential meaning of individual terms and the contextual meaning of larger linguistic units. Context corrupts even correspondence claims.

Granting this point has an interesting corollary: no particular semantic context can be arbitrarily isolated from the broader contexts of which it is a part. Let us put *this* claim in context. Its more distant source is the theological hermeneutics of Friedrich Schleiermacher. In addition to anticipating Frege's understanding of the distinction between *Sinn* and *Bedeutung*, Schleiermacher presented a sophisticated theory of context, centered around the claim that "the meaning (*Sinn*) of any given word at a particular location must be determined according to its context or fit (*Zusammenhang*) with those words that surround it."[22] In explicating his context-based hermeneutic, Schleiermacher discovered a certain immanent tendency toward broader and broader contexts, such that, ultimately, "the individual can only be understood with reference to the whole" (36).

What we saw in Wilhelm Dilthey was essentially this same discovery. In developing his contextual theory of meaning, Dilthey defended the immanent movement through word and sentence and on to the whole of history. Indeed, it would seem arbitrary to appeal to contextual considerations up to some level n, and then to deny that n's meaning must in turn rely on some yet broader context. Hence, granting the irreducibly contextual element in meaning theory means acknowledging that any given stopping point will be provisional and open to still broader contexts of evaluation.

Do we uncover a similar phenomenon when we reflect on theories of truth? Here, in fact, analogous arguments can be made, though I do not yet find them to hold the same compulsion as they do in the theory of meaning. To begin, one has to be convinced that there are serious problems with correspondence theories of truth. Often cited are the difficulties with making sense of what a correspondence between words and world might be; the inconceivability of finding a place from which to address the question (from within language? from the standpoint of "reality itself"?); and the inability of even a viable definition of correspondence to guide us at all in knowing *what* is true.

The second step, after one has become suspicious of correspondence claims, is to show that a coherence theory can do all the work that the concept of correspondence actually does. The correspondence claim nicely does justice to our intuition that a true sentence should represent in words the way things actually are. Could a coherence theory plausibly (coherently) include a place for correspondence? In fact, as I suggested earlier, there is reason to think that it can. Recall that I defended coherence as an umbrella criterion of which other criteria are specifications. In particular, correspondence can be redefined as expressing the coherence of sentences with facts, for example, with observation sentences that represent the world (and our predictions about it) within our theoretical discourse. As a result, we can speak of the evaluation of a theory in science in terms of the coherence of its prediction set with the set of statements accepted by (a relevant subset of) the scientific community. Likewise, the consensus criterion specifies the desirability of a coherence of scientific opinion; and similar moves can be made with pragmatic, consistency, and comprehensiveness criteria.

This process of redefining the various truth criteria in terms of coherence is especially helpful in the case of philosophical explanations. Here, where the empirical reference of terms is much less clear (think of notions like substance or justice) and empirical checking well nigh impossible, the case for coherence as the ultimate court of appeal is, if anything, easier to make. According to the redefinition that I am proposing, what we mean by asserting that a philosophical explanation is true is simply that it is consistent, comprehensive, pragmatically useful, fits with widely (universally?) accepted beliefs, intuitions, and practices—in short, that it is coherent in the widest sense of the term. To say that we also want it to correspond to the world is not to say anything additional at all.

This coherentialist restatement of the traditional correspondence theory of truth avoids, I believe, the difficulties in elucidating the alleged word/world relationship, as well as the difficulty of linking a correspondence definition of truth with noncorrespondence criteria of truth.[23] The broader task would be to show in detail exactly how the other major criteria can be conceptually wedded in coherential terms. If a decent case can be made for this claim, we will have a broad structure that is able to link together the concepts of truth and of meaning through a formally similar appeal to coherence. The attractiveness of this notion of a coherence or context principle of rationality lies in its ability to unify (at least at one level) discussions of such diverse questions as the problem of meaning, of understanding, of explanation, and of truth.

Such unification has importance in light of a query that one might raise about a contextualist theory of explanation like the one developed in these pages: "So you have a coherent explanation, held hypothetically, that answers a why-question. Why think that it is for that reason true, or has anything true about it?" This query *might* concern a philosopher who holds that his attempts at philosophical rigor and consistency are something more than entertaining. It *must* concern a religious person, for whom faith and the formulation of religious explanations is not just an academic exercise. If the notion of coherence can be spelled out in sufficient clarity, and if a coherence theory of truth is a viable option philosophically, we would be justified in taking explanatory success as in some measure truth indicative.

I should conclude this reflection with one caveat regarding the criterion of comprehensiveness. Although reaching the most comprehensive context is an ideal desideratum, I do not believe that one is justified in claiming that sentences are *false* apart from explicit reference to the broadest possible context. The tendency to deny full significance to the parts except within the explicit horizon of the whole is visible in some of the idealists such as Bradley and may underlie Pannenberg's assertion that one can finally understand the meaning (*Bedeutung*) of the word *rose* only in the context of the whole of history.[24] There may be an immanent movement toward more comprehensive contexts of meaning; yet this does not make somehow false the understanding that takes place at intermediate levels. And there may be contexts—arguably, each scientific discipline is one—in which it is methodologically desirable *not* to incorporate the perspective of broader frameworks.

The central point is rather that the impetus toward a continual expansion of semantic scope reveals no inherent qualitative breaks, such that everything becomes irrational or meaningless after a certain level. From the perspective of a coherence theory of meaning, a philosophical (or religious) explanation is not a different breed from a lower-level explanation. The individual who begins to reflect on the meaning of a portion of her experience can, by placing the question within ever broader contexts, progress along a continuum to the context of the whole of her experience, which in turn can become the question of the whole of *human* experience or even that of all possible experience.

The individual who follows this chain of reflection through to its end raises meaning questions in the broadest possible semantic context. I am tempted to label this broadest context *religious*, though others have defended it as metaphysical, aesthetic, or ethical. At any rate, one is involved at this level with the attempt *to make sense of total experience*. It seems fairly clear that this project, in the form of a task for reflection, is the goal of explanatory attempts in at least a significant portion of traditional philosophy. The metaphysical tradition in philosophy from Thales onward has dealt explicitly with the nature of all that is. Indeed, the quest for an ultimate principle or *archē* is precisely the search for a systematic principle that is able to synthesize all more limited contexts (or disciplines) under its purview. Even the more analytic traditions in philosophy, despite their suspicion about broadly synthetic systems, have always with time rejected attempts to circumscribe the range of philosophical explanations. The debate over and rejection of the verificationist criterion in this century is a good example of this interplay of analytic and synthetic tendencies. These three tasks—to synthesize, systematize, and analyze—remain indispensable aspects of the philosophical attempt to make experience meaningful, to make sense of it.

CHAPTER FIVE

Religious Beliefs as Explanations

A challenging array of difficulties faces the methodologist when she turns from the philosophy of science to the study of religion, even given the general reflections on philosophical rationality presented in the excursus. Only if a long list of potential difficulties can be resolved will we be justified in treating explanation in religion in a manner similar to that outlined in the previous chapters: (1) it must be possible to specify what a religious context is if the term *religious explanation* is to make any sense at all; (2) religious beliefs must be shown to have some explanatory function, and the nature of this function must be specified; (3) the particular difficulties facing religious explanations must be discussed and any resultant restrictions on their use noted; (4) religious explanations must exhibit some similarity to explanations in other areas of human experience if the term *explanation* is not to be equivocal; yet (5) if the similarity demanded by (4) is overemphasized, one can easily overlook the factors that differentiate religious explanations from explanations in other areas of human experience.

Though the gravity of these difficulties should not be underestimated, to refuse a priori all comparisons between religious and nonreligious explanations is equally unjustified. The objects of religious belief and experience may well lie beyond human grasp, but complexes of religious meaning and belief need not. Believers speak at length of what they believe in and what its significance for them is, even when the ultimate referent of their language is ineffable or transcends the world. We may well be able to reconstruct the development of these complexes of meaning, specifying the manner in which religious beliefs function as explanations for believers. If we can compare the process of the creation or appropriation of religious meaning with similar processes in more mundane social contexts, then it

113

should be possible to draw out the methodological implications of their similarities and differences. One might call our project in this chapter a phenomenology of religious meaning-construction, if this phrase is understood in the (not necessarily Husserlian) sense of a description of how individuals come to accept and utilize particular religious beliefs to make sense of their world.

The goal of this chapter, then, is to consider the appropriateness (and implications) of viewing religious beliefs as explanations, beginning with a description of the formation of religious meaning. The manner in which I propose to approach this study evidences some significant parallels with the project pursued in earlier chapters. Specifically, the reference to complexes of meaning underscores the connections with the phenomenology of the social world. In other words, instead of focusing on religious beliefs from the start as cognitive truth claims, I suggest we view them first in the context of the individual's project of making sense of his experience. Otherwise, we run the risk of neglecting Giddens's double hermeneutic for the human sciences, forgetting (as the formalists did) that both researcher and object of research are subjects who are trying to construct a meaningful world. Thus, the semantic nature of religious worlds or traditions forces us to approach religious explanations only through a discussion of individual meaning-construction on the social level (as in chap. 3). One can compare scientific and religious *theories* directly; but understanding the *appropriation* of religious beliefs requires a detour through the problem of meaning.

Studying Religion

In order to make progress with this project, we need to make explicit the disciplinary viewpoint from which we will observe religious experience, beliefs, and explanations. The study of religion and theology represent two significantly different perspectives which are currently available. The former discipline will provide the framework or second-order language in this chapter as we discuss first-order religious language and practice. Chapter 6 then considers religious explanations from the perspective of the discipline of theology, including the question of whether and to what extent theology can be viewed as an academic discipline analogous to the study of religion.

Very roughly, I use the term *study of religion* to describe a second-order discourse concerned with the religious phenomenon in all its manifestations: religious experience, practices, beliefs, language, institutions. A variety of social scientific disciplines contribute to this undertaking, including the psychology, sociology, anthropology, and history of religion. As mentioned above, I will draw especially from the phenomenology of religion, which I take to express two important methodological guidelines for the study of religion. First, one must begin with a description of general features of the religious phenomenon. One need not ascribe transcendental status to these suggestions; each is dependent on the outcome of actual research with religious communities and practices. Second, such descriptions bracket questions of the ultimate truth of the claims involved. When I say "religion originates in an encounter with the divine," I am not claiming to know the existence of a god or gods. Each such sentence is prefaced, by implication, with the words "As the believer sees it" or "As implied by religious language and practice." Of course, this bracketing by no means implies that believers do not care about the truth issue, only that the phenomenologist must set it aside long enough to understand their claims and practices. In this chapter, one might say, we ask about the nature of the religious perspective; in the next, about methods for evaluating it when it takes theological form.

My thesis will be that the same reciprocal relationship of explanation and understanding can be detected with respect both to the believer and the student of religion. Regarding the first, one can view the religious person as involved in the quest of making sense of his world, that is, the totality of his (direct and indirect) experience.[1] In this attempt to make sense, two separate elements can be distinguished: that of intuitive *understanding*, or the inner sense of an overall coherence of his experienced world, and the element of rational *explanation*, or the reasoned quest for an overall coherence of his (or his group's) beliefs and attitudes in the theoretical sphere. Although the explanation/understanding distinction tends to break down at some levels of religious experience, both elements play a vital role in analyzing the religious phenomenon.

The student of religion then repeats in a more abstract manner this same twofold process in her effort to explicate or make sense of her object of study. Just as we found sociological or anthropological theorizing to require an understanding of the social object, so also one precondition for adequate theories of religion is some *understanding* of the religious dimension. Religious believers have long insisted that researchers who lack understanding of the religious form of life will not be able adequately to evaluate religious practices and attitudes. This understanding may include some personal religious experience, though this is not in itself sufficient and may not even be necessary. Also required is an openness to believers' ways of thinking and perceiving and a willingness to consider religious phenomena nonreductionistically (without naturalistic assumptions)—or at least some value-neutrality in approaching forms of life different from one's own. After understanding the practices or beliefs in question, the student of religion is then able to formulate certain hypotheses or *explanations* aimed at making theoretical sense of the religious phenomena. It is her task not just to describe what beliefs and practices are characteristic of a religion, but also to explain why they occur as they do and how they are tied together as components of a religious whole. These explanations may include formulations of particular underemphasized or unexpressed beliefs, the introduction of interpretive concepts not present in the community itself, or evaluations of the mutual fit of beliefs or their consistency with other areas of experience.

Through the account that follows, I attempt to show that intersubjective explanations in the study of religion need not be reductionist in spirit, countenancing an explanatory account only if it explains away the beliefs in question. Indeed, whether the spotlight is on believers or students of religion, I regard the attempt to explain as an integral part of the study of religion. But we will see that explanation in religion is very closely linked to the broader semantic effort at making sense of one's existence, in a manner reminiscent of Henry Duméry's definition of understanding as the attempt "to recover from its structures the origin and establishment of meaning."[2] To the extent that we can view the religious quest as a semantic project, it can be studied with the methods and within the framework already developed in the social sciences. The discovery of meaningfulness through the religious life is yet another form that the human search for meaning can take—albeit a unique form, and possibly the most comprehensive one of all.

As I emphasized in the discussion of social meaning-construction, the attempt to trace the genesis and development of complexes of meaning, religious or otherwise, from the synthesizing activity of the individual need reflect no more than a heuristic or methodological starting point. It is manifestly false to claim that religious meaning is primarily an individual phenomenon; such a claim would neglect the important influence of preexisting societal and communal beliefs, structures of meaning, expectations, doctrinal systems, liturgy, praxis. As became clear in the discussion of Schütz above, he and Husserl (and those phenomenologists of religion who follow too closely in their tradition) stand guilty of absolutizing one moment in the reciprocal interaction of pregiven context and individual synthesis. Nonetheless, it remains essential for one to examine the process by which the individual appropriates existing traditions and beliefs in his quest to make sense of his world, especially in a highly individualized civilization such as the contemporary West. Whatever the influences on the religious individual, every time he appropriates the tradition he becomes anew a locus of religious meaning.

The Centrality of the Meaning Dimension in Religion

First, why begin with the question of meaning rather than, say, rational warrant in religion? Doing so serves as a corrective: whatever role we find reason to play in the initiation or maintenance of religious belief, there is no point in analyzing religious beliefs as if they originated as consciously rational arguments.[3] Even if some religious apologetic or systematic theological approaches will consider only those beliefs that are advanced according to objective criteria, a phenomenology of religious belief can make no such move. In reality, a vast array of nonrational factors exert their influence in actual cases of religious commitment. The recent school of Reformed epistemology, for instance, has made an interesting attempt to explain in a nonfoundationalist manner the believer's relation to his beliefs. Plantinga now speaks of "basic beliefs," or beliefs that one does not accept on the basis of any other beliefs.[4] Certainly Plantinga is right that many religious persons actually hold beliefs in this manner. One *may* step into a religious belief system as into a new world, without prior reflection or by means of a sudden conversion from one way of seeing to another (Wittgenstein's thesis); further, there is often an intimate connection between one's practice and the beliefs one holds.

The phrase "the meaning dimension" draws attention to an even greater disanalogy with scientific practice: religious faith or practice may not be primarily propositional. To begin a treatment of the religious life in an exclusively propositional framework[5] obscures this fact. Taking the lead from the methodology of the interpretive social sciences (chap. 3), I will instead begin with a *semantic* analysis of religious belief. Only from this perspective can we move on to speak of the rationality of religious explanations without fear of drawing artificial analogies between explanations in religion and science.

In short: in those areas where rational analyses of propositions are of little help in explaining religious beliefs, a phenomenology of religious meaning may still have much to offer. Not all religious belief is of this variety; however, in cases dominated by noncognitive factors, a phenomenology of religion may still be able to analyze the understanding and explanation components of belief. The believer may still be conscious of the fit of his beliefs together; at least there is strong empirical evidence for holding that believers actively seek to avoid cognitive dissonance.[6] Where phenomenological study does not reveal any rational grounds for an individual's entering or continuing in a religious tradition, it may still reveal his behavior to be motivated by a sense of the meaningfulness or personal disclosure value of a given belief or set of beliefs.

Religious Meaning-Sketches

I have argued that the first context for approaching religious explanations is not epistemological but semantic. An important task is posed by the
need to view one's life as meaningful, and religious explanations are in the
first place (but not solely) responses to this task. As students of religion we
seek to rationally reconstruct the semantic dimension in religion by providing theoretical accounts that make second-order sense of first-order explanatory efforts in religion. In this section we consider several accounts of the
semantic dimension, employing the notion of religious meaning-sketches.
Although I overlook questions of the epistemic justification or truth of
religious meaning-structures for the time being, we will find these issues
inevitably arising as we continue.

My thesis is that religious beliefs are grounded at the outset in their
ability to make the experience of an individual or group meaningful. The
believer understands the world in a certain way; that is to say, he perceives
a significance in certain (or all) objects or situations that others do not.
Significance here can be understood with Hick as "that fundamental and
all-pervasive characteristic of our conscious experience which *de facto*
constitutes it for us [as] the experience of a 'world' and not of a mere empty
void or churning."[7] As our earlier discussions suggested, this is a hermeneutic question, a matter of interpretation. The believer has a sense of
the cohesion of his religious beliefs with his nonreligious concepts and life
experiences; although he may not be able to express how it is the case, they
create a world or totality of meaning for him. By stressing some aspects of
his experience and deemphasizing or explaining away others, he constructs
a unique complex of significance relationships, including a particular interpretation of the tradition in which he finds himself, in a manner similar to
our discussion of the individual agent in the social sphere. The coherence
theory of meaning suggests that the different elements of his world—his
mental, social, and religious experience—will receive their meaning from
the network of interrelationships that structures that world. Although religious believers and unbelievers may at times evidence an underlying
disagreement about facts, about whether or not a given event occurred, at
other times this need not even be the case.[8]

How then are judgments of meaning made within this religious dimension? One portrayal of the grounding of beliefs in a semantic context is
provided by John Hick. Hick appeals to Cardinal Newman's notion of the
"illative sense," or the sense of certitude that the mind has of the meaning
and truth of a judgment. Beliefs, which for Hick arise on occasions in which
one does not know, are a matter of "appreciating the drift of a miscellaneous
mass of evidence" (81). It is thus possible to speak of the various reasons for

adopting a religious belief or set of beliefs and of factors which impede such acceptance. For instance, we may believe "because the belief coheres with the mass of our other beliefs and is not contradicted by any item of our experience."[9] Still, even allowing for reasons for believing, there obviously remains a more subjective element in religious belief than in knowledge claims in many other fields. Religious beliefs supplement claims to knowledge with a general, holistic sense of fit or meaningfulness. In this connection, Hick's appeal to the illative sense draws attention to the level of "global impressions" or interpretations.[10] Indeed, the comprehensive claims typically found among religious beliefs suggest that they are operative at a rather global level to integrate the total experience of the believer.

How might we characterize these vague, possibly nonpropositional, semantic judgments that have emerged as important in the religious sphere? I suggest that it is theoretically fruitful for the student of religion to examine these worlds of religious belief and practice as structures of meaning or *meaning-sketches*. The word *structure* carries the connotation of something constructed and enduring. In the present context, the constructing refers to a subjective process. Yet it nonetheless involves identifiable semantic structures that can potentially be isolated and analyzed theoretically. In van der Leeuw's words, a structure is "an organic whole which cannot be analyzed into its own constituents . . . ; a fabric of particulars, not to be compounded by the addition of these . . . but again only *understood* as a whole. . . . Structure is reality significantly organized."[11]

Two of van der Leeuw's comments on structure are especially relevant here. On the one hand, the objective element in these semantic structures allows the student of human action (the historian or phenomenologist) to pursue the activity of reconstructing meaning-structures in her theoretical work. Rational reconstructions require a shift of levels, a movement from observing the phenomena to formulating and analyzing them. On the other hand, an individual world is too complex to recreate in its entirety. This limitation is not overcome through an appeal to the subjective process of recreating, that is, the historian's imaginative "living himself into" (*Einleben*) the lives of past persons, as advocated by Dilthey and Collingwood.[12] At best we can engage in the "sketching of an outline within the chaotic maze of so-called 'reality'" (672).

Second, the significance involved in the study of meaning is neither purely subjective nor purely objective: "the sphere of meaning is a third realm, subsisting above mere subjectivity and mere objectivity," although meaning is "experienced" by understanding (673). Van der Leeuw's "realm" terminology may be misleading, but the point is clear: the old subjective/objective dichotomy is transcended if religious meaning, with its subjective overtones, is understood in terms of structured complexes of attitudes, beliefs, and practices. It is this structural approach to meaning that I wish to condone with the term *meaning-sketches*.

Meaning, understood in the contextual or coherential sense, leads for the religious person in an immanent movement to ever broader contexts of meaning:

> [Man] arranges life into a significant whole: and thus culture arises. . . . But he never halts; he seeks ever further for constantly deeper and wider *meaning*. When he realizes that a flower is beautiful and bears fruit, he enquires for its ampler, ultimate significance. . . .
> The religious significance of things, therefore, is that on which no wider nor deeper meaning whatever can follow. It is the meaning of the whole.[13]

Hick, like van der Leeuw, has defined religious significance as "the believer's experience as a whole." To attain it, one performs an act of "total interpretation."[14] We return to this theme in the following section.

The notion of meaning-sketches invokes a number of other associations that cohere well with our discussion of the religious dimension. The term suggests a certain preliminary (not fully articulated) form; it invokes the artistic analogy (nonrational elements); it carries connotations of an outline, the blurring of details under the bold strokes of a basic idea. Meaning-sketches are, with Nygren, "outlines of the totality of meaning that is presupposed in all individual experience."[15] Similarly, John Kekes speaks of them as "metaphysical visions."[16]

As my references to the illative sense implied, we find here an important discontinuity with theories, be they scientific or metaphysical; for theories are analyzed within discursive contexts that do not fully capture the immediate nature of these religious connections. Nonetheless, the existence of a dimension of meaning that is sui generis does not invalidate treatment of religious phenomena in propositional or epistemic terms, either by believers themselves or by theorists of religion. In fact, one notes some interesting connections with metaphysical beliefs. Both types of belief tend to be broad or all-inclusive. When one attempts to give didactic (as opposed to, say, poetic) expression to a meaning-sketch, it may well take the form of a metaphysical theory.[17] And, as Kekes notes,

> Metaphysical theories share an important feature not just with aesthetic and mystical visions but also with such large-scale scientific theories as cosmological speculations about the expanding universe, the theory of evolution, the conservation of parity, and the theory of relativity. This shared feature is the *goal of offering a comprehensive*

explanation of what there is . . . Metaphysical theories explain by providing schemes in terms of which phenomena, whatever they may turn out to be, could be explained.[18]

In other words, to the extent that religious meaning-sketches perform an explanatory function, they also share a kinship with metaphysical theories. Both approaches may be based on a "root metaphor," a fundamental framework for interpreting the world, even if the metaphor is interpreted more epistemically in metaphysics, more semantically in religion.[19] One could even call religious meaning-sketches hypothetical, in the sense that they remain preliminary, that they have *some* empirical implications (though there are difficulties with this in the case of very general religious beliefs), and that they require constructive activity on the part of the individual.

The Quest for the Total Context

As I have construed them, meaning-sketches constitute one of the areas in which philosophy and religion share some common ground. In many respects the comparison of religion and philosophy is simply a category mistake; still, on at least one level similarities obtain. The religious believer who attempts to find a coherent formulation for his religious experiences, his community's practice, or the teachings of his sacred scripture, engages in an activity not entirely dissimilar to the philosopher engaging in metaphysical speculation. The believer's activity has other than epistemological goals; his is not solely an endeavor to know. Yet we have already been able to speak of both efforts as quests to make sense of one's world in either a philosophical or a religious context.

Tillich, after noting that "spirit (*Geist*) is always [the medium for] the actualization of meaning (*Sinnvollzug*), and the thing intended by the spirit is a systematic interconnection of meaning,"[20] proceeds to define philosophy as "the theory of the structure of meaning-reality" (57). Again, there is good reason to be cautious of attempts to equate the philosophical and religious motivations: philosophy must necessarily define its questions within a conceptual framework (e.g., the quest for an *archē*), while religion often posits the negation (or at least the *Aufhebung*) of the philosophical perspective into a higher or deeper religious whole. Even Tillich insists that philosophy or "culture" is directed toward particular forms of meaning and their unity, whereas only religion is "directed toward the unconditioned meaning, toward the import of meaning. . . . Religion is directedness toward the Unconditional" (59). It may be, as Schleiermacher maintains, that philosophy is occupied with things (including metaphysical entities) and their interrelationships, "whereas the religious consciousness grasps finite realities as grounded in the Infinite and Whole, thus intuiting the Infinite itself within finite things."[21] Nonetheless, such differentiations of content leave room for various important parallels to be drawn. Natural theologians, for instance, have employed philosophical methods and terms in the process of formulating religious givens, whereas a number of philosophers have insisted on basic intuitions or the practices of individual or community as the starting point for philosophical reflection.

The similarities between the religious and philosophical impulses can best be expressed, then, in full cognizance of the differences that remain, when one begins with a semantic rather than an epistemological context. I have already posited a gradual continuum of ever broader contexts of meaning. Placing the chapters of this book on that continuum, we might say summarily that in natural scientific practice questions of meaning are unthematized but present; the social sciences then thematize them explicitly but always with reference to a specific, circumscribed social context. In philosophy proper no limitations of scope are countenanced and no higher level of reflection remains outside its purview: reflection on philosophy *is* philosophy. Perhaps in some traditions of philosophy,[22] but certainly in the religious consciousness, the horizon of the meaning of experience as a whole is at least implicitly present. Note that when philosophy does thematize the whole of reality, it is as its final achievement or telos (as in Aristotle or Hegel). By comparison, "the religious dimension *means* the concern for the ultimate ground and goal of existence."[23] Not every person asks about the totality of his experience, any more than one would say that all persons are religious. But when one does act, conceptualize, or symbolize with reference to the meaning of the whole, one has in some sense entered the religious dimension.

It is helpful to conclude this section with a case study. Anders Nygren has made a remarkable contribution toward an adequate theory of meaning in religion in his important *Meaning and Method*, using coherence and context arguments similar to those presented in previous chapters.[24] His description of the semantic movement toward a total context is exactly correct; yet, inexplicably, he draws back from the apparent implications of his own position.

As prerequisites for addressing the question of meaning, Nygren analyzes scientific argumentation (chap. 4), discusses the metaphysical and scientific tendencies in philosophy (chap. 3), and ultimately construes philosophy itself as "analysis of meaning" (chap. 5). He is also able to demonstrate a role for coherential meaning at the heart of debates about validity, philosophical argumentation, and the analysis of presuppositions, providing evidence that problems of meaning are indeed as central to the philosophical enterprise as I have claimed. Nygren's analysis of the nature of "contexts of meaning" (chaps. 9–11) again underscores the indispensability of context for meaningfulness. He warns of the dangers of "logicism," in which "minute attention is paid to the parts while the whole, the context, is neglected. In other words, we get an 'analysis of meaning' which ignores the very thing that gives a statement its meaning" (149). Most crucially, Nygren's various arguments show that talk of contexts of meaning leads inevitably to the notion of a "total context": "Thus the question of 'meaning and method' leads on to that of diverse, comprehensive 'contexts of meaning', with regard to which the final and decisive question is how these contexts, each determined by its own basic presuppositions, are related to one another, how they differ from one another, and how possibly in the last resort they are dependent on one another" (228).

After his excellent exposition of the relationship of meaning and context, however, Nygren does not pursue the logic of his own argument into the realm of religion. One would expect that religion would be linked in some way to the total context that he posits as the telos of his theory of meaning. Yet instead of addressing the religious dimension in terms of this "final and decisive question" of the ultimate interdependence and interrelationship of all other contexts, he simply places the study of religion alongside all the other contexts of meaning: "It is the business of the philosophy of religion to investigate the religious context of meaning with regard to its basic presuppositions, its distinctive character and meaning in relation to other contexts of meaning, and its connection with these other contexts" (228). The book peters out with treatments of the different motif contexts in the various fields of science, ethics, aesthetics, and religion. Since each field is "free and independent" of the others, they can be compared but never placed in a hierarchy, for "each is autonomous and must be judged according to its own laws" (276). Now Nygren is right in insisting that "scientific philosophy" begin with existing contexts of meaning, as he is in claiming that "none of them needs to justify itself in another's eyes or to be measured by its standards" (278). But this is a separate issue from the nature of the religious dimension as involving believed access to an all-encompassing context of meaning. Nygren's own thought should have brought him to this conclusion regarding religion, since he has argued convincingly for a compelling movement in the notion of context that drives one always to a more encompassing perspective.[25]

How has Nygren avoided the holistic impulse evident in like-minded thinkers such as Schleiermacher and Dilthey, as well as in statements of his own such as "the concept of meaning (*Sinn*) is not, as has often been supposed, only a historical category, but is of universal significance" (236)? The answer lies in his final equation of contexts of meaning with Wittgensteinian language games (253f), together with his acceptance of Wittgenstein's definition of meaning: "the use of an expression, or the way it functions in its context, *is* its meaning" (262). Though Wittgenstein showed his awareness of the transcending impulse in religious belief in the *Tractatus*, neither the *Philosophical Investigations* nor the lectures on religion[26] treat religion as anything more than another form of life. But this internalist approach is diametrically opposed to the synthetic movement to ever broader contexts that Nygren has so masterfully demonstrated.

Sociologically considered, religion may be one among a multiplicity of forms of life; but to view religion sociologically is not necessarily to view it religiously. As the phenomenology of religion has shown, the religious impulse is to move beyond any limited context to the most comprehensive or synthetic viewpoint possible.[27] For instance, the religious person may well grant the authority of science in its sphere while asserting that "God transcends even science" or, with the early Wittgenstein, "The sense of the world must lie outside the world."[28] Religion's refusal to remain just another form of life is even more obvious in the Eastern religions, where the paradoxes arising in science and ethics (or Kant-like antinomies between scientific and religious truths) traditionally provide the occasion for enlightenment and the true entrance into the religious dimension.[29]

Toward a Theory of Religious Explanation

We have considered in sufficient detail the semantic level on which religious beliefs occur and the general nature of the meaning question that motivates them. What now is the relation between the project of making sense of one's total experience and the specific details of individual religious experience and belief? What role, if any, does the notion of explanation play in this process? Obviously, the locus of explanations in religion will be the set of beliefs held by persons or communities. In many cases the explanans (the explanatory account) or its warrants may include non-religious beliefs: that the universe actually did begin at a particular moment in time; that I indeed recovered after the rite was performed; that a necessary being explains the existence of contingent beings. But most religious explanations are couched in terms of distinctively religious beliefs. Let us turn then to examine the explanatory function of religious beliefs.

Religious Belief as Explanation

Religious belief originates in an initial encounter with the divine. Natural theologians speak of revelation through Nature, Durkheim of an encounter with the sacred, van der Leeuw of an attitude of awe, Otto of the sense of the holy.[30] The response of the persons involved is characterized by intense respect (worship) and great attraction (Otto's *mysterium tremendum et fascinans*); by a sense of contingency, finiteness, or sinfulness; and by a reorientation of values and priorities. Often associated with this encounter are extraordinary or charismatic phenomena. Weber has analyzed these phenomena in the context of the founding of religious traditions and their prophetic renewal, using the ideal-type of the charismatic leader. He defines charisma as "a certain quality of an individual personality by virtue of which he is set apart from ordinary men and treated as endowed with supernatural, superhuman, or at least specifically exceptional powers or qualities."[31] Whether directly or mediated by the chosen or enlightened leader (Moses, the Buddha), the followers then sense the possibility of closeness to the transcendent, the potential for their own private religious experience, and the obligation of holiness that stems from encounter with the Holy.

Out of this initial encounter with or self-revelation of the divine, lasting possibly over a long period of time, the transition takes place to a more stable period, which Weber labels the institutionalization of charisma. In "normal religion" (to paraphrase Kuhn) relatively stable patterns of belief, feeling, and worship emerge: a set of stories, a scripture, a cultus with rites and rituals, a priestly caste, organizational structures for education, reinforcement, and control. Now it might be thought that individuals inheriting a tradition that has been institutionally transmitted in this way would also inherit, ready-made, a pregiven complex of meaning, and hence that the stress I have placed on the individual semantic project in religion is inappropriate for believers at a historical distance from their tradition's founding. In a sense this is true: a given sacred cosmogony, for instance, makes sense of the world in a distinctive manner; a specific rite such as the Roman Catholic Mass predisposes to (and possibly determines) the sort of religious experiences that may accompany it.

Nonetheless, a given moment of the religious experience, a given religious interpretation or practice, always remains the experience of an individual, similar to "my seeing this vision" or "my feeling this joy." It may be simultaneously a communal rite or ritual, yet it is experienced by a given person. Each individual's experience of his religious tradition is idiosyncratic and reflects a unique constellation of feelings, attitudes, and life-experiences. In this sense each individual reappropriates his tradition in his religious experience and understanding, making it his own. Admittedly, the amount of individual synthetic creativity in this process varies greatly between individuals (the prophet or great teacher as opposed to the uncreative "man in the pew") and between traditional and nontraditional cultures (the limited belief options of the tribesperson as opposed to the smorgasbord of alternatives facing the North American believer). Yet if, as we claimed above, each individual world is a unique synthesis of particular experiences and perceptions, then the appropriation of a given religious tradition and its symbols, the manner in which it makes sense of one's personal world, will also vary between individuals. Hence, it is true that "the religious experience of individuals and their reflection upon it has been not only the origin of religious beliefs and practices but also a source of their continuation from age to age and of the transformations they have undergone in every religious community."[32] It is precisely the importance of the semantic dimension in religion that confirms the frequent stress on religious *experience* in the philosophy and phenomenology of religion.

For the purposes of relating religious beliefs and explanation, then, we can most profitably define religious belief as a reciprocal relationship between *an inherited tradition* of institutionalized belief, practice, and experience on the one hand, and *an individual's unique world*, personal appropriation or reinterpretation of the tradition, and individual religious experiences on the other. In suggesting this definition, I disagree by implication with Tillich's view that *any* object of "ultimate concern" is a religious object for the individual.[33] Some reference to a religious tradition is necessary, if only as that which the individual rejects in formulating his own complex of belief. Conversely, I also question purely sociological treatments of religious meaning that dwell on the details of the story told to the exclusion of the horizon of appropriation.[34]

Though neither of the two poles can be treated in abstraction, the locus of the individual is a helpful means for incorporating both the traditionally given component *and* that modification or creative appropriation that is vital if a religious tradition is to avoid becoming old and dry, a "dead" tradition. It is the necessity of meaningful personal appropriation that has been underscored, for example, by Luther in his insistence on the *pro nobis* of personal faith. Likewise, the same emphasis stands at the heart of Schleiermacher's critique of natural religion in the *Speeches*: "Single perceptions and feelings are, as you know, the elements of religion, and it can never lead to the character of any one religion to regard them as a mere heap, tossed together without regard to number, kind or purpose."[35] Whatever other standards can in the end be applied to religious explanations, they at least depend upon the personal disclosure value of the beliefs in which they are expressed.[36]

It should be clear that I am treating religious beliefs and (personal or communal) religious experience as standing in a reciprocal relationship. That is, a system of beliefs suggests a type of experience while, conversely, certain experiences tend to give rise to particular types of belief. The experience of power in the natural or social realm may find expression in a belief-system of animism or monotheism (the creator god); that of personal concern or nurture may lead to a personalistic theism; that of unity with nature, to some form of pantheism or panentheism; that of God's love, to a highly-developed doctrine of divine providence. It has often been pointed out how well the experience of pointless suffering is described by the karmic notion of the cycle of death and rebirth. In fact, instead of the reciprocal relationship that I am defending, some students of religion prefer to speak of the synthesis of religious belief and experience in a (or the) "religious attitude."[37] However, even those who wish to analyze the religious life from a synthetic perspective such as that of the religious attitude would presumably be willing to distinguish between the cognitive content and the experiential or affective elements in the religious phenomenon. That it is sometimes difficult to isolate experience and belief in practice does not imply that it is impossible for a phenomenology of religion to describe the characteristics of each. Even when one views them as facets of a deeper reality, the descriptions of religious belief and experience may vary: they evidence different "logics."

Given that we can in fact discuss the content of religious beliefs despite their imbeddedness in a personal or communal project of meaning-construction, it is now possible to gather the threads of this discussion into a theory of religious explanation. I have presented religious beliefs as that portion of the religious phenomenon that can be propositionally formulated, described, and in some cases critically evaluated. In virtually all traditions religious explanations are formulated in terms of such beliefs. Such explanations are the theoretical outworking of the quest for coherence or overall meaningfulness on the part of the religious believer. They are the reasoned attempt to achieve a nondissonant fit, a relationship of mutual implication, between one's beliefs and attitudes.

In explaining, the believer enters into a form of theoretical discourse, however tentatively and however strong his continuing commitment to the attitudinal aspects of his faith. As in other forms of theoretical discourse, here also various why-questions are formulated—why do I exist? why did this experience occur? why is the world the way it is?—which a religious tradition attempts to answer by means of its belief-structure. Question and answer do not necessarily represent a chronological progression, of course, but rather a logical relationship. It may well be that specific religious explanations give rise, after the fact, to their own particular set of why-questions. Still, as the striving for systematic consistency from the Christian church fathers to Advaita Vedanta Hinduism, from the elaboration of tribal creation myths to creation science shows, the same quest for a far-reaching coherence is manifested on the religious-theoretical level as has been pursued on the level of individual religious meaning-sketches.

Taken together, I suggest, the individual beliefs accepted by the believer provide a coherent explanation of the world known to him. As noted, the religious tradition in which he has been socialized plays no small role in telling him what questions ought to be asked and what sorts of answers are likely to be accepted as explanatorily adequate. The explanation may not arise out of disinterested speculation and the evidence for the explanans may not be purely objective. Religious explanations are not paradigm-independent. Nonetheless, the ruling religious tradition must offer answers to the queries that preoccupy the individual if it is to integrate his various experiences into a meaningful whole.

The penalty for explanatory failure is cognitive dissonance, a sense of tension between one's nonreligious intellectual (moral, affective) experience and the religious account of it. Such explanatory inadequacy *may* not lead to an immediate rejection of a religious tradition, since participation in a religious community serves other functions in addition to making sense of one's experienced world. It will, however, limit the ability of the individual to appropriate the tradition in question, as well as threaten the attempt of that tradition to perform its integrative semantic role ("making sense of total experience"). This failure may occur whether or not the tradition explicitly grants a place for formulating and questioning its basic explanatory accounts. [38]

Levels of Explanation in Religion

Forms and functions of religious explanations are as numerous as types of religious belief. They vary from the extremely personal function of explaining a given religious experience undergone by an individual, to justifying social mores or a societal structure of authority, to explaining "why there is something rather than nothing." We will turn to the question of evaluating religious explanations in the following section. First, however, it is important to clarify the relationship between religious explanation and understanding as it varies according to the various levels of religious experience.

We might distinguish between a narrow and a broad conception of religious experience—and, correspondingly, of religious belief[39]—as long as these are taken as expressing not a dichotomy but opposite ends of a continuum. According to the narrow conception, specific experiences are tied to specific beliefs about the world and God. The divine, understood as having a particular form and content that is (at least partially) knowable, is encountered in individual experiences and moments of the believer's life. Certain times and places (Passover, the Temple), and certain of his actions (prayer), are interpreted as more spiritual than others. Beyond this, either in pure form or as a tendency within the narrow conception, the broad conception of religious experience sees all of life as falling under the control of the divine, everything as making it present, every action as a response to it. Religion in this broad sense is the clearest expression of that inherent movement to the broadest context that emerged in our discussion of meaning above. Yet even in the narrower conception the divine being or sacred truth that is manifested is one whose significance is understood to be universal.

These two conceptions of religious experience shed light on different tendencies in the religious impulse. The narrow conception has the specificity required for religious belief and practice: it allows for a creed or story and ethical maxims to live by, for a community of like-believing persons as a socialization and support network, and for a cultus to express the shared belief. Such needs have spawned and maintained the so-called positive religions as the major loci of religious experience and belief in all cultures. Nonetheless, in tension with this component, the broader religious impulse resists any ultimate compartmentalization. "Your God is too small!" claims one popular religious author; "you can't put God in a box," cries another. Visible in its purest form in mystical experience and negative theology, the synthetic tendency transcends creeds and the boundaries of positive religion, necessary as they may be in day-to-day practice, moving into an ultimately united realm where all distinctions fall away.[40]

I believe that the distinction between these two conceptions of religious experience requires a certain limitation of scope for all theories of religious belief and explanation. In the social sciences we found some tension between the broad explanatory power of higher-level theories and the explanatory detail of lower-level theories; the same tension returns with a vengence in religion. In virtually all religions the divine is perceived in or through particular objects or events, while transcending all limiting words and contexts. Jewish and Christian theologies stress God's salvation-history as the particular locus of his self-manifestation, for example, without wishing to give up the notion that God is Lord also of universal-history.[41]

I suggest that this phenomenon necessitates a multilevel account of religious explanations, one that distinguishes the project of making sense at more concrete levels of experience from making sense at the level of the whole of experience. At the narrowest level, the believer will take a particular complex of experience and belief to constitute an explanation for some particular event or events: Yahweh caused the Flood to punish the people's sinfulness; God allowed the flat tire to teach me patience. A religious explanation of the events in question will include reference to the activity of the divine in or behind the event. For the believer the explanation will be true if the divine actually acted in the way claimed. Such assertions, which appear to contain empirical claims, may not be immediately testable. However, internal contradictions within the believer's account, empirical predictions that are falsified, and tensions with, say, naturalistic explanations of the same event may in some cases count against his explanation. [42]

Even at a somewhat broader level, why-questions can still be formulated: why did God create the world? why is the circle of death and rebirth perpetuated? Here also doctrinal answers are given, usually by higher-order theological statements referring to the creation of the world or "God's plan in history." The reference is now to history as a whole. Truth is claimed for the belief that God exists or that *samsara* will end when amassed karma no longer causes another cycle, although there may be no particular event in the present that could falsify these truth-claims. They function to explain for believers why their life is as it is, yet they do so by providing an overarching interpretation of experience that seems more to describe the whole than to explain any particular part of it.

Here we begin to see a shading over from explanations of experience to attitudes toward experience. One might claim that explanatory accounts still have empirical entailments at this level, but they will be of only the most attenuated sort. Perhaps there should not be suffering in the world if an omnipotent, omniscient, omnibenevolent being exists, or at least not a balance of evil over good—at least not in the long run. Definitive falsifications seem rather unlikely, insofar as these explanations extend over large periods of human (or divine) history; more appropriate is an appeal to "eschatological verification" or falsification (cf. n. 8 above). Nonetheless, broader religious accounts still evidence what we might call *explanatory coherence*: they attempt to explain human experience in the most general terms at which an explanation can still be formulated. As a result, certain types of incoherence might still provide a basis for intersubjective criticism at this level.

At the *broadest* level of religious experience, however, one can speak of explanation, if at all, only in a rather different sense from its meaning elsewhere in this book. Indeed, recalling our overall attempt to pursue the theory of explanation from physics to theology, here we face perhaps the greatest hiatus of all. Any explanation at this level is so different from scientific explanations that equivocation threatens any attempt at comparison. The existence of this level in religion underscores the element of truth in the appeal to "total interpretation" by thinkers like John Hick and W. Cantwell Smith. (That it is only one aspect of the religious life represents the element of truth in their opponents' positions.)

Understood at the level of total experience, faith is "an uncompelled mode of 'experiencing as'. . . . No *way* of accounting for the data can be said

to be, in any objectively ascertainable sense, more probable than another."[43] When concerned with the meaningfulness of the whole, basic
intuitions are more at home than arguments; one speaks symbolically, if at
all; and religious experience becomes undifferentiated, in the sense that
meaning is ascribed directly to the whole and only by derivation to each of
its parts. No wonder thinkers like Nygren, who wish to defend philosophy
of religion as a process of linguistic analysis and clarification, rope in their
theories of meaning short of this point by considering the religious context
only to the extent that it can be accounted for in purely propositional and
epistemic terms.

At this level the believer's fundamental religious intuition makes sense
of his experience as a whole more in the manner of an immediate aesthetic
sense of beauty than in the manner of propositional analysis. The believer
or mystic senses ("sees") that things fit together, that there is an underlying
coherence, that "All shall be well, and / All manner of thing shall be well."[44]
Here at the borders of propositionality scant analogy remains with explanatory projects elsewhere. Intuitive understanding is no longer a precondition for explanation but seems to supersede it. The best the student of
religion can offer is the semantic line from limited to broadest contexts of
meaning that has structured this chapter up to now; and even this line is
more posited than observed. That is, we could say that this highest level,
the making sense of total experience, is the limiting case for efforts to
explain at other levels. Here the believer or mystic claims to have a final
coherence, an ultimate, comprehensive fit. Here he may speak of harmo-
ny, or unity, or the acceptance of all that is. But the elements that typified
explanations in our earlier discussions are now absent: no problem-situation can be specified, no field delimited, since the explanation encompasses everything; no why-question can be formulated; no distinction between general law and specific instances remains. The reference (if subject
and object, intuition and reference, can be separated any longer) is not an
item in the world but the world as a whole, its relationship to the transcendent as totally other. In an important sense, the entire explanatory effort
has been left behind or transcended; understanding supersedes explanation.

Interestingly, this limiting case of religious explanation works its way
back into the more concrete explanations that one finds within religious
belief systems. I have already defended the interconnection of the broad
and narrow conceptions of religion in most actual religious systems. A
corollary of this reciprocity is that one finds a holistic component even in
those religious explanations that are more limited in scope. Even in those
traditions that are willing to speak in univocal or analogous terms about
their god or cosmic principles, one often finds some reference to a tran-

scendent or wholly other standing outside all language. The tacit presence of this final horizon, in which all distinctions are absolved, circles back to cast a preliminary or tentative pall onto the realm where distinctions *are* drawn, rendering their status finite and provisional, perhaps even hypothetical.

For all of these reasons, we can never reduce religion to a matter of the mere formulation and evaluation of explanations. Religious statements are never completely free of their telos in the whole or beyond; their explanatory role is consequently only part of their religious use. As we saw, the semantic or interpretive element is not so constrained. Since explanation fades over into understanding at the highest reaches of religious belief and experience, this process can by anticipation be said to be already at work, albeit in a less obvious way, in more limited religious contexts. It is unjustified to overlook the explanatory or epistemic element in religion because of its concern with meaning. It is equally unjustified to countenance only explanatory considerations.

The Rationality of Religious Explanations

In the remainder of this chapter we explore whether religious explanations can be rationally evaluated and, if so, under what conditions. We will not ask about the rationality of specific religious explanations, although the conclusions suggest a place for such apologetic efforts. Nor will I settle the question of how rational it is to appeal to religious explanations in the modern world. The task here is rather more modest, namely, to specify what would be required for religious beliefs to pass as rational, in the sense of being intersubjectively criticizable. I shall argue that there are in fact some requirements, that the term *rational* cannot be understood in a merely subjective manner. Admittedly, in light of the difficulties and limitations acknowledged in this chapter, the rational evaluation of religious explanations will be a difficult and at best partially successful task. Nonetheless, no argument yet presented warrants the conclusion that the very notion of rational religious explanations is untenable.

Our examination of religious belief and meaning has shown, among other things, that it is impossible to evaluate religious beliefs individually. This initial condition for any rational discussion of religious beliefs should not come as a surprise. Contextual constraints emerged already in our discussion of the natural sciences, where I considered them under the rubric of the context principle of rationality; they were then underscored in the treatment of social scientific and philosophical rationality. When one focuses on religious beliefs as explanations and seeks to evaluate their rational adequacy—whatever common criteria for evaluation may or may not emerge—one must evaluate at the level of systems or groups of beliefs.

Even where this stipulation is accepted, there remains disagreement as to the sorts of belief-systems to be evaluated. In the effort to avoid comparisons between abstract philosophical systems and religious belief-systems, some thinkers have insisted that as religious beliefs we should take only the teachings of the major world religions, that is, those longstanding religious traditions that include the rites and practices found in religious communities. Although there are reasons for focusing on practicing religious communities, I do not find sufficient warrant for limiting the religious sphere exclusively to them. It is perfectly conceivable that Whiteheadian philosophy (or Teilhardian, or Swedenborgian) could provide the content for a comprehensive theory of human existence. That a "mere philosophy" appears devotionally inadequate to many has not prohibited its passionate avowal by others. There is a creative ability in humans and an openness in the fabric of history that should discourage us from excluding new religions or systems of religious belief.

The major existing religious traditions, however, have withstood the test of time: they have helped to structure worlds of meaning for large numbers of persons for centuries, and their rational potential, the possibility of building them into coherent intellectual systems, has been explored by thinkers through a number of successive historical contexts. There is therefore at least prima facie justification for beginning with them when the question of the rationality of religious belief is raised. Moreover, focusing on existing religious traditions helps to avoid many of the pseudo-connections that are often drawn between science and religion. A number of writers have sought to use physics as a religion or as the direct source for a religious position.[45] Such approaches might be helpful as apologetics for existing religious traditions, to show that they are not incompatible with contemporary science (though I am doubtful of their value for this as well). But to attempt to build religion out of science without consideration of the individual's project of world-construction (as discussed in chap. 3) may lead one to assert far-reaching continuities between explanation in science and religion where in fact important discontinuities obtain.

What constitutes a religious tradition? Thomas Luckmann defines religions as "specific historical institutionalizations of symbolic universes."[46] We might understand "symbolic universes" as developed and shared versions of the meaning-sketches presented above. As Luckmann's definition suggests, it is possible for the believer or the student of religion to distinguish the symbolic universe of a specific religion from its particular institutional form at a given time. Indeed, the prophets of the various faiths have often done just this, calling for the modification of institutional structures or practices in light of the alleged original meaning of the religion in question. Nevertheless, the explanatory adequacy of a religious system for each of its adherents may well be closely tied to its present institutional and doctrinal form. Each individual will be concerned, as I have maintained, to achieve a coherence between his own life experience (intellectual, ethical, aesthetic, and explicitly religious) and the beliefs and practices of the tradition.

Beyond the Inside/Outside Dichotomy

The question of the rationality of religious belief can only be answered by distinguishing the two explanatory levels introduced at the outset of this chapter. When we devote a phenomenological inquiry to individual believers, we may be satisfied with the conclusion that the religious tradition in question helps *them* make sense of their experience, adequately interpreting or explaining it *for them*. Indeed, it is almost tautological to say that beliefs need to provide only as much warrant as the individual demands of them in order for him to consider them warranted. Surely the history of religious belief gives ample evidence that persons will accept beliefs as rationally satisfactory that are somewhat less than rationally compelling to others. There may be general, conceptual criteria that label these explanations rationally lacking; but that is no justification for dismissing them as *religiously* inadequate.

By contrast, when we move to the level of the study of religion, reevaluation is called for. The student of religion works to analyze the world-constructing activities of religious individuals and groups. By broadening the domain of experience (the evidence) to which her explanatory efforts must be adequate, she also broadens the standards of adequacy and inadequacy. Moreover, by extending the opportunity for critical response to those outside the religious community, she commits herself to providing descriptions and arguments that are intersubjective, that is, accessible in principle to any informed reader. But must we really draw a qualitative distinction between the explanatory projects of the believer and the student of religion?

My response to this question can be illustrated with the help of an extended parable. We might imagine a particular student of religion whose concerns include those of the social scientific study of religion (anthropology, psychology) and of the philosophy of religion. Let us assume her to be engaged in studying the religious beliefs of an Indonesian tribe, the Ajunyee, who worship a warrior god Tzojov. The anthropologist learns that Tzojov created the world, that is, the island inhabited by the Ajunyee and the surrounding islands of which they have knowledge, by pulling them up from a mythical netherworld using his fishing string and bone hook. Further, Tzojov is considered worthy of worship because he is more powerful than the dangerous ancestor-spirits and because he grants victory in war over neighboring cannibalistic tribes when presented with proper and sufficient offerings.

The Ajunyee cosmogony is explanatorily adequate to Ajunyee believers, since it explains the objective and social world known to them and does so in terms that they can appropriate. It answers the relevant why-questions in a way that makes sense of their world to them. Moreover, Tzojov is worthy of worship because he has the power to supply those things needed or esteemed by an Ajunyee. Nevertheless, when she moves from description to evaluation of these beliefs, the philosophically minded anthropologist is inclined to fault the Ajunyee cosmogony for not being able to explain additional facts and institutions unknown to the Ajunyee (Iowa City, McDonald's). She also has trouble believing in their god (questions of proving his existence aside) because he is utterly lacking in certain ethical qualities (justice, benevolence) and is not powerful enough, even in theory, to address the central concerns of her world (cross-cultural communication, tenure). If one has difficulties with the Ajunyee example, one can reflect on the loss of religious adequacy of the Greek gods, or the contemporary claims that Thomas Aquinas's notion of God as omnipotent *esse subsistens* is incompatible with the loving Father of the New Testament and is hence no longer a viable object of worship.[47]

When religious explanation is conceived as in this example, an interesting possibility begins to come to light. The distinction between the levels, between believer and the student of religion, need not be absolute. *Both* can be involved in the critical process of accepting or rejecting explanations on the basis of reasons. Instead of positing an American anthropologist who finds Ajunyee beliefs to be explanatorily inadequate, we can just as well imagine a widely traveled Ajunyee undergoing a similar reaction. Picture, for instance, an Ajunyee tribesman who, while out fishing, was carried by a hurricane to Jakarta, where he settled and was trained to assemble microchips. The tribesman might well come to the same conclusions about the inadequacy of Ajunyee religion and for reasons very similar to the anthropologist.

In stressing the parallels between believer and student of religion, I am emphatically not reducing religion to rational reflection. It is not necessary to presuppose that the rejection of a belief system will follow automatically from its effective criticism, even when the domain of experience to be explained is broadened and the requirement of intersubjective criticizability has been followed. The believer or community may introduce ad hoc modifications or may interpret the status of the beliefs in a different way to insulate them from the difficulties. The prodigal tribesman may return to his island without altering his religious beliefs. Perhaps he will decide that Tzojov's power was more extensive than he had been taught as a child, or that the Ajunyee religion is still aesthetically pleasing for him when interpreted symbolically. Or maybe the fear of social ostracism, or of being turned over to the cannibalistic warriors of a neighboring tribe as punishment for heresy, will keep him from abandoning his beliefs. But that the believer does not always allow rational assessment full sway is no proof that religious belief and a questioning or critical attitude need be incompatible. Social scientists also are not pancritical, though more of them agree that they ought to be, and they are so to a greater degree. The phenomenon of the anthropologist "going native," for example, and uncritically accepting parts or the whole of a native cosmology is well known. In such cases the assessments of the anthropologist may well be less critical or objective than those of the native believers themselves.

I am suggesting, in other words, that the distinction between the levels, between believer and student of religion, need not be taken as final. One is not always locked inside, the other outside. The student of religion may understand as well as, or better than, the actual believers and participants. For their part, believers can, and often do, evaluate their religious explanations in light of apparently countervening evidence and according to criteria not drawn directly from their interpretive system. When the scope of the believer's relevant experience is broadened, as in the Ajunyee fisherman example, the semantic and explanatory demands on his religious paradigm increase. An explanation he once judged rationally adequate may be modified or rejected because it cannot account for new data in a coherent manner—again, given that he chooses to consider such data and to reflect on external problems raised by other experiences or disciplines.

In these cases *there is no longer a sharp line between religious explanations and those found more typically in the philosophy of religion.* Put differently, the lines between involved adherent to (or critic of) a religious tradition and the objective ideal analyst of its rational strengths and weaknesses need not be drawn using a participant/non-participant schema. Many religious statements will presumably have meaning only within a given religious framework, as the Wittgensteinians insist. But those internalist accounts of religious belief that hold that external critical assessment can have no place in religious belief-systems do not have the last word. The believer can play the role of objective analyst and vice versa.

In Defense of the Secular Believer

We have seen that the inside/outside distinction is relative: it can be, and often is, transcended by religious believers. This fact will play a crucial role for the view of religious beliefs, explanations, and the theological enterprise advocated in the remaining pages of this book. We apply it first to religious belief: specifically, to the oft-voiced reservation that failure to delineate a clearly religion-internal realm of discourse will result in the reduction of religion to ethics, psychology, or fiction. My thesis is that allowing free movement between the levels of belief and reflection about belief need not reduce religious beliefs to something nonreligious, though it may entail an openness to revising them if necessary.

It is helpful to field the criticism of reductionism using a distinction recently advanced by Wayne Proudfoot. Proudfoot rejects the use of *descriptive reductions*, or "the failure to identify an emotion, practice, or experience under the description by which the subject identifies it."[48] This insistence is surely correct. Our earlier demonstration of the importance of understanding in social science, as well as the work of the great phenomenologists of religion in this century, have underscored the need for accurate, internal description if we are to understand the phenomena in question.

Proudfoot does however advocate *explanatory reduction*, which "consists in offering an explanation of an experience in terms that are not those of the subject and that might not meet with his approval" (197). Proudfoot's chapter on explanation is a successful defense of this latter move as necessary in accounting for religious experience. It is basic to the study of religion, he asserts, to offer competing explanations of the activities and perspectives of the believer. For religious experiences themselves assume concepts and beliefs that are not distinctively religious. This is the noetic element in religious experience that Proudfoot accuses Schleiermacher of disregarding when he maintained that religion was an autonomous moment of human experience, and which, he correctly claims, arguments for "religion without explanation" ignore.[49]

More crucial for my thesis, when we explain other parts of *our own* experience, we invariably do so with the aid of such external explanations. Because of the plurality of competing explanations, it is illicit to use a "protective strategy" (233) to rule out examination of the other possible explanations of the experience.

At first blush, Proudfoot's advocacy of explanatory reduction would seem to leave insufficient room for theology and the thought life of individual believers.[50] How shall we understand the process whereby believers attempt to redescribe their experience in different terms and concepts than the primary language of their worship or scriptures, yet still in terms that are internal to (within the framework of) their tradition? Does Proudfoot's explanatory reduction allow for believers' own reconstructions of their beliefs in nonreductionistic (belief-internal) terms? Such activity appears to lie in a gray area between his two categories: it is not mere intuitive understanding, nor is it meant as complete explanation. The redescription of his faith in belief-internal terms may still represent, *from the perspective of the individual concerned,* a full or partial explanation of his faith. Redescription may be a full explanation for those individuals or in those societies where education and socialization do not provide a significant secular perspective and, conversely, an only partial explanation for most educated persons in Europe and many in North America for whom it does. When the individual claims that an internal redescription makes adequate sense of his first-order beliefs and experiences, it would be gratuitous to dismiss his claim completely as unwarranted. Internal explanation is not a nonsensical concept.

Internal explanations, however, have become epistemically unsatisfactory for a large number of believers in contemporary culture. Let us call this type of person a *secular believer.* For such persons, not uncommon in the developed West, secular perspectives and ways of thinking—scientific, political, ethical—coexist alongside religious experiences and/or active participation in the "form of life" of a church or synagogue. For these persons, Wittgenstein's approach to religious belief is of very little applicability: "Suppose that someone believed in the Last Judgment. . . . He has what you might call an unshakable belief. It will show, not by reasoning or by appeal to ordinary grounds for belief, but rather by regulating for [him] in all his life. . . . This in one sense must be called the firmest of all beliefs."[51] This group of contemporary believers does not leap with Kierkegaard or begin its rational reflections from the standpoint of the certain knowledge of God's existence with Barth's Anselm. Even the traditional *fides quaerens intellectum* (faith seeking understanding), with its underlying assumption of a linear progression from unbelief to faith to intellectual understanding, is less accurate for these persons than a more hermeneutical model of personal dialogue between religious and secular modes of thought.

The secular believer may address skepticism using the formulations of his religious tradition. But, because doubts are no longer external to his religious belief, the effort to answer them in a generally acceptable manner becomes an intrinsic part of the life of faith. Recall the focus in chapter 1 on intersubjective explanation as the attempt to offer reasons that are acceptable also to those outside one's own form of life or belief community. The point here is that this effort does not need to be external or reductionistic to religious belief, but it can instead be internal to the dynamic of belief. Secular believers might take the well-known quote from Diderot as their motto: "Doubts in the matter of religion, far from being acts of impiety, ought to be seen as good works, when they belong to a man who humbly recognizes his ignorance and is motivated by the fear of displeasing God by the abuse of reason."[52]

Interestingly, what has become true for many contemporary believers, at least in western culture, is also reflected in the history of the formulation of religious beliefs in the West. There is no need to argue the process in detail, since it is accepted precisely by those who most deplore the developments. The process of thinking a God whose existence was unproblematic, typical of the medieval and Reformation periods, became the effort to defend the existence of the God of religion in the Enlightenment and after. The process of retelling the biblical story became the historical-critical task of culling the kernel of what could still be believed from the chaff of premodern miracle stories and other embellishments, or the philosophical task of discovering the (philosophical) meaning underlying the traditional narratives.[53] Ninian Smart concludes that "there is an assimilation of the results of Religion ['Religion' he defines as the study of religion] into the making of Theology."[54] But more strongly, one could say that in the western tradition, especially the tradition of Christian reflection, the philosophy of religion has become an element of theology, as has not been the case in many nonwestern religious traditions.

Obviously, at least two courses of action are available in the face of this generally acknowledged fact. One can propose that we return to a pre-Enlightenment or (what amounts to the same thing) postmodern way of thinking. We can seek to comb the philosophical impurities out of religious reflection like burrs out of cotton, allowing belief to stand not on the foundation of secular disciplines but "nonfoundationally" on the strength of its personal disclosure value or the weight of its tradition alone. Yet the human appropriation of meaning just does not work this way. As we saw in chapter 3, the meaning of a belief for an individual depends upon its place within his personally synthesized semantic world. Thus the meaning of a given religious tradition with its beliefs and practices will be different for the contemporary individual than for the believer living in the first, fifth, or thirteenth century. So, for instance, Ninian Smart writes, "In uttering a New Testament Theology (e.g., Paul's Theology) am I actually Expressing the [first-century] picture? The reason for doubt is that the terms I use have a new significance in *my* twentieth-century milieu. For example, if I affirm a miracle in this scientific age am I *making the same point* as was originally being made? We may call this the phenomenon of milieu-transformation."[55]

Though there is no point in denying that there are individuals who can live within the first-century stories, it also seems clear that there are many who can read and appropriate them only through a fusion with the twentieth-century perspective. It is emphatically not the case, as Cornelius Van

Til's "metaphysical presuppositionalism" holds, that one thinks within a presuppositional world, that there are no points of contact and no common criteria between worlds, and that the Christian proclaims a world as a whole that the secular mind of the twentieth century must either jump into and appropriate as a whole or not at all.[56]

Those who attempt to include a place for rational doubt within their theories of religious explanation are correct, therefore, at least with regard to the type of person in contemporary western culture I call the secular believer. George Thomas's statements provide a good picture of this type of faith: "Since [religious experiences] are not self-authenticating, we must subject them to *critical examination* to determine whether they are supported by other religious experiences and by experience as a whole. If they are not supported by the religious experiences of others and are not consistent with other kinds of experience, they are bound to be regarded as doubtful, if not false."[57] This is a valid requirement for the rationality of religious belief for the secular believer, though not necessarily for the member of a traditional culture for whom questioning and multiple options are not a part of his belief or for the Christian fully enough socialized into the Christian tradition that such doubts do not occur.

In this context the untenability of the distinction between "decisive assent" and "interim assent," recently proposed by Gary Gutting, should be obvious.[58] Decisive assent is defined by the fact that "it terminates the process of inquiry into the truth of p": "This does not mean that I no longer think about p, but my thoughts are concerned with developing its significance (analyzing its meaning, determining its implications) rather than establishing its truth" (105). Interim assent, by contrast, "accepts p but without terminating inquiry into the truth of p. Its effect is to put me on the side of p in disputes about its truth" (105). Gutting's own conclusion is unambiguous: "Religious belief requires decisive, not just interim, assent" (106).

I think he is mistaken. Nothing inherent in the nature of religious belief requires us to disallow an interim component to religious assent, and the widespread phenomenon of the secular believer suggests the viability of this notion. Because Gutting's position is typical of many in contemporary discussions, let us use his three claims to orient our discussion. *Claim 1*: "Religious belief represents *the (relative) end* of a quest for emotional and intellectual satisfaction" (106, emph. mine). Gutting is correct in viewing a given set of beliefs as a relative end, a (short- or long-term) resting point, but wrong to imply that it must close the door on the truth question. Religious belief is not equivalent to the offering of hypotheses in science; Ian Barbour has correctly emphasized that religious beliefs are held with greater subjective involvement than scientific beliefs.[59] Yet it is hardly obvious that only those persons can be defined as believers who are "entirely confident."[60]

Claim 2: "A merely interim assent is inconsistent with the typically religious attitude toward nonbelief" (108). It may be the case that believers are typically impatient and judgmental concerning those who do not share their convictions; it hardly follows that they *ought* to be so. Although secular believers lack the unquestioning conviction with which saints have inspired believers through the centuries, it may be that their continuing openness to other positions provides a better model in the contemporary setting of religious pluralism and dialogue. Alone the political consequences of the fundamentalist attitude toward unbelief, whether in the Middle East or in Southern school districts, should be enough to encourage some revision here.

Claim 3: Religious belief requires "a total commitment to its implications for action that is incompatible with continuing reflection on its truth" (107). But, unless one *defines* as religious only those beliefs that flow from total commitment, I believe this stipulation is arbitrary. One regularly acts in accord with beliefs that remain open to revision. Indeed, does Gutting not grant just this possibility when he admits that "I can rightly give my life for a belief that I acknowledge as merely probable and that I admit I might give up on the basis of new evidence" (107)? What is the difference between this *rational* action and the "simply foolish" move of "giving up everything for a belief that I think requires further discussion and evaluation" (108)?

Still, claim 3 implicitly raises two other objections to the notion of the secular believer that we must consider, namely, the questions of obedience and of faith. First, does a continuing openness to criticism not make religious obedience impossible? How can the secular believer commit himself to religious observance when the truth question has not been settled once and for all? In fact, as William James has shown, if one admits religious belief to be a "forced option," where not to decide is to decide, one can do nothing else *but* act on inconclusive evidence.[61] Assume for the moment that a given secular believer has worked out the lifestyle demands of his religion and thinks it likely that his religion is true. Clearly, at least in ordinary ethical decisions where the cost of religious observance is not extreme, his grounds for belief seem sufficient to support observance.

But what of so-called momentous ethical contexts: how would the secular believer hold out if forced to pay homage to another god or die? For he has not decided the truth of his religion once and for all. The answer must be: when a new context of decision is introduced, reevaluation will take place for the secular believer, *just as it does for traditional believers*. The only difference is that the perspective I am defending refuses to dichotomize inside and outside, belief and doubt. So, in the martyrdom example, secular believers may decide that the costs of observance are now too great and abandon their religious commitment. Or, like any believer, they may rethink the lifestyle demands of their religion—think of Jews in sixteenth-century Spain who practiced Christian rituals once unthinkable for a Jew, yet continued their Jewish observance through newly invented codes, symbolic songs, and so forth. Or the doubting believer could even choose martyrdom, for a variety of consistent reasons: because his religion seemed truer than its rivals, because the values it embodied were preferable to those of its opponents, because obedience had become an unconscious habit despite doubts, and so on.

In fact, I think these options for decision exactly represent the stance of many believers in the developed West today. Think, for instance, of the Roman Catholic church in the United States; Protestant examples could be adduced as well. There is a widespread resistance to clear papal guidelines, from birth control and in vitro fertilization, through classical doctrinal teachings such as transubstantiation and the role of women in the Church, to contemporary issues such as homosexual ordination, married clergy, nuclear armaments, liberation theologies. And yet many remain committed Catholics in their observance and individual self-understanding. This combination of sincere religious belief and secular (or at least nontraditional) doubts and objections is precisely the double identity I am ascribing to the secular believer. A similar phenomenon affects Jewish belief and observance, albeit less distinctly, given the different relationship between practice and belief in Judaism and the cultural and political elements that for many are equally central to their Jewish identity.

The second objection that I mentioned concerns the nature of religious faith. How can faith not be total commitment that presupposes the truth of a set of beliefs? In this chapter's gradual movement from religious meaning to beliefs to explanations to their assessment, have we not excluded any place for faith? On this question too, I am not convinced that the theory of the secular believer requires major revisions of traditional western religious thought. Faith has generally been taken to involve a subjective attitude of commitment, trust, or hope in response to a set of beliefs. The western theological traditions have always acknowledged that their beliefs were not rationally certain; yet they have rightly defended the possibility of subjective certainty and committed response by the individual or community. There is no reason why a secular believer should be in a different position on this matter. He *may* be more inconsistent in actual practice, but this need not be the case. For the degree of subjective response has no necessary relation to more objective philosophical, historical, or scientific warrants: I may be uncertain of special relativity or a geometrical proof and be certain that a future event will occur or that God exists.

However, the theory of the secular believer *does* stand in opposition to one misconstrual of religious faith that occasionally crops up, namely, the claim that faith can serve as evidence for the truth of religious propositions. Faith is a religious virtue in many traditions, a sign of one's acknowledgement of and trust in the object of one's belief. From the religious perspective, it may represent the heart of religion. No part of this section need challenge that view. Nonetheless, faith is not an *epistemic* virtue (nor an epistemic vice!). In the context of argumentation and defense, it does not make the object of faith more probable. We turn now to this final issue.

The Rationality of Religious Belief

Undeniably, a discussion of the rationality of religious belief using the model of interim assent goes against more familiar notions of religious belief as the "infinite passion of inwardness" (Kierkegaard) or "the certainty that excludes all doubt." Yet its revisionary implications need not invalidate the notion. We have adequately specified the core of the religious attitude in terms of parameters such as meaning, scope, and coherence, so that its distinctiveness does not need to be insured by the subjective strength of the individual's avowals. Not surprisingly, a treatment of religious rationality informed by an understanding of scientific rationality will tend to stress the context of justification over the context of discovery. In other words, it is not the subjective criteria of *how* one believes that alone determine the belief as religious (though they play an important role in the phenomenology of religion); the formal and substantial factors regarding *what* one believes must be considered as well.

Regarding the issue of *why* one believes—the issue most germane to the rationality of religious belief—I would thus allow for two possibilities. The premodern and postmodern model conceives of belief based on the givenness of the tradition, that is, based on nothing outside that tradition itself. The rationality of such belief may be described nonfoundationally in terms of the coherence of the beliefs with the believer's own life-experience, with themselves, or with the founding narratives and doxological practice of the religious tradition.[62] However, for the type of contemporary believers I have labeled "secular believers," religious rationality may be understood (equally nonfoundationally) as requiring relationships of coherence outside the religious tradition as well, hence with the life-experience of one's nonbelieving peers and with otherwise accepted scientific or ethical truths. Put differently: the cognitive dissonance that is the product of incoherence is viewed in the former case as stemming solely from difficulties within the tradition (intratextual incoherence), in the latter as the product of incompatibilities or tensions between traditions (intertraditional incoherence).

To specify the rationality of religious belief based on the process of intertraditional comparison and evaluation is similar to a proposal advanced by Wolfhart Pannenberg in a variety of contexts. "It belongs . . . to the finitude of theological knowledge," he argues, "that the concept of God remains hypothetical even within theology. It recedes before the human experience of the world and of the self, from which it must find its confirmation."[63] Admittedly, Pannenberg's desire to avoid a *Glaubenssubjektivismus* stems from other concerns than the phenomenon of the secular believer here described. Specifically, he defends the historicity of reality, which he claims is widely accepted in modern thought, and develops an understanding of theology consistent with this metaphysical starting point:

> The reality of God is available at any given time only through subjective anticipations of the totality of reality, through sketches (*Entwürfen*) of that totality of meaning that is posited along with all individual experience. These sketches for their own part are historical; that is, they remain vulnerable to confirmation or destruction through the progress of experience. The notion of anticipation thus always contains the notion of the hypothetical as well. (312–13)

But the conclusion is the same: even for the believer the contents of faith can remain disputable (*strittig*). Religious experience and religious practice may bespeak—and at times create—certainty,[64] but it is possible for religious beliefs to be held hypothetically, in continued dialogue with other religious and nonreligious positions and in conscious openness to criticisms of formulation and content. From the perspective of religious experience, religious beliefs may be viewed as self-authenticating.[65] However, this does not make the search for broader epistemic warrants any less essential if the believer is to achieve an overall coherence of his experience. For "from other perspectives, namely from those of theoretical reflection, even the truth claim of religious experience and tradition must be judged as hypothetical and the certainty of faith as a subjective anticipation."[66]

We discussed scientific rationality in chapter 2 in terms of hypothetical solutions to specified problem-situations. We now see that a similar structure is, with suitable modifications, not inappropriate to the believer's effort to elucidate his faith. This effort may take the form of a redescription of experience and practice in belief-internal terms; but it may also include calling belief-statements into question in a dialogue with other perspectives that becomes vital to the belief itself. The context principle of rationality which emerged in chapters 2 and 3 plays an even greater role in philosophical discourse (chap. 4), and serves as a reminder that religious belief, experience, and practice arise in the context of—or in reaction to—a given religious tradition. However, the indispensable role of the individual in synthesizing elements of his tradition into a unique whole or "world" for him (chap. 3) prevents us from viewing traditions or forms of life as monolithic and nonnegotiable givens. The fusion of comprehensiveness and coherence in the religious dimension (e.g., in the broad conception of religious experience) militates against a compartmentalization of religious truth-claims and offers some guidelines for intertraditional dialogue. Although the interim status of religious claims for the secular believer does not characterize the belief of all religious persons, it is at least a viable option for religious believers in contemporary culture.

How then should the discipline of theology be understood? Who is its audience and what is the breadth of its validity claims? We may expect some continuity between the way religious explanations function for individuals and their more formal place in theological discourse. Yet certain unique difficulties arise if theology is to be pursued as an academic endeavor in the university setting. How can theology bridge the gap between the publics of Jerusalem and Athens, of church and academy? Can it be understood in continuity with a concept of rationality adapted from the sciences, or is it an endeavor of faith responsible to no notion of rationality but its own? We turn to these issues in the final chapter.

CHAPTER SIX

Theology as Explanation and the Question of Theological Method

Theology as Explanation

We have devoted an entire chapter to the way in which the individual—or a group of individuals in a religious community—makes sense of his personal and communal experience. In our analysis of religious experience we found explanation and understanding to work together in the case of both believers and students of religion. We were not able to unearth any underlying formal structure common to religious explanations. But these explanations did evidence the general characteristic of accounting for the believer's experience (making it meaningful) rather than merely repeating or describing it, and they did this by seeking to tie disparate elements into a coherent whole, as in the construction of religious meaning-sketches.

Paralleling the contextualist shift in natural science, then, the analysis of religious explanations shows them to be characterized more by the quest for coherence than by some universal structure. Unlike the natural sciences, though, they are concerned with *semantic* coherence, the meaningfulness of a coherently constructed world-picture that constitutes its personal disclosure value. Further, the process may involve making sense in a way that is accessible only to the individual. Finally, a certain impulse in the religious project itself propels it toward the realm of ineffability, threatening to reduce the explanatory project to the wordlessness of immediate understanding. These characteristics of religious explanations are too frequently ignored by comparative treatments of religion and science; each one is sufficient to block facile parallel-drawing.

146

In the present chapter we turn from the individual's semantic project to the more formal discipline of systematic theology, in which claims are made to more than personal disclosure value. In comparison with this new task, the previous chapter seems to have presented the less difficult problems. In retrospect, it is not surprising that the religious individual would construct a semantic world and attempt to make it coherent in ways similar to the individual in society. Hence, it should not have been surprising that we were able to find some broad links between the phenomenology of individual world-construction and the phenomenology of religious experience. Indeed, we could also don sociologist's garb and develop even closer parallels between religious and nonreligious communities than has been done here. For a religious community is a social community and as such exemplifies the characteristic features of all human communities. Without reviewing the literature in detail, we may grant the thesis stressed by sociologists of religion: explanations serve similar social functions in both religious and nonreligious groups. Communities, like individuals, attempt to make sense of a specified range of experience, intermingling explanatory beliefs with intuitive understanding, greater or lesser amounts of doubt or cognitive dissonance, and nonreflective action or practice.

Even the level-two reflection of the study of religion did not present insurmountable problems for comprehension. Although a higher degree of abstraction is involved than in level-one religious phenomena, and although the explanation/understanding relation would have to be spelled out here as in chapter 3, still the general nature of this discipline is not unclear. The study of religion is a second-level discipline, dealing with the phenomenon of religion or specified elements thereof. It has a factual or descriptive component, the task of describing the relevant religious beliefs and practices, and an explanatory component, the task of explaining why individuals (or communities) believe and act as they do and how their beliefs form a coherent whole for them.

But the student of religion can bracket one question that the believer or religious community cannot: that of the truth of the religious beliefs. I can explain how a witch doctor's beliefs form a coherent whole within his religious world-picture even if I know that certain of his beliefs are mistaken—just as a philosopher of science can explain the experiments of the alchemist while rejecting the truth of his premises. In either case one can portray the individual being studied as a rational agent without sharing his beliefs about the world. This freedom is not available to the believer or to the theologian, however we finally construe their relationship. Both of these persons appear to be committed to the truth of their religious beliefs, or at least to act in accordance with those beliefs—or, at the very least, to be concerned about whether or not the beliefs in question are true. This requirement places a unique demand on the discipline of theology: like the study of religion, it is a second-level discipline, reflecting on particular aspects of a given religion; yet, like the believer or religious community, theology cannot proceed simply by bracketing all questions of truth. To clarify the nature of explanations in this discipline that appears to be both fish and fowl, and in the process to specify what sort of a discipline it is (i.e., to address the question of theological rationality), will be the task of this concluding chapter.

The initial formulation of the task already suggests two parameters for our consideration of theology. On the one hand, theology is not equivalent to the study of religion; it is not just another social science. For instance, we can agree with David Tracy that Christian theology must in some way serve the "public" of the Church, along with the publics of Academy and Society.[1] No such religious constraint pertains in the social sciences, even if thinkers like Geertz and Winch are right in believing that the social scientist must immerse herself in the culture or community that she is studying. On the other hand, there remains some distinction of levels between the theologian and the religious believer, insofar as theological inquiry takes as its object either the believer or the content of his beliefs or the actions of the religious community. It is not yet clear how sharp a distinction must be drawn between theological inquiry and its object, or even how this object is to be construed. One of our goals will be to specify precisely what this distinction of levels amounts to in the case of theology. Still, however it is developed, an adequate account of theology will have to preserve the conceptual distinction between theology as discourse-about and that which it is about.

What then are theological explanations? As I have suggested, part of the answer to this question has been given already in our discussion of religious explanations in previous chapters. That is, theological explanations are composed of groups of statements that are answers to why-questions. But these why-questions, as contextualists in the philosophy of science have realized with regard to their disciplines, vary greatly in subject matter and function. Some answer questions in terms internal to a particular religion ("we study Torah to learn the Commandments of G-d" or "Jesus is the second person of the Trinity"), while other why-questions require answers that are phrased in terms shared by the religious community and outsiders ("the Judeo-Christian God is the source of all that is" or "God acts justly" or simply "God exists").

An analysis of the functions of theological explanations must make reference in a similar manner to factors both internal and external to the religious tradition. Viewed functionally, theological explanations attempt to establish a link between the inherited beliefs and practices of a given religious tradition and the contemporary experience of its practitioners. Theology's explanations can be phrased in terms of traditional doctrines, the practices (rites, rituals, liturgies) of the religious community, or its norms or codes of behavior. But they may also be drawn primarily from the broader (social, ethical, intellectual) life-experience of believers, from a particular psychological theory or political agenda, or from believers' more general religious sensibilities. Whatever their source, theological explanations function in continually insuring the tradition's relevance to the challenges posed by contemporary questions (e.g., the tradition's answers to evolution, abortion and euthanasia, atomic weapons, miniskirts).

Obviously, the debate with the sciences concerning the nature of theology is an extensive one. Throughout its history, theologians have attempted to clarify its status in regard to science. A full treatment of the Christian tradition would have to present, inter alia, the position of Thomas and the medievals concerning *scientia*, the post-Reformation debates about theology as a science, the influence of the Enlightenment and Newtonian models of science, and a multitude of nineteenth- and twentieth-century options. Moreover, this entire dispute is arguably a mere facet of the broader debate concerning the relationship of faith and reason, which in turn leads to questions of christology, revelation, the church, the fall, salvation.

Obviously, we will not lay all of these questions to rest in this chapter. Instead of pursuing a historical survey or even a typology of positions, I will address the question from the standpoint of the contemporary discussion of rationality across the academic disciplines. Doing so will aid in focusing the discussion and will insure some coherence with earlier chapters. Conversely, because so much will be omitted, there is justification for advancing these proposals in only rather tentative terms. At most I can claim that my position is one viable way of construing theology, a hypothesis worthy of further discussion. But the lack of a complete survey or typology means that there may be other internally consistent construals of the term *theology*. One could, for example, remove theology from among the academic disciplines or define it as primarily descriptive (first-order) rather than explanatory (second-order). I think there are good reasons for theology to pursue academic excellence and explanatory adequacy; but there does not seem to be intrinsic necessity on either side.

An important terminological clarification: I use *scientific* in this chapter in the broader sense of *scientia* or *Wissenschaft*, in conscious opposition to its usual natural scientific connotations. I intend it to denote any explanatory discipline, empirical or otherwise. It is not synonymous with *rational*, for nonexplanatory activities (painting, washing) may still have rational methods of their own. The term includes a *descriptive* component, as a name for any academic discipline. It also contains a *normative* element: a discipline deserves to be called scientific by accepting, perhaps implicitly, certain standards of scientificness. The former is an inclusive, the latter an exclusive, category. That is, the former prohibits the limitation of the label *scientific* to a given discipline, a move which we might call the positivist fallacy. The latter draws attention to the existence of some set of standards. What sorts of standards, then, apply to theology as a science?

Theology as a Science

If a cross-disciplinary, context-free theory of science existed, capable of definitively separating acceptable from unacceptable claimants to scientific laurels, our discussion would be brief. But we have chronicled the failure of such purely formalist programs in earlier chapters. A theory of science must now include reference to contextual and pragmatic factors, even if these are broad enough to apply to whole fields of the scientific endeavor. Consequently, we must turn to the actual practice of science across the academic disciplines in order to give shape to our inquiry into theology as a science.

Beyond Foundationalism

The context for formulating the question of theological methodology has changed radically in the last years, in part because of developments in the philosophy of natural and social science. Before the advent of the newer models of rationality, attempts to include questions about the truth of the tradition *within* systematic theology itself ran the serious risk of sacrificing theology's disciplinary integrity. For under the epistemological framework then operative, now critically labeled *foundationalism*, giving rational support for the assertions of a discipline meant a de facto reduction of that discipline to another discipline in terms of which, or on the foundation of which, rational justification was to be given. Will the epistemological framework here developed enable us to avoid the inherent flaws of foundationalism?

Students of the nineteenth century are perhaps most familiar with the once widespread tendency to reduce theology to another discipline. Kant found a place for theology under the rubric of practical reason, at the cost of reducing Jesus to the prime exemplar of a religio-moral ideal.[2] Schleiermacher is said to have reduced Christian experience to a particular form of the universal sense of absolute dependence. Hegel, and D. F. Strauss in his later work,[3] found a place for theology, but as the penultimate moment in a system that was finally a philosophy of Absolute Spirit rather than a theology. Gradually and for diverse reasons, the functional role that the various thinkers attributed to God became dysfunctional—and the conclusion of the story in Feuerbach, Marx, Durkheim and Freud is too well known to require reciting here.

But the recent developments in the philosophy of science surveyed in this book have led to an entirely new approach to redeeming the validity claims of theology. First, the distinction between contexts of discovery and contexts of justification[4] prevents the validity of religious truth-claims from being challenged simply because of their source. Whether an assertion stems from personal experience, a divine revelation in history, or the tradition of a community is irrelevant to judgments of its epistemic merit. Next, the contextualist shift justifies us in taking not isolated assertions but whole religious systems as hypotheses or programs for research (Lakatos). This satisfies, I believe, a central concern of antifoundationalists, namely, that a foreign authority not be allowed to sift randomly through the beliefs of a theological tradition, rejecting particular ones because the evidence for them is insufficient. Finally, the verificationism of the logical positivists has received at the hands of Popper and others as complete a refutation as one will ever find in such debates. Rejecting it allows us to dismiss as illicit any demands for a point-by-point verification of theological assertions. Developments such as these do not divorce theology from the general standards of scientific discourse, but they do soften and contextualize the standards that remain. The guidelines proposed by a thinker like Lakatos no longer rest on the presuppositions of empiricism or natural scientific positivism; rather, they represent only the minimal conditions of any academic discourse, without which critical inquiry in the academy would be impossible.

These developments have caused a flurry of methodological activity in a number of fields. If one takes seriously the ongoing, presumably inherent tension between theology's religious and academic commitments, one will address theological method with particular care. Efforts to reduce theology to a "faith science" (*Glaubenswissenschaft*) on the one hand, an abstract "science of God" on the other, easily skew the delicate balance. As a result, I believe that the recent methodological developments have an indispensable role to play in the self-understanding and self-presentation of theology as a discipline.

But to hold this position is not equivalent to espousing the foundationalist demand, namely, that one use an external source to establish definitively the meaning and truth of theological assertions before theological work can be carried out. Instead, the formulation of theological explanations and the evaluation of their truth can still proceed before the demands of its two publics are fully integrated; better: the material work of theology can be pursued *while* the project of integrating church and academy is being carried out and in reciprocal interaction with it.

However, to reject foundationalism is not to fall automatically into the waiting arms of the antifoundationalists, who claim that theology can be pursued without attention to the nature and epistemic status of its truth claims. To the contrary, the whole debate between foundationalism and antifoundationalism is probably based on the false dichotomy of an outdated epistemological dilemma. The shift to a fallibilist epistemology avoids, I believe, the alleged necessity of being either a foundationalist or an antifoundationalist.

Leaving behind the dichotomy that structured the older faith/reason debate must have a major impact on theological methodology. Specifically, it is no longer necessary to hold that the traditional project of theological prolegomena is ancillary to theology, functioning (as in fundamental theology) as a foundation to be settled at the outset and assumed in what follows. Yet nor are its epistemological and comparative questions to be dispensed with. Instead, I will argue, *the project of theological prolegomena can now be included as part of an ongoing inquiry within the practice of theology itself.* To the extent that it operates as a science, theology will formulate explanations that are open to criticism (and revision) by both church and academy. Approached in this way, theology can be understood by analogy to explanatory efforts in the sciences, for which, as we have seen, universal criticizability is the rule. No statement can be advanced without a justification that is (as far as possible) open to all; but every formulation remains open to criticism and revision in light of the continuing discussion.

This proposal for theological method is integrally linked to the stance developed in this book as a whole. Recall that the project has focused on contextual features that vary by discipline and subject matter, as well as on a few more general qualities that seem to serve as regulative ideals for all such inquiry. We have approached the more specific explanation debate in light of broader theories of rationality, and these in turn through the rationality of the various academic disciplines. With most of the inquiry behind us, it is perhaps appropriate to pause here and formulate the postfoundationalist approach to the rationality question that I have advocated and attempted to employ.

Ultimately, the task requires a sort of phenomenology of scientific inquiry, which I take to imply two complementary tasks, one primarily descriptive-sociological, the other more formal or (perhaps) transcendental. First, one must examine academic disciplines in the university setting. When approached sociologically, this has involved specifying disciplinary subgroups, discussing journals and conferences and their role in fostering communication, and hypothesizing about the cognitive, affective, and sub-cultural components of opinion change. The work of thinkers such as Stephen Toulmin, Thomas Kuhn, and Gerald Holton provides a useful model for such an analysis. Habermas's phenomenology of the ideal speech situation is a further instance of this endeavor.

The analysis can be conducted in a nonreductionistic manner, as I have argued, by exploring pragmatic relations without downplaying the content of beliefs and arguments. The point is to avoid the mistake of the social scientist seminar participant described by Karl Popper, who completely ignored the content of the speakers' arguments in order to concentrate on the social dynamics, for example, on "the manner in which one or the other attempted to dominate the group . . . [and how] a hierarchical order and a group-ritual of verbalization developed."[5] The 1979 Oxford Symposium on science and theology offers some painful examples of approaches to the question that completely disregard the content of arguments in their concentration on sociological analyses.[6]

To provide a full account of scientific argumentation, then, the sociological approach has to be supplemented by a detailed analysis of the ways in which arguments contribute to rational persuasion in academic discourse. This requires a transition from the descriptive to the normative. Basic features of discursive rationality then begin to emerge. Among these I would include: the free and public exchange of ideas, use and acknowledgement of sources, reasoned and criticizable discussions of others' ideas, and the ideals of clarity, objectivity, and criticizability. These general characteristics must characterize each of the explanatory disciplines, including theology, although their application will be affected by the specific issues that arise in each unique disciplinary context. Therefore, despite criticisms by Barth and others, Heinrich Scholz's three "minimal requirements" (*Mindestforderungen*) for the discipline of theology, or something like them, remain useful as models for theological rationality.[7]

The second, formal or transcendental task also plays a role in a phenomenology of scientific inquiry, albeit a more limited one. Some progress can be made via a conceptual analysis of the concept of science itself. For instance, we can ask what must be the case such that scientific research can be carried out, replicated, tested. Admittedly, the conclusions regarding the transcendental arguments of Habermas and Apel in chapter 3 were largely negative: the obscurity of the logic of transcendental argumentation easily leads to inflated claims on behalf of allegedly definitive conclusions. Still, if one recognizes that analyses of this type are never purely a priori, that the descriptive and formal approaches are more accurately two facets of a single project, some place may remain for the latter type of analysis.[8]

Theology Among the Academic Disciplines

According to the stipulation first suggested above, to label theology a science is to say at least two things. Theology is an explanatory discipline, practiced in the university setting; this is a descriptive statement presumably beyond dispute. But it is also to say that theology faces whatever formal requirements accrue to membership among the sciences. These might be extremely minimal, even to the point of scarcely affecting theological activity. After all, the university community is an exceptionally broad collection of different pursuits and interests. Still, it is significant that one engages in theology in university classrooms, where one does not pray or (ideally) preach. What has the tradition implied by labeling theology a science? If the label is not an empty one, we can expect theology to share the general characteristics and requirements that pertain to all sciences as sciences. As it turns out, the treatment of theology as a science evidences some interesting parallels with our earlier discussions of explanation and rationality in the natural and social sciences.

The situation with regard to theology is complicated by theology's accountability to two publics, those of church and academy. It is of course possible to remove one of the two—the historical precedents are numerous!—either by abolishing the link to the church (theology as a philosophical discussion among scholars) or by removing theology from the university (theology as a church activity). I shall, however, take theology's two publics for granted.[9] The result is that theology faces two competing sets of demands, those from the religious community (already alluded to in the preceding section), and those pertaining to the academy. Since service to these two publics is essential to theology as we know it, we are justified in taking their injunctions not as incidental to theology but as part of its basic nature. As a result, I suggest that the theological endeavor must include the questions of its place within and responsibilities to the religious community. Likewise, it includes the disputes over theology's academic status—questions such as the nature of theological explanations, the criteria for theological rationality, and the specific characteristics and goals of theology as a science. Only in this way can justice be done to the urgency of theology's self-definition in the contemporary discussion. The debate over theology as a science, often taken as *external* to the theological endeavor, should, I suggest, be taken up *internally* into our account of the nature of the discipline. Clearly, this position is a natural outworking of my arguments for abolishing the inside/outside dichotomy in the study of religion.

What does it mean to say that theology includes the search for (and specification of) the criteria that accrue to it as an academic discipline? For one, the debate over scientific rationality is not foreign to theology. This is true at various levels. Theologians are to be included in the debate over general criteria for scientific explanation (as in the concluding sections of chap. 2). They can contribute to and are affected by discussions concerning the criteria for those sciences that research complexes of meaning (chap. 3). Traditionally, they have been active with philosophers in addressing the methodological problems of theories having to do with experience as a whole (chap. 4). Finally, they have an especially important role to play in methodological discussions surrounding the disciplines that study *religious* experience, as opposed to inquiries into social, moral or aesthetic experience.

But theology faces methodological dilemmas of its own. Perhaps the most crucial is the struggle between functional and semantic approaches to religious belief. I have argued that functional analyses of religious explanations need to be supplemented by a consideration of their content and supporting arguments. Functional approaches to explanation ask how dogmas (belief-that statements) function within a given community in terms independent of the content of the belief in question—for example, how they foster group solidarity, what noncognitive attitudinal or affective factors they represent, or how they serve as norms or "grammatical rules" for the community. Such an approach begins with the religious community as an existing social entity or cultural unit, independent of the truth or falsity of its beliefs, and evaluates theological explanations in terms of their function within the community. Starting at the level of groups necessitates that the discussion of religious explanations will be primarily sociological.[10] The propositional content of beliefs, if thematized at all, will be secondary, derivative from and explicable in terms of the sociological analyses.

The analysis of scientific explanation and rationality defended in this book, by contrast, suggests that theological inquiry begin with the content of the community's belief-assertions as primary data. Such a starting point involves several assumptions about explanation and the believer. (1) Religions involve "beliefs about" that *as such* are of vital concern to believers. (2) Although an adequate analysis will examine religious beliefs in a variety of contexts (emotive, social, ethical), this should never be done at the expense of their actual content. A theory of religion that reduces these beliefs to products, for example, epiphenomena of a primarily sociological reality, has not done justice to the belief-that component of religious belief. (3) Some comparison between religions may be possible on the level of doctrinal content. Religions intend to formulate statements about the world that, whether or not interreligiously criticizable, make assertions that conflict or agree in principle.

The exposition in chapter 4 was meant to provide support for viewing belief statements as forming a world-picture of some sort.[11] A religion involves a distinctive view of one's environment or experience. What makes it religious is, among other things, the breadth of the view: religious beliefs thematize our world as a whole, the totality of our experience. A body of religious belief attempts in some way to make sense of this world. Now there is no need to deny the incredible diversity of ways in which religious beliefs "make meaningful." Yet, as Ninian Smart's *Worldviews* illustrates, even agreeing to view religions as interpretations of or statements about the world allows us to compare them in one significant respect.[12] It may be that the development of such a worldview into a theology is unlikely to occur in many nonwestern religions, at least not without outside influence.[13] Nonetheless, I believe that a theological inquiry into the content of these beliefs, one which does not reduce them to community-internal functioning or use, is both mandated by, and is possible because of, the role that beliefs inevitably serve as part of a religious world-picture.

If the argumentation to this point is sound, it should now be possible to specify more precisely the relationship between religious beliefs and the theological task within a tradition. Let us consider Christian theology in particular. According to the approach here advocated, Christian theology will be concerned, among other things, with Christian beliefs as components of a Christian explanatory system, a more or less coherent set of beliefs about the world. Theology's reflective element, the moment of abstraction from immediate religious practice and belief, demands that it be understood as a level-two discipline.[14] To the extent that we can consider it a science, theology is the science *about* the beliefs *about* the world (humans, God) held within the Christian tradition.

The distinction of levels hearkens back to my defense of theoretical discourse in the context of Habermas's theory of rationality. Although we examined the different senses of rationality and truth pertaining to theoretical, regulative, and expressive discourse, it became clear that explanations could only be evaluated in the context of regulative or constative discourse. Likewise, theology as level-two discourse will involve a certain *distancing* from the immediate involvement of belief statements in their original context. It has the *descriptive* (in this sense, phenomenological) task of making clear what level-one statements say and how they function. But it also has the *systematic-explanatory* function of revealing the interconnections of such statements and demonstrating their systematic fit. The latter is a creative (synthetic) as well as an analytic task for theologians: formulations of systematic theologies or encompassing understandings of Christianity cannot be "read off" directly from experiential contexts of faith or worship.

The moment of distancing is likewise evident in the revisionary component of theology. Each theological proposal construes the Christian faith and tradition in a particular way. Of course, the construal is not arbitrary; a testing process is involved. Specific systematic theological proposals that are deemed formally adequate (consistent, coherent, sufficiently comprehensive) can be weighed against belief statements in level-one contexts to assess their material adequacy, namely, their degree of correspondence with or deviance from the tradition. It may be that some revisions are so drastic that their credentials as Christian will be challenged.[15] However, as Brian Gerrish has shown, it belongs to the nature of the transmission of Christian tradition that it modify the tradition in appropriating it.[16]

It is within this context that one must frame the question of theological rationality. It is, most generally, a question about the nature of the process involved in constructing and evaluating theological statements, and about the nature of the statements so constructed. More specifically, it includes: (1) the relationship of these theological statements to level-one statements, that is, how a person moves from the one to the other, how level-one and level-two discourse are different, and what the relative priorities of the two are; (2) the question of the criteria for theology stemming from its publics of church and academy; (3) the issues arising in a comparison of systematic theology with other disciplines, for instance, is the process involved in systematic theology best understood by comparing it to hermeneutics, anthropology, philosophy, or pastoral counseling? Under (3) one is also asking about theology as a discipline in the university: what similarities does it have with the other disciplines? What separates it from them? Are there interdependencies between theology and any other disciplines? How is its use of, say, philosophy different from its borrowings from anthropology or clinical psychology?

I have stressed the systematic element in theological explanations. But it is essential to distinguish this concept of systematization from some of the traditional notions of system that have been employed in the history of the discipline. The system concept was introduced explicitly into theology by B. Keckermann in 1600 in connection with the analytic method.[17] In its use in the seventeenth century the term connoted a scholastic or academic approach to theology.[18] The notion of systematization underwent a corresponding change, however, as the circumference of systematic theology was enlarged. The demonstration of quasi-deductive relationships that was possible for Keckermann, working just with the classical theological loci, became inconceivable as systematic theology became a broader conglomerate of methodologically and materially unrelated disciplines and sub-disciplines during the following three centuries. In one sense, Planck's definition still represents a helpful ideal for theological systematization:

> Systematic theology is the essence of the very same truths of religion
> that are contained in the Bible. But here they are developed further in
> light of their presuppositions and consequences, and are placed into
> the context that is appropriate to their various interrelationships. In
> other words, in theology the biblical truths are placed in an order in
> which each one either confirms and explains, or limits and more pre-
> cisely defines, the others.[19]

Of course, our concept of these interrelationships and contexts must be
freed from any remaining deductive or a priori connotations. Systematic
theology can give expression to its concepts in an orderly, coherent manner
without needing to employ a mathematical model of axiomatization.

Theology may have rejected the earlier goals of system-building inherited from scholastic metaphysics. Still, it remains committed to thematizing the beliefs of the religious tradition in a systematic manner. We have
already discussed the *individual* project of making sense of one's world in
order to explain it coherently. An exactly parallel project recurs on a *corpo-
rate* level in theological discourse—but now in explicitly theoretical terms
and with the demand of intersubjective criticizability. Here the project of
making sense, while still essentially parallel to the individual's project,
shares the minimal criteria of theoretical discourse in general. Here,
though, instead of adequacy to his experience alone, the theologian strives
for adequacy to the experience of the community, in the present as well as
through history. This dual allegiance accounts for the tension that characterizes theology as theoretical *and* religious discourse.

It is of great importance to isolate and understand these two countervail-
ing tendencies that historically have formed and enlivened the theological
project, for the adequacy of specific suggestions for theological method can
only be assessed in light of them. Theology remains bound to its religious
tradition. A metaphysical system can begin and end with whatever basic
principles recommend themselves to the metaphysician; not so theology.
The subject matter it addresses, the concepts it employs, have their source
in the existing beliefs of a religious community. Further, theologians remain accountable to the community's beliefs when they work to reconstruct the logic of the tradition, for the applicability of a theological paradigm to the tradition must be demonstrable.[20] Here we see the underlying
truth in appeals to theology as a faith science: the conceptual schemes
employed in level-two theories must be appropriate to the types of beliefs
and practices found in religion. Hence the kernel of truth in the dictum,
"The object of inquiry determines the method of inquiry": a system must
not be imposed on the object that is foreign to it.

Of course, this stipulation still leaves much latitude regarding the relation between religious belief and theological reflection. I have already argued that the movement into reflective discourse involves constructive or creative thought. Drawing from our discussion of scientific positivism above, we must view those positions that oppose this claim as forms of *theological positivism*. Theological positivists tell us that theology only needs to redescribe or make explicit a preexisting content or "grammar" that is already inherent in religious life and practice. Although their method represents the correct direction of movement, it neglects the creative work required for the rational reconstruction of level-one beliefs in any explanatory discipline. For example, we cannot accept the position, sometimes attributed to Schleiermacher, that theology can move directly from the religious (or Christian) consciousness to theological assertions. More is involved than a simple formulation of the meaning of religious practice. There is no "essence of worshipfulness" that we can read directly out of acts of worship through some sort of "intuition of essences." Such claims to immediate understanding bypass the element of tentativeness and fallibility that emerges in any interpretive explanatory discourse.[21]

Therefore, there is need to concentrate on the minimal requirements inherent in the theoretical task. The project of systematizing one's data and explaining an area of experience involves as such certain basic requirements that go beyond the data in question. Here the "object determines method" dictum stands in need of a corrective.[22] Science, in the broadest sense of intellectual or academic inquiry, is not adequately captured in the rather empty description, "a form of human verbal activity in which the object determines the activity." Indeed, to see this one need only ask, What is the level on which this claim is made? What is its status? Arguments about the nature of theological method (e.g., the claim that one religious tradition is incommensurable with another), if they are not to be meaningless, already imply the existence of a level of theoretical discourse—however limited, biased, or problematic it may be. Unless we are willing literally to forego any statements about the nature of religion, it is incumbent upon us to reflect upon the nature of this discourse. Given the developments in the understanding of scientific rationality that we have examined in earlier chapters, it may be possible to delineate more precisely what it means for theology to inquire into, and so to systematize, a body of religious beliefs and practices.[23]

Now it may be that theology as critical discourse is impossible. Perhaps the well-known dilemma is insoluble: either theology is about a transcendent being, in which case all human language about the divine is equivocal, or it is (as Feuerbach argued) about humankind, in which case the transcendence is illusory. Or perhaps the openness to criticism and revision involved in hypotheses is psychologically or spiritually incompatible with religious belief. The academic ideal of objectivity may finally prove to be irreconcilable with the personal, existential commitment that permeates the believer's attitude toward his beliefs and religious community. Tillich has presented very clearly the tension between the existential ultimate concern that locks the thinking believer into a "theological circle" and the demands of a "scientific theology."[24] Maybe his claim, "No one can call himself a theologian, even if he is called to be a teacher of theology" (10), is to be understood in this context. When Tillich denies the possibility of scientific theology his case deserves careful attention, for the possibility that a level-two discussion of Christian belief will obscure the distinction between theology and the philosophy of religion (ibid.) cannot be ruled out.

Or it may also be, as the requirements of an academic discipline become plainer, that Christians will simply choose to remove theology from the academic context of critical inquiries, stipulating that it is to be no different from level-one discourse. A good case can be made that this was the goal of Barth's work, in which the revealed Word stands above and beyond the reach of philosophy and even religion. But it may also be true of Schleiermacher. Ernst Troeltsch thought that Schleiermacher had brought about the transition from dogmatics to a "doctrine of faith" (*Glaubenslehre*), in which statements are made only about the believing consciousness. And Troeltsch himself, after handling the history of religions aspects of Christianity in part 1 of his *Glaubenslehre*, devotes part 2 to explicating the content of Christian experience in the present.[25]

Admittedly, the divorce of theology from science, or from religion, has been the goal of many great theologians; I make no claim to have presented fully, much less to have refuted, this long tradition. However, one fear frequently expressed by the tradition is, I believe, mistaken. There is no a priori reason why applying insights on explanation and rationality gleaned from the discussion of other fields should be seen as an illicit attempt at dominion over theology or as placing Lockean strictures on revelation. Level-two reflections have no essential authority over the community's level-one practice and use of language, nor over the believer's religious experience. Individual believers are free not to attempt a discursive explication of their beliefs, not to move from level one to level two. The community has the same freedom. In choosing not to enter the arena of critical discourse, one would naturally remain exempt from any external requirements.

On the other hand, to misquote Wittgenstein, "if you want to play the (discursive) game, you have to follow the rules." Theology faces a choice. If it wishes to engage in level-two activities such as explaining in intercommunal terms the status of its language, or explicating or arguing for the meaning and truth of its assertions—and, more obviously, if it wishes to do so in an academic setting—it must take into account the general characteristics of academic discourse. Here the normative elements of the philosophy of science (again, *science* in the broadest sense) do become relevant. This normativity does not stem from some arbitrary stipulation of the theology/philosophy relation, but from the decision to seek a systematic conceptual expression of Christian belief. It is significant that, in actual fact, theologians present arguments for their positions and would like to view their endeavor as rational. Even those who claim freedom from the constraint of the law of noncontradiction do not consciously contradict themselves in their argumentation and regard self-contradiction as a fault in their fellows. Similarly, few would be willing to remove theology from the university setting (most are professors), in practice accepting for their discipline academic ideals such as criticizability and the quest for objectivity. As long as this choice is made in practice, its implications for theory must be drawn; work on the definition of and method in theology needs to reflect the accepted constraints of academic theology.

Toward a Methodological Definition of Theology as a Science

In order to ground the following methodological proposal, let us review the conclusions to which our inquiry has led. We have seen, first of all, that rational discourse is oriented around specifiable *explanatory problems* of various types. In the light of a given problem, proposals of an explanation or problem-solution are formulated, criticized, and modified or rejected as a result. The nature of this discursive process sets certain requirements on potential explanations. (*a*) They must be open to intersubjective examination and criticism. (*b*) No in-principle limits can be set on who can participate in this examination, even though some may more qualify as experts than others. As argued in chapter 1, intersubjective testability connotes pansubjective accessibility.

(*c*) No solution can be grounded by privileged premises. Clearly, we hold certain basic beliefs on which we base other beliefs but for which we do not possess arguments. There is nothing irrational in appealing to these beliefs during the course of disputes with others who share them. But when basic beliefs are called into question, rational discourse requires that reasons be given on their behalf. Where this is impossible, no epistemic merit, expressed or implied, continues to accrue to the beliefs in question. (*d*) Consequently, *all* beliefs in a discursive context must ultimately be treated as *hypotheses*. As hypotheses they must be internally coherent (consistent)

and clearly criticizable; as attempts to explain broad areas of human experience, they need to be adequately comprehensive if they are to answer the
why-questions raised with regard to their domain.

These conclusions provide the basis for a viable methodological definition of theology as a science. (*a*) As an academic discipline, theology formulates explanations that should be intersubjectively criticizable. (*b*) The
results of research in other disciplines are relevant; as part of her task, the
theologian will be concerned with objections from natural scientists, social
scientists, historians, philosophers. (*c*) Where basic theological beliefs are
disputed by others in the discussion, some warrant must be given for
assuming their truth in arguments in the intersubjective explanatory context. The psychologist would not normally be expected to defend the use of
cognitive dissonance or rationalization as explanatory categories, but
should they be called into question, she is obligated to defend the explanatory value of such theoretical terms.

Finally, (*d*) theology's claims must be taken as hypothetical in the academic context. The context of argumentation may lead to revisions in the
models and assertions that a theologian brings to her task. Note that the
revisability of theological assertions does not mean that they are always
experienced as hypothetical by the theologian-cum-believer. That is, room
remains for faith's "assurance of things hoped for and conviction of things
unseen" (Heb. 11:1). However, in theology as in any discipline, there need
not be a direct correspondence between the degree of personal subjective
commitment to a statement and the epistemic status that the discipline
ascribes to it. Indeed, one can as easily find theologians taking a *more*
critical stance toward their discipline than scientists, as one can find theologians whose subjective commitment is stronger.

In short: as in other disciplines claims are made without an ultimate
assurance of finality, so also theology as an academic discipline can include
within itself this element of openness. In fact, given the plurality of contemporary religious (and nonreligious) options, an element of doubt or
openness to revision is already intermingled with belief for a large number
of believers today. This was the point of my defense of the secular believer.
Theology can hold dogmas in the sense of distinctively Christian teachings,
without needing to condone dogmatism in the sense of immunity from
criticism.

The four requirements just listed are the basic building blocks for a
methodological definition of theology as a science. However, it is important now to look at several specific theologians as examples, in order to see
concretely what form these proposals take in actual theological reflection. I
use three thinkers who have concentrated on methodological problems,
two in recent years, to illustrate the implications of my position: Schleier-

macher, Ian Barbour, and Wolfhart Pannenberg. We must ask: does the use of minimal standards for scientific discourse conflict irremediably with the theological tradition? Or are their theories of rationality compatible with consistent and constructive work within theology proper?

There is no thinker more important for contemporary discussions of our question than Friedrich Schleiermacher, though no one else raises more problems of interpretation and has been used as model by more competing camps than he. More than anyone else, the father of modern theology grasped the need for theology to be level-two theoretical discourse as well as the language of the church in the service of the church. As level-two reflection, theology shares the academic method of the scientific disciplines; yet as reflection on "faith assertions" (*Glaubensaussagen*), it is part of the life of the church. Schleiermacher clearly believed that these two approaches could be harmoniously related in a correlation without subordination. However, as Hans Frei once noted, "general agreement among commentators ever since his day has been that he failed at nothing more succinctly than this attempt."[26] Still, Schleiermacher was absolutely correct in holding to both poles of the dilemma without compromise. Because he did so, his work remains programmatic for contemporary theology. We may wish to substitute for his key concept of God-consciousness another systematic concept; we may turn to a more eclectic pluralism of themes and models; or we may declare the entire project as impossible (though in what language could we do so?). But we cannot preserve the epistemic status of theology as an academic discipline unless we continue to address Schleiermacher's task.

There is no doubt that Schleiermacher meant theology to be an activity for the church. The *Kurze Darstellung* labels it a "positive science" in the first paragraph.[27] Schleiermacher stipulates: "Christian theology is therefore the essence of those scientific (*wissenschaftlichen*) knowledge-assertions and rules of proceeding, without the use and possession of which a harmonious leadership of the Christian church—that is, a Christian authority of the church—would not be possible" (par. 5). Likewise, Schleiermacher asserts in the early pages of his dogmatics, "Since Dogmatics is a theological discipline, *and thus pertains solely to the Christian Church*, we can only explain what it is when we have become clear as to the conception of the Christian Church."[28]

In actual practice, however, Schleiermacher seeks to link each concept in his exposition to a general notion or conceptuality not shared by Christianity alone. In the *Speeches* it is the feeling of absolute dependence, which he believes even the "cultured despisers" are aware of; in *The Christian Faith*, the general notion is that of a universal God- or Christ-consciousness. But Schleiermacher's link of general with specific, external with internal, is not just carried out at one level; it works its way into each specific doctrine. Thus Jesus's God-consciousness determines Schleiermacher's christology, that in turn his anthropology. Inevitably the dogmatic position represents a particularization of a more general feeling, concept, or ideal, as in the heart of Schleiermacher's christology: "As an individual historical being [the Redeemer] must have been at the same time ideal (*urbildlich*); that is, the ideal must have become fully historical in him, and his every historical moment must at the same time have carried in it the ideal" (*Christian Faith*, par. 93). As Gerrish summarizes, "that 'the Word became flesh' (probably Schleiermacher's favourite text) means that in Christ the ideal became historical."[29]

Again, no sooner has Schleiermacher made the Christian church normative for dogmatics in *The Christian Faith* then he asserts that the concept of the Christian church "itself can properly be reached only through the conception of 'Church' in general, together with a proper comprehension of the peculiarity of the Christian Church" (par. 2). This attempt to connect the theological particular with the religious general, which is paradigmatic for the methodology that I am advocating, has been taken up again and again by modern theologians, albeit sometimes with somewhat less concern for the particular. As long as it remains a genuine attempt to formulate the particular in general terms, the Schleiermacherian method expresses the essence of the theological task: to preserve the uniqueness of its own tradition without sacrificing the intersubjective (intercommunal) accessibility required of it as a science.

Unfortunately, despite his programmatic formulation of the task of theological methodology, Schleiermacher did not succeed in reconciling the demands of the church and the academy. The reason for his failure lies, I believe, in the appeal to "God-consciousness" as his central tenet. The genius of the appeal stems from the fact that it appeared to connect the Christianity-external feeling of absolute dependence, with which presumably all would be familiar, with the experiential knowledge that the redeemed had of their own Redeemer, thereby linking external and internal within one conceptual framework. But both camps have rejected the stratagem. Among philosophers of religion, the appeal to a "feeling of absolute dependence" passes for unmitigated subjectivism, whereas internalist theologians oppose Schleiermacher for imposing a systematic philosophical framework on theology, and neofundamentalist thinkers find in him the root of all modern evil (i.e., liberalism).[30] The systematic ambiguity in the notion of God-consciousness makes it possible for Schleiermacher to be simultaneously castigated by both camps. For the concept has not been able to perform the synthesis claimed for it; like Wittgenstein's duck/rabbit, it seems to shift back and forth from a purely philosophical to a purely church-internal concept. Schleiermacher interpreters continue to debate about which side predominated in Schleiermacher's thought, while apparently all agreeing that he was not successful in achieving a conceptual marriage of the two sides.

Ian Barbour has utilized recent developments in the philosophy of science to overcome the tension between the traditional self-understanding of theology and the more general requirements of scientific rationality. His success demonstrates the methodological fruitfulness of the contextualist shift in science in its complete reconstrual of the traditional faith/reason debate. In order to integrate the demand for intersubjectively valid arguments with the presence of contextual or pragmatic factors, Barbour focuses on the use, in both science and religion, of models and paradigms or exemplars. Note his definition of theology:

> Theology is the systematic and self-critical reflection of a paradigm community concerning its beliefs. The theologian traces the ways in which the memory of historical exemplars has shaped the life and thought of the community. He explores the relationships among its central models and doctrines and the implications of its view of nature, man and God.[31]

Certainly Barbour cannot be faulted for inadequate regard for the practicing community and its practices. His starting point is the actual beliefs of the religious community, and he considers at length how these historical exemplars actually function to unify particular religious traditions. Nonetheless, he continues to characterize theological reflection as systematic and self-critical. What can these scientific requirements mean within the context of theology? The former term suggests regarding theological statements as expressing the inner coherence between belief statements ("relationships among . . . central models and doctrines"), *as well as* their relationship to tenets of natural science, anthropology and philosophical theology ("implications of its views of nature, man and God"). The term *self-critical* stems ineluctably from the former: the dialogue with other disciplines requires some form of critical control over the process. Interdisciplinary debate implies interdisciplinary standards for discussion.

I suggest that Barbour's definition of theology offers a way of overcoming Schleiermacher's unresolved dilemma between church and academy. The philosophy of science notion of paradigms allows us to mediate, as he argues, between "external description" and "internal self-description" (26). Theology remains "reflection of a paradigm community"; hence its particularity. Yet while it differentiates, the paradigm notion is at the same time a general model shared by all academic disciplines. Even Kuhn, who (I believe falsely) stresses the incommensurability of paradigms, is willing to grant that there are broadly shared epistemic values among disparate disciplines. Such values serve as criteria for theology as long as it remains a member of the broader academic community. Barbour correctly derives from his treatment of the paradigm notion at least five requirements for theological reflection: systematic consistency, criticizability, trueness to one's religious tradition as well as current thought and practice, coherence of paradigm beliefs, and correlation with paradigm-external disciplines.

There is hope, then, that Schleiermacher's project can be consistently carried out using a framework drawn from contemporary philosophy of science. We should therefore pause to highlight more explicitly the major implications of uniting internal with external in the manner I have proposed as a model for theology. I conclude with the methodological proposal of Wolfhart Pannenberg, in order to demonstrate two of these implications: (1) theological science must be construed as the science of God or the science of, for example, Christianity rather than a faith science; (2) its statements must remain open to revision in the light of further research and discussion.

(1) Pannenberg's specification of theology as the "science of God"[32] is already well known. Given the emphasis on tradition and the particularity of the Christian community that seem to be essential for Christian theology, many have been suspicious that Pannenberg's move will ultimately threaten theology's link with the community of Christian believers. Moreover, his understanding of God as "the all-determining reality" (*die alles bestimmende Wirklichkeit*) has led some to worry that theology will be sublated within, say, classical metaphysics or Enlightenment rationalism, divorced from the actual historical religion and contemporary existential concerns of Christianity.

This is not, however, the case. Pannenberg argues that in the first place *the historical religions*, not philosophy, are "the place in which the experience of the self-proclamation of God (or divine reality in general) is articulated in the reality of the world as a whole" (313). The only sublation then, despite popular misconstruals, is the "sublation (*Aufhebung*) of the formal definition of God, understood as the ground or source of reality as a whole, into the historicity of the positive religions."[33] In fact, Pannenberg demotes "the general philosophy of religion" to the role of a "propaedeutic" (419). In order to understand the phenomenon of religion, "the abstraction of the general concept of religion, which is unavoidable as a starting point, must be transcended-yet-preserved (*aufgehoben*) within the multiplicity of the religions in their historical reality" (ibid.).

These are difficult issues. Our position requires that theology, understood in the broadest sense, be construed as the science of God. A variety of factors can contribute to carrying out theological research on this question: study in comparative religions, human religious experience, the question of meaning, the course of history. Clearly, the basic focus is on the content of theological beliefs rather than on subjective response or appropriation. At a more specific level, Christian theology can be understood as "the science of Christianity" (314). In this case we can freely begin with one particular religious tradition and the way in which its beliefs and practices have developed through time. Still, even here we focus on Christianity as a historical phenomenon and not exclusively on the subjective or communal experience of being Christian. By means of this emphasis, we can avoid an anthropomorphizing of Christianity that would reduce its primary reference to the internal (sociological) dynamics of Christian communities. Adequate place is thereby preserved for the belief-about element in the Christian religion, including a discussion of the claims to divine revelation and the consequent truth claims involved.

(2) Pannenberg has also become famous for arguing that theological assertions remain preliminary and open to revision.[34] This position too is revisionary, to the extent that theology has been taken to presuppose the truth of its central beliefs or, at least, to argue for them by means of prolegomena or apologetics that were essentially separate from the theological enterprise itself. But the truth of theological explanations cannot be definitively settled in advance; it is a question that must remain open to continuing work in the discipline. For the present, anyway, theological truth is hypothetical truth.

Let me now summarize the position on theological methodology and rationality that has emerged in this section. Although these comments should hold for the theology of any religious tradition that wishes to be acknowledged as an academic discipline, I will formulate them specifically in terms of Christian theology. I have suggested that Christian theology can be understood as level-two discourse concerning level-one beliefs, attitudes, and practices of the Christian community. As critical inquiry, it is concerned with redescribing the level-one data in a systematic and self-critical manner; it is therefore methodologically related to critical inquiry in other disciplines. Because theology results in clarification of beliefs and practice, it is of vital concern and assistance to the church, and may in this sense be said to work in the service of the church. Yet because this clarification of Christian belief necessarily involves dependence on categories not drawn from the Christian tradition, as well as the use of general notions such as truth, meaning, and reference, Christian theology will also find itself in vital discourse concerning material issues with science, philosophy, and other theologies.

The Truth Claims of Theology

It remains now to confront a perplexing issue that has only been skirted up to this point: the question of the truth of theology. What is the connection between explanation and truth? Is theology conceivable without the sort of truth claims associated with the explanatory disciplines? If not, how strongly and in what manner should theologians state their claim to truth?

Theology without Explanation?

There is no direct road from critical inquiry to truth, nor from hermeneutics to truth theory—this our contemporaries know well. Along with the (attempted) avoidance of metaphysics in this century has come the avoidance of classical epistemology with its talk of reference and truth conditions. Thinkers are vitally concerned with science, its methodology and manner of justification; yet if this concern is epistemological, it is not so in the classical sense. Epistemology reduced to the question of warranted assertability within a specified linguistic or pragmatic context becomes philosophy of science or philosophy of language.

As philosophers began to delve into the structure of language, their studies revealed insuperable difficulties with simple and direct views of the language/world relationship, such as the picture theory of the early Wittgenstein. As significant as Wittgenstein's *Philosophical Investigations*, which argued that many uses of language are not meant and cannot be construed as referential, were Quine's now widely-repeated doctrines of underdeterminism and the inscrutability of reference. In arguing for the inscrutability of reference, Quine insisted that we have no access to the entities to which our words intend to refer. The evidence we have underdetermines our statements about the world, so that it is impossible to know which of the various possible ontological interpretations of our language is correct. In one of several creative examples Quine argues, "We can systematically reconstruct our neighbor's references to squirrels as references to squirrel-stages, and his apparent references to formulas as references to Gödel numbers, and vice versa."[35] More recently, Bruce Hauptli has fleshed out the epistemological implications of the Quinean position, arguing for a "disappearance theory of truth": if there are no evidential arbitrators between two different theories for determining which one is true, then the traditional notion of truth is meaningless. "What it means when one says that a theory or statement is true is that it is indeed the theory held by the theory's supporters."[36]

The arguments presented by Wittgenstein and Quine raise severe difficulties for traditional theories of truth. And they continue to be influential.

In an important work, Hilary Putnam has moved from Quinean under-determinism to a wide-ranging critique of metaphysical realism and the "God's eye point of view."[37] Similar to the more radical position held by Nelson Goodman, Putnam argues for a multitude of worlds, of references, of truths, and of rationalities. Mary Hesse has likewise combined Quine's doctrine of underdeterminism with recent work in the sociology of knowl-edge in order to reduce the natural sciences to the equivalent of social sciences and to reduce both to products of our culture with no unique epistemological merit.[38] Her forthcoming Stanton lectures on the philoso-phy of religion[39] argue for a theology that eschews metaphysics and the truth claims of "metaphysical realism." As I noted in chapter 1, similar moves to avoid referential language in religion are familiar to students of the philosophy of religion in the period following the publication of A. J. Ayer's *Language, Truth and Logic*.[40]

If philosophers of science are bracketing the truth issue and epistemolo-gists are widely skeptical about maintaining even a modified form of the correspondence theory of truth, would it then be safer to remove theology from the gaping jaws of this dispute? Does theology as a discipline require a referential theory of truth? Certainly it is not uncommon to find theolo-gians who insist that neither theology as theoretical discourse nor theology as a hermeneutical inquiry requires an extratheological account of the correspondence relation. That is, many believe that it is possible to present an internally coherent view of theology that bypasses the problems of a referential theory of truth. These thinkers seek therefore to leave aside the external question of the objective truth of Christianity, arguing that it is presupposed by believers anyway, and deal only with the ways in which Christian statements function within the believing community.

In the following section I will defend a very different understanding of the discipline of theology. However, I no longer think that it is necessary to reject the academic credentials of the internalist construal of theology: it may still be rational in the sense of meeting the standards of (some of the disciplines of) the academy. To give a full exposition of the particular attributes of this model of theology would involve explicating the nature of rationality in several disciplines not explored in this book, in particular those dealing with literary studies and the arts.[41] Note that these academic disciplines do not attempt to *explain* some subject matter, but to offer various construals of it.[42] To use a recently much discussed label, we might speak of them as being characterized by "intratextuality."[43] In literary criticism one may be concerned with explicating meanings of texts (leaving aside the question of where that meaning is to be located), without thematizing the issue of their truth outside of that context. Activities such as textual interpretation, the interpretation of music or the visual arts, and the creation of such artistic works themselves may be rational, goal-directed activities, pursuing goals of their own (beauty, political effectiveness, a personally enlightening reading), without referring to a correspondence relation with extratextual states of affairs. [44]

More strongly, consideration of such activities can lead one to speak of multiple kinds of truth corresponding to the variety of such activities. We saw already in chapter 3 that Habermas proposes a variety of categories to correspond to the varieties of validity claims advanced in different types of communicative action. For instance, Wolfgang Kayser has spoken of "the truth of the poets," and a recent book by Kurt Hübner attempts to define a distinctive "truth of myth." Many of these efforts stem directly from Heidegger's critique of the hegemony of truth as correspondence and his attempts in his later work to offer a phenomenology of truth broad enough to incorporate the truth of art and the truth of things. [45]

Construed according to some such truth theory, "theology without explanation" would become literary theory or aesthetics or existentialist philosophy. [46] If theologians choose to wed their discipline to one of these disciplines in this manner, the methodologist of science cannot rule out their move as invalid. Of course, there are reasons to resist choosing such bedfellows. The recent spate of publications on narrative theology, even if methodologically allowable, may disturb the theologian with their thoroughgoing narrativizing of theology's traditional self-understanding. Theologians may fear for the autonomy of their discipline when its predicates and truth claims are consistently clothed in the garments of structural or narrative theory. The rejection of narrative categories in favor of scripture's literal sense by the author of *The Eclipse of Biblical Narrative* appears to be one such instance. [47] Frei's later work reflected the insistence that theology not consist of a collection of literary truths, nor of philosophical truths, but of theological truths.

Some of the most influential theological expressions today involve the marriage of theology to another discipline or contemporary movement: in narrative theology, to literary theory; in liberation theology, to Marxist political science, and so forth. If these theologies are to be rejected as unhelpful to theology's own project—and it is still too early to tell whether this will be the judgment—the argument will have to come from the viewpoint of theology as religious discourse. That is, as long as the members of the religious community believe that their concerns are being advanced through such approaches, there is no way that the methodologist can fault them. But theological resistance to certain disciplinary marriages proposed for it could betoken fear for the loss of theology's religious usefulness, as for example in some recent criticisms of process theology. Again, we face the tension of the two poles of theology: how much can theology utilize other disciplines for its disciplinary identity without being reduced to something different? How can it wed internal and external?

If the two poles cannot be unified, they can at least be mediated. I assume that some formulation of theological methodology is allowable and desirable. Naturally, every such formulation orders the data in some way. Any stipulative definition of theology, any statement on the nature of doctrine, will affect how we read and interpret past theological proposals, for theology has a pluralistic history encompassing a number of irreconcilable self-understandings. For example, though I think there are strong reasons for doing so, theology does not have to be construed as an explanatory discipline, nor even as an academic discipline at all. The methodological conclusions arrived at in this study do not prohibit a self-understanding of theology based upon activities such as literary theory, poetry, or the arts. Each of these represents an activity with its own truths and criteria, its own structures, rules, and categories. They may not be explanatory disciplines; their goal is not to explain anything in the world (or the world as a whole), but to describe or represent it in various forms. In such cases, the level-one/level-two distinction may be impossible to draw.

Likewise, other lines of argument, not pursued here, might lead to different conclusions. One could argue that theology is a universal science that, because it subsumes all other sciences under itself, has no need to move outside its own disciplinary boundaries. Classical Thomism, and some of its modern-day representatives, appear to be committed to some such position. Or one could deny that there is anything undesirable about a wholesale reduction of theology to another discipline. Since I have not surveyed such positions here, I cannot claim to have refuted them.

Nonetheless, we have found some reasons for preferring an intersubjectivist methodological proposal. It is therefore appropriate to follow out the stance toward the question of its own truth that might be taken by theology as an explanatory discipline, a program of research in which referential truth claims are made, explicated, and defended. In these last few pages I concentrate on this particular model of theology, one based on the central methodological themes of this book: the context principle of rationality, the coherential theory of meaning, and the universal nature of religious truth.

Theology and the Quest to Know

Can theology be *pure* theology and produce purely theological truths without reliance on any other disciplines? I do not think that it can. The universal nature of religious truth claims make it impossible for theology to stay within strictly defined disciplinary boundaries. "Limiting oneself to theological truths" is an oxymoron, at least in the monotheistic traditions in which the term *God* means the creator of all that is. By the very nature of its claims, theology will find itself in dialogue with explanatory disciplines across the academic spectrum. If this is true, then should we not build into our understanding of theology both the impact of these disciplines and the need to find a means for adjudicating between them?

In fact, it appears that the traditional self-understanding of theology is modified the least when its assertions are understood propositionally as claiming to be true of God and the created world. The view of theology as advancing claims that can conform or conflict with other statements in science, metaphysics, or the philosophy of religion is in conformity with the majority of its history, with the present belief and practice of most religious communities, and with the consciousness of many contemporary religious individuals. The propositional model can therefore be defended as a viable option in the debate over models for theology.

In order to give place to the comprehensive and propositional nature of theology, I propose a methodology for theology that includes the question of its objective truth *within the theological endeavor itself*. Theology is not just about the coherence and application in practice of a number of statements whose ultimate truth status is either presupposed or left unaddressed. Rather, as theology thematizes the question of the inner logic of and relations between various statements within the tradition, it can at the same time address the issue of their truth. At least five lines of argument lead in the direction of this understanding of theology.

(1) The nature of assertions is to refer to extralinguistic states of affairs. In asserting, one asserts something *about* something. Now an analysis of language may show that the assertion of religious explanations does other, nonassertorical things as well; explanatory assertions may also have an affective, performative, or doxological illocutionary force in the broader context of discourse, as our treatment of Habermas showed. Indeed, the discussion in chapter 5 revealed the importance of personal disclosure value to the individual believer. Moreover, how one formulates one's assertions or doctrines is bound historically to specific situations in the life of the religious community. But to remove completely their intended ontological reference is to deny that believers use assertions *as* assertions. One may in the end wish to be skeptical about the knowability of the intended reference and may thus attempt to reduce theological statements to something different from what they seem to be, for example, to emotive expressions or to basic value judgments of some kind. But in the meantime it seems strange for theologians to rush in to reduce their own discipline to another. Surely it is a desideratum for an account of theology to modify as

little as possible the appearance that here we have to do with assertions of actual states of affairs.

(2) The argument in (1) can be supported by drawing attention to the objectifying or representational function of assertions in language. Since it is part of the function of linguistic assertions to (claim to) represent something nonlinguistic, we must reject any construal of language in general (and theology in particular) that denies to statements their representational function. Consider, as a negative example, the hermeneutics of Hans-Georg Gadamer, who has continually downplayed the role to objectification in language.[48] Emilio Betti has rightly complained that Gadamer's hermeneutics tends to obscure the fact that texts are "meaningful forms" that in their historical distance from us stand in need of interpretation.[49] However, insofar as Gadamer acknowledges that the Other's horizon may strike us as alien, is not even he committed to allowing some place for the notion of objectification—at least in the sense of the distinction between my own subjectivity and the objects of my consciousness or knowledge? As Pannenberg argues, granting this does not entail the return to a purely objectivist epistemology: "'Objectivity'. . . obviously cannot mean a complete independence of the interpretation from the interpreter's position, but only that for every such position the thing to be interpreted must be distinguishable from the subjectivity of the interpreter, and that its distinctness must be given full weight."[50] If these critics of Gadamer are correct, we are justified in maintaining in principle the objective function of language for representing nonlinguistic states of affairs verbally. Although the verification of the word/world relationship remains problematic, the compulsion to eliminate or explain away the relationship is thereby mitigated. An intrinsic aim of our language is to represent states of affairs; it is not necessary to translate representational truth into the truth of personal disclosure or communal identity.

(3) The content of theistic belief involves truth claims about the way things are. For instance, when one believes in God, one believes that there is a being with such-and-such qualities that actually exists. Acknowledging this is not a return to natural theology. Our language may make reference claims about God that are not amenable to the classical theistic proofs; nevertheless, in some cases the existential entailments of a doctrine of God can be fleshed out.[51] Christians assert that God has power over events that occur in the world, that God is directing the course of events toward a specified end. Such statements make claims that extend beyond the borders of the particular religious community. In both form and content they are assertions that claim intersubjective validity. Although we may have particular motives for wishing to treat religious explanations in other

than their apparent sense, I believe the burden lies on the side of revisionist interpretations to demonstrate that theological language should not be taken at its face value.

In the remaining arguments we turn to considerations that are more specific to Christian theology. (4) Christianity is a historical religion. Its identity is built around the life of a historical individual and around specific events that the Christian scriptures claim actually occurred at specific times and places in the past. Although historical claims involving the birth, death, and resurrection of Jesus also have existential implications for believers, their surface structure at least is factual. The truth of these historical claims is certainly presupposed in their personal and communal use. Moreover, the Christian narrative seems to commit Christians to beliefs about other historical events occurring before and after the New Testament events. Of course, theologians have worked for centuries to reinterpret or demythologize some or all of these historical claims. Still, at least the *issue* of their truth or falsity must remain of vital concern to those who attempt to explain the world in terms of the Christian narrative.

(5) Positions that reject or downplay external truth often claim that Christian assumptions should be presupposed without any external grounding. But is not a presuppositional approach to the question of the truth of Christianity more appropriate for epochs in which that truth is generally assumed? When Augustine defined *assensus* as assenting to the propositions of Christian belief on the basis of evidences, it was sufficient for him to appeal for evidence to the authority of the Church that had faithfully preserved the words of the initial witnesses up to his day. Concerned with the disbelief of the Gentiles, by contrast, Aquinas had to extend his evidence for the Christian faith to arguments for the existence of God; yet it was sufficient for him to conclude his metaphysical proofs with the words "et hoc omnes intelligunt Deum."[52] In each case the apologists could gloss over potential conceptual difficulties that were not difficulties for their readers and instead direct themselves to the difficulties that were actual threats to those whose faith was seeking understanding. In our time the plurality of live religious and secular options now forms the context for deciding what can and cannot be credibly presupposed.

We can now try to specify the position suggested by these considerations. What implications does the breakdown of the theology/apologetics distinction have for the Christian thinker in the twentieth century, in a "post-Christian era"? In "The Will to Believe," James writes of "living" and "dead" hypotheses, depending on whether a belief-claim is a live option for a given person or group.[53] We might adapt his terminology slightly and speak of living and dead doubts, of those that are live options for the potential (or actual) believer and those with which she does not in fact concern herself. The breadth and severity of the live doubts that most contemporary believers face would, I think, prove to be startling. To then argue, either as description or by stipulation, that believers do or should presuppose the truth of their Christianity as unproblematic seems psychologically unlikely and conceptually inadvisable. Too many of those still actively involved in religious life are secular believers in the sense outlined in chapter 5.

The threat that some may see lurking behind my approach is that Christianity's uniqueness will be lost, and that it will be subordinated to a foreign authority, most regrettably that of philosophy. I believe this fear to be ungrounded, for reasons to be adduced below. More importantly, the major attempts to make the dialogue with other disciplines less essential run into serious problems. We have already examined some difficulties with internalist approaches. Another strategy, often employed by conservative theologians, is to appeal to a completed and self-interpreting revelation of God, which one holds to guarantee the truth of Christian belief and practice. However, this strategy also runs into trouble on evidential grounds. We might call it "Locke's Dilemma": either the revelation itself (e.g., biblical statements) is simply presupposed as true, in which case no intersubjective evidence claims are being made, or it must be shown to be true. In the first case we have only moved the presupposition back one step, from self-authenticating religious beliefs to self-authenticating revelation, whereas in the second the revelation will only be as strong as the arguments for it.

In fact, appeals to intratextuality or self-authenticating revelation are not the only ways to preserve the theological endeavor. Other options are available by means of which one can allow debate concerning the truth of Christianity into theology without thereby reducing theology to some other discipline. One option is to opt with Pannenberg for the specificity of the Christian faith over the general issues addressed by the philosopher of religion.[54] He *begins with* Christianity as "the history which receives its impetus from the investigation of the truth of the Christian faith" (417), and argues throughout his work for the hypothetical status (*Strittigkeit*) of Christianity's truth. Yet he rejects any "universal theory of Christianity," maintaining that "*the essence of Christianity is this history* from the advent of God's future in Jesus to the future of the kingdom of God" (418, emph. mine). Though much is appealing in this proposal, I am not sure that Pannenberg's approach solves the problem of the language with which to discuss the truth of Christianity as a unique historical entity. If he used purely Christianity-internal terms, he would indeed do justice to its historical uniqueness, while being unable to communicate its hypothetical or scientific status in general terms as he would like. To speak nonhistorically

of the truth of a historical phenomenon would seem to require a broader
framework and terms that are more accessible than internal Christian
descriptions.[55]

Once again we have run up against the twofold requirement faced by
theology: the theologian needs to thematize the general issues raised by
Christian truth claims without sacrificing the specificity of the Christian
tradition. I have defined theology as level-two discourse concerning level-
one beliefs, attitudes, and practices. This stipulation reflects on the one
hand theology's concern with the language and situation of its own religious
tradition. On the other, it indicates the systematic and critical nature of
level-two discourse. In theology one works toward an explanation of the
phenomena of belief and practice in a metalanguage rich enough to thematize the question of the objective truth of these phenomena. In entering
into the latter debate, one is not wreaking havoc on theology's distinctiveness as a discipline, but merely making explicit the implications of claims
already made by Christian level-one statements and practices.

Here, as in chapter 4, the theories of truth and of meaning come together. The truth-theoretical component of theology (in the externalist
sense) is by no means incompatible with the religious project of "making
sense out of total experience." We have observed that religious believers
are occupied with attaining a meaningful understanding of their world, and
that religions generally offer an explanation of its meaning at the broadest
possible level. The beliefs of Christianity constitute one such unique picture of the world. In the theoretical discourse of theology, this explanation
is systematized and subjected to critical analysis: its various aspects are
explored, further details and substantiations are provided by way of other
areas of human knowledge, and a formally consistent formulation is sought.
But Christian explanations can only make sense of the world if believers can
believe that they are actually true, that what they claim is the case. Areas in
which the truth of Christian claims seems unlikely may well become problem areas.

To apply an insight from Lakatos's work on research programs, if no rival
is a live option, one may well remain with a clearly inadequate explanatory
system. Obviously, believers bring to their religious belief more commitment (and less readiness to modify their beliefs) than a scientist would. But
today there are many live options. The theologian, as here defended, is
committed to engaging the other positions in serious and open dialogue. If
a rival view can offer a more satisfactory explanation, it will merit rational
consideration and may either be incorporated within or replace an existing
explanatory system. Therefore, at this level the questions of meaning and
of truth coincide in Christian thought: I cannot feel that the Christian

explanation makes sense of my total experience unless I also believe that it is true of the world.

In summary: if the arguments given in this section for an objective referential function of assertorical language are valid, we are justified, more skeptical positions in the philosophy of language notwithstanding, in continuing to speak of the possible objective truth of a given belief system. Where recent skeptical work cannot be disregarded, however, is in its critique of the appeal to correspondence in justificatory contexts. Assuming the inadequacy of appeals to direct evidence or intuition, there is no direct way to verify the word/world relationship in the case of any given claim to knowledge (i.e., to truth). It follows that, even if the correspondence theory remains an indispensable part of any definition of truth, it can no longer be claimed an adequate *criterion* of truth. Yet, if we are unable to defend the truth-indicativeness of *any* criterion for truth, do my arguments for the incorporation of truth considerations into theology not represent an empty victory?[56]

I am not convinced that definition of *sans* criteria for the success of theology would indeed represent so pointless an attainment. Even in the absence of any adequately defended truth criterion, a valid definition can serve a useful function. To return to the thinker with whom we began our analysis in chapter 2, Karl Popper defends a notion of truth in science as a regulative or limiting-case concept. Truth represents the ideal limit of scientific inquiry, regardless of the fact that we cannot say of any given theory that it is true (though we may be able to say that it is less false). Among others, Pannenberg has criticized Popper's position.[57] Both thinkers admit that we have no privileged point of view from which to verify correspondence claims; yet the theologian finds Popper's truth theory unnecessarily weak. However, a regulative theory of truth is only weak in comparison to a specified alternative, such as Pannenberg's own anticipatory theory of truth. Should the latter fall short of the claims made for it,[58] the greater skepticism of a purely regulative notion of truth may prove justified.

Let us review the general requirements for an ideal explanation. Its statements will be systematically interconnected in relationships of mutual entailment (ideal coherence) and will correctly reflect the way the world is (ideal correspondence). (We might also wish to stipulate that it makes maximal sense of the world for its advocates or believers [disclosure value], although the truth-indicativeness of this criterion is more difficult to defend.) We cannot know that such an ideal explanation would be true of the world, for we lack a "God's eye point of view" (H. Putnam) from which to verify its correspondence. But we can *posit* the link between ideal explanations and truth. The suggestion is to accept that systematic, critical re-flection (science in its broadest sense) must aim toward ideal explanations, and then to posit that such explanations, were we to achieve them, be taken as true as well.

In order to conceive of this possibility, we have to construe the notion of ideal coherence in an explanation as contributing more than epistemic justification; it would have to be truth-indicative as well. But this is pre-cisely what the link of coherence and correspondence in chapter 4 entails. In other words, a case can be made—giving a Kantian twist to arguments advanced by Bradley and Brand Blanshard—for selecting the coherent system of statements that has the greatest possible comprehensiveness and *treating it as true*, that is, as representing the way things actually are. One (also Kantian) argument for this move is a negative one: if our best justified system of statements is not for that reason true (or: more likely to be true), then justification and truth have no link. But this would make all intellec-tual inquiry pointless from the point of view of the truth question. There-fore, if we wish to continue with truth-seeking intellectual activity, we must posit that perfect justification is truth-related. In this manner, with-out having achieved our goal we can still posit the ideal and then mold our academic inquiry to correspond with it. For *ex hypothesi*, the explanation that best approximates the ideal qualities of a scientific explanation is the one which is the most likely to be true.

Now such a regulative theory of truth does not allow us to defend the truth of any particular statement or explanatory scheme as settled, nor to maintain, for instance, that science or theology is progressively approx-imating truth. Yet it does, I believe, provide a context within which our continued utilization of the notion of truth in the context of religious expla-nations is not only justified, but also mandated, in order to make sense of the knowledge quest at all.

I think that a theory of truth and meaning developed along coherential lines makes some headway against the skeptical problems; at any rate, recent work on the subject has much to recommend it.[59] We have already looked at its ability to unify various of the other criteria proposed in the discussion of theories of truth. Recall that correspondence could be viewed as the coherence of different sorts of linguistic units (e.g., of the observa-tion set with the theory set). Similarly, Habermas' consensus theory of truth may be inadequate when taken alone, but there is potential for combining it with a coherence criterion: as the latter connotes the coherence of a group of statements, consensus can be viewed as the coherence of a group of persons or opinions.

I will not pause here to detail the specific implications for theology of this line of argumentation, since the more difficult task in the current discussion is to defend the inclusion of the ontological truth quesion at all. More-over, the fact that one theologian tends to rely more on traditional meta-physical defenses, another on work in comparative religions, another on the methodology and results of contemporary science, militates against pinning theology down to any particular approach to its ontological truth. Perhaps some ordering of and gradual transition between the various theo-logical subdisciplines could be derived by conjoining a regulative theory of truth with the just-completed analysis of scientific rationality and explana-tion. For instance, the level-one/level-two distinction suggests that theol-ogy begin with the history of the Church's thought and practice up to the present day; that it then seek to systematize these beliefs in the most coherent fashion and in a manner that allows for criticism and revision; and finally that it pursue the inquiry in light of the question of the truth of those beliefs under discussion. Though this approach involves supplementing a praxis-oriented version of theology with nonpragmatic concerns, it need not get in the way of the ongoing practice of the religious community. Indeed, in an age in which the believer can no longer be expected to presuppose unproblematically the truth of beliefs held (recall again the concept of the secular believer), this approach would expand the theologi-cal task to include precisely those doubts and questions with which believ-ers may be assumed to be wrestling. Arguably the result is a treatment of religious explanations that in the final analysis is not destructive to religious beliefs and practice, but offers a constructive option both for the discipline of theology and for the efforts of individual believers to make sense of their world.

Notes

Chapter 1

1. Robin Horton might be taken as advocating this position; he has recently (in Bryan Wilson, ed., *Rationality* [1970], chap. 7) portrayed the African religious traditions as monolithic in comparison to the western religions with their highly developed emphasis on choice. The stress on magic, however, might be taken as an early form of scientific verificationism: tribal believers may well take their beliefs to be objectively warranted by external events.

2. See John M. Koller, *Oriental Philosophies* (1970), 105–45; Ninian Smart, *Doctrine and Argument in Indian Philosophy* (1964), 97–105.

3. It must be stressed that private explanations may be quite comprehensive in scope, accounting for broad areas of human experience. I focus here only on their epistemic basis.

4. Søren Kierkegaard, *Concluding Unscientific Postscript* (1941), 182.

5. See Ludwig Wittgenstein, *Lectures and Conversations on Aesthetics, Psychology and Religious Belief* (1966), in addition to the *Philosophical Investigations* (1953).

6. Cf. David Burrell, "Religious Belief and Rationality," in C. F. Delaney, ed., *Rationality and Religious Belief* (1979), 84–115; Louis Dupré, *The Other Dimension: A Search for the Meaning of Religious Attitudes* (1979), 71.

7. For instance, if truth is defined as correspondence, issue (1) seems to reduce to (2); if one defines truth as some kind of coherence or fit between statements, the relationship between truth and the ideal of rationality (4) is underscored.

8. Hilary Putnam, "Realism and Reason," *Realism and Reason* (1983), 202.

9. See Theodore Geraets's introduction to the Ottawa Symposium, published as Geraets, ed., *Symposium on Rationality To-day* (1979), xi.

10. C. F. Delaney, in Delaney, ed., *Rationality and Religious Belief*, intro., 1.

11. For a modern-day restatement of this position see Cornelius Van Til, *The Defense of the Faith* (1955), and the essays in E. R. Geehan, ed., *Jerusalem and Athens* (1974). Van Til calls his position *metaphysical presuppositionalism*, since

the uniqueness of the Christian metaphysic eliminates *all* common ground with other worldviews.

12. Calvin, "The Knowledge of God Has Been Naturally Implanted in the Minds of Men," *Institutes*, book I, chap. 3.

13. There is, however, some reason to dispute this interpretation. Clement believed that philosophy was able adequately to conceptualize Christian truths, and he highly praised pre-Christian Greek thinkers, especially Plato, for their insights into matters later to be revealed. He might thus better be understood as teaching an equal authority of faith and reason. Nonetheless, he seems ultimately to acknowledge the superiority of faith.

14. Augustine, *Confessions* (1972), XI, xi.

15. Anselm says that it was written as "an example of meditation on the grounds of faith" (*Proslogium*, in *Basic Writings* [1962], preface) and that only after writing it and reflecting on what he had written did he see "that it was put together as a long chain of arguments" (ibid.).

16. John E. Smith has called it "the one avenue of approach whereby a form of rationality and intelligibility can be recovered within the sphere of religious belief," in "Faith, Belief and the Problem of Rationality in Religion," in Delaney, ed., *Rationality and Religious Belief*, 42–64, quote on 59.

17. Troeltsch divides the interests of the "theological sciences": "One part serves pure science and only indirectly the practical-religious life, the other serves the Church and praxis" ("Rückblick auf ein halbes Jahrhundert der theologischen Wissenschaft," *Gesammelte Schriften*, vol. 2 [1913], 198). For his part, Tillich distinguishes between the "profane-rational view of theology," i.e., the "science of religion," and the "religious-heteronomous" view that makes theology the "science of God" ("Theonome Systematik," *Das System der Wissenschaften nach Gegenständen und Methoden* [1923], in *Gesammelte Werke*, vol. 1 [1959], 274–75).

18. The work of Paul Holmer is paradigmatic in this regard; see, among many articles, his "Nygren and Linguistic Analysis: Language and Meaning," in Charles W. Kegley, ed., *The Philosophy and Theology of Anders Nygren* (1970), 70–94. Among philosophers of religion, D. Z. Phillips is probably the chief spokesman for the use of the later Wittgenstein; see his *Religion and Understanding* (1967); *Faith and Philosophical Enquiry* (1970); and *Religion Without Explanation* (1976).

19. Karl Barth, *Church Dogmatics* (1961), e.g., IV.2, 123.

20. *Christliche Dogmatik* (1927), 115, against H. H. Wendt, *System der christlichen Lehre* (1906), 2–3.

21. T. F. Torrance, *Theological Science* (1969).

22. See Scholz, "Wie ist eine evangelische Theologie als Wissenschaft möglich?" *Zwischen den Zeiten* 9 (1931):8–53.

23. *Kirchliche Dogmatik*, I.1, 6; cf. *Church Dogmatics*, I.1, 7.

24. See (respectively) Juan Luis Segundo, *The Liberation of Theology* (1976); John B. Cobb, Jr., and David Ray Griffin, *Process Theology* (1976); and Helmut Peukert, *Science, Action and Fundamental Theology: Toward a Theology of Communicative Action* (1984).

25. The works of Brian A. Gerrish make this historical progression especially clear. See *The Old Protestantism and the New: Essays on the Reformation Heritage* (1982); *A Prince of the Church: Schleiermacher and the Beginnings of Modern Theology* (1984); and *Tradition and the Modern World: Reformed Theology in the Nineteenth Century* (1978).

26. Wolfhart Pannenberg, *Jesus—God and Man* (1977), 109. See also his *Theology and the Philosophy of Science* (1976), chap. 5, for the definition of theology as the general "science of God" (*Wissenschaft von Gott*).

27. Pannenberg, "Der Gott der Geschichte," *Grundfragen systematischer Theologie*, vol. 2 (1980).

28. See Carnell, *An Introduction to Christian Apologetics* (1948); Ramm, *Varieties of Christian Apologetics* (1961); and the survey of different positions in Lewis, *Testing Christianity's Truth Claims* (1976).

29. On the "Metaphysicals" see the collection of essays, Basil Mitchell, ed., *Faith and Logic: Oxford Essays in Philosophical Theology* (1957). See also Swinburne, *Faith and Reason* (1981) and Mitchell, *The Justification of Religious Belief* (1973). The tradition is continued in the recent collection, William J. Abraham and Steven W. Holtzer, eds., *The Rationality of Religious Belief: Essays in Honor of Basil Mitchell* (1987).

30. This debate, often called the "University Discussion," asked whether religious beliefs could be cognitively meaningful at all if nothing could ever verify or falsify them. The central articles are contained, e.g., in Baruch A. Brody, ed., *Readings in the Philosophy of Religion: An Analytic Approach* (1974), 308ff. Brody's anthology also contains a representative selection from recent work on the theistic proofs and the problem of evil.

31. For a recent statement of this position see the essays in Alvin Plantinga and Nicholas Wolterstorff, eds., *Faith and Philosophy: Reason and Belief in God* (1983).

32. However, Wolterstorff's attempts to appropriate the common-sense realism of David Reid in " ", sjf, may represent a more overt form of what I am claiming is implicit in Plantinga's approach as well. I also suspect that the parallels between the Plantinga school and the epistemological work of William Alston and Roderick Chisholm are stronger than may appear at first glance.

33. See Alfred North Whitehead, *Science and the Modern World* (1948); and Stephen C. Pepper, *World Hypotheses: A Study in Evidence* (1961). Pepper's four basic categories are formism, mechanism, contextualism, and organicism.

34. Consider the mingling of levels and terms in a sentence such as, "In this chapter and in the one following, the methods of religion will be compared with the methods of science" (Ian Barbour, *Issues in Science and Religion* [1966], 207).

Chapter 2

1. The major stream of influence flowed in the *opposite* direction, i.e., from theology to science, at the time of the birth of most of the modern sciences. In these instances, religious or metaphysical beliefs were more often the causal factor,

scientific method or theories the result. See Edwin A. Burtt, *The Metaphysical Foundations of Modern Science* (1951).

2. A. J. Ayer, *Language, Truth and Logic* (1946), 5.

3. Or: for those treating religious statements as rational truth-claims. The dilemma does not concern some theologians and does vitally concern many students of religion who are nontheologians.

4. See, among many recent examples, G. Radnitzky and G. Andersson, eds., *Progress and Rationality in Science* (1978), and W. H. Newton-Smith, *The Rationality of Science* (1981).

5. See (respectively) W. W. Bartley, *The Retreat to Commitment* (1962), and Hans Albert, *Traktat über kritische Vernunft* (1969; 1978); Helmut Peukert, *Science, Action and Fundamental Theology: Toward a Theology of Communicative Action* (1976; 1984); and "Sociological Critique," in A. R. Peacocke, ed., *The Sciences and Theology in the Twentieth Century* (1981), part 4.

6. Clark Glymour, "Explanation and Realism" (1984), 173, emphasis mine.

7. See Frederick Suppe's excellent summary of the developments in Frederick Suppe, ed., *The Structure of Scientific Theories* (1977), intro.

8. Karl Popper, *The Logic of Scientific Discovery* (1935; 1959), 59; cf. his *Objective Knowledge: An Evolutionary Approach* (1972; 1979), 103.

9. It is interesting that *Logic* represents Popper's preoccupation with the problem of induction as the primary one, with the demarcation problem (viz., how to separate science from metaphysics) then stemming from it (e.g., 35), while *Conjectures and Refutations* (1963) dates his concern with demarcation to 1919, or four years before he "bec[a]me interested in the problem of induction" (*Conjectures*, 42; cf. 255). Albrecht Wellmer, who claims that Popper "came upon the problem of induction in the first place independently of the demarcation problem" through his occupation with Hume (A. Wellmer, *Methodologie als Erkenntnistheorie* [1967], 30), has unfortunately overseen Popper's own chronology. Nonetheless, the *Logic* presentation correctly reports the *logical* order: the failure of induction reopens the demarcation question for the natural sciences.

10. See also Karl Popper, *The Open Society and Its Enemies* (1945), chap. 25, esp. n. 7.

11. That is, concepts in which proper names are indispensible; see Popper, *Logic*, 66.

12. Popper, *Logic*, 61.

13. Popper, *Conjectures*, 63.

14. Karl Popper, *The Poverty of Historicism* (1957), 124.

15. Popper explicitly opposed the demand for ultimate explanations in *Conjectures*, 104–5; cf. *Objective Knowledge*, 194ff.

16. Popper, *Objective Knowledge*, 195.

17. *Conjectures*, 199.

18. Hans Albert, *Traktat über kritische Vernunft* (1969; 1978), 155; English

translation: *Treatise on Critical Reason* (1985), 195. Page references are to the English edition, though I have altered some of the translations.

19. The term stems from W. W. Bartley; see his "Rationality *versus* the Theory of Rationality," in M. Bunge, ed., *The Critical Approach to Science and Philosophy* (1964), 3–31; and "On the Criticizability of Logic," *Philosophy of the Social Sciences* 10 (1980):67–77.

20. Albert, *Treatise*, 19.

21. Albert, *Treatise*, 46. It is not as though Popper himself failed to realize that his approach had broader implications, e.g., for addressing philosophical questions. See "The Nature of Philosophical Problems and Their Roots in Science" and "On the Status of Science and of Metaphysics," in *Conjectures*. Yet, whereas Popper always remained a philosopher of science, his followers have been more ready to develop his approach beyond the borders of natural science. Thus Albert has castigated, inter alia, Marxism and analytic philosophy (*Treatise*, chaps. 4 and 6), modern Catholic theology (*Das Elend der Theologie. Kritische Auseinandersetzung mit Hans Küng* [1979]), Protestant theology (*Theologische Holzwege. Gerhard Ebeling und der rechte Gebrauch der Vernunft* [1973]), "transcendental pragmatics" in social scientific theory (*Transzendentale Träumereien. Karl-Otto Apels Sprachspiele und sein hermeneutischer Gott* [1975]), and the entire hermeneutical tradition (*Plädoyer für kritische Rationalismus* [1971]). Somewhat less casuistic efforts in the same direction include J. W. N. Watkins, "Confirmable and Influential Metaphysics," *Mind* 67 (1958):344–65, and William Bartley, *The Retreat to Commitment* (1962).

22. The publication in 1979 of his *Die beiden Grundprobleme der Erkenntnis,* "based on manuscripts from the years 1930–1933," and the three volumes of *The Postscript to the Logic of Scientific Discovery* in 1983 (*Realism and the Aim of Science, The Open Universe*, and *Quantum Theory and the Schism in Physics*), virtually unchanged from the galleys and notations of 1962, is ample evidence that Popper's encounter with Lakatos, Kuhn, and others did not lead to any major modifications or retractions.

23. On (3) see Popper, *Logic*, 102. A number of other labels have been used for the thinkers in this category. Glymour speaks of their "purely logical theories" ("Explanation and Realism," 178); many others label it the "covering law" or "deductive-nomological" approach, although I believe this label to be too narrow. Carl Hempel at one point calls his position the quest for "a general analytic theory" of explanation and prediction; see his "Deductive-Nomological versus Statistical Explanation," in Feigl and Maxwell, eds., *Scientific Explanation, Space, and Time,* (1962), 167. It was already called a formal analysis of explanation by Feyerabend in the same collection (28).

It is tempting to place these positions under the heading of structuralist theories of explanation, in light of their preoccupation with structural considerations. The term *structuralist* nicely draws attention to their claim that there is universally shared structure in scientific explanations (and thus in the world), as in Rudolf Carnap, *The Logical Structure of the World* (1928; 1967) and Ernest Nagel, *The*

Structure of Science: Problems in the Logic of Scientific Explanation (1961). But structuralism has a very different meaning in social scientific theory. Moreover, the concern with structures has continued in nonformalist philosophy of science (as in T. S. Kuhn, *The Structure of Scientific Revolutions* [1962]), now with the sense of *pragmatic* structures.

24. R. B. Braithwaite, *Scientific Explanation* (1953), ix.

25. Carl G. Hempel and Paul Oppenheim, "Studies in the Logic of Explanation," *Philosophy of Science* 15 (1948):135–75; page references are to the reprint with a 1964 postscript in Carl G. Hempel, *Aspects of Scientific Explanation* (1965), 245–95.

26. Even Ernst Nagel, *The Structure of Science*, 49, is aware of this difficulty.

27. Hempel had already made strong claims for deductive-nomological explanation in historical studies in his early "The Function of General Laws in History," *Journal of Philosophy* 39 (1942):35–48, reprinted in Hempel, *Aspects*, 231–43, e.g.: "The necessity, in historical inquiry, to make extensive use of universal hypotheses . . . is just one of the aspects of what may be called the methodological unity of empirical science" (243).

28. See Popper, *Logic*, secs. 13–15, 62–70. Wesley Salmon notes that Popper's *Logic* contains an "important anticipation" of the deductive-nomological model of explanation, though still belonging to the "prehistory" of the subject; see his *Scientific Explanation and the Causal Structure of the World* (1984), 21n9.

29. Wesley Salmon, "Carl G. Hempel on the Rationality of Science," *Journal of Philosophy* 80 (1983):555–62, quote on 555.

30. That Hempel was aware of many of these problems in the later years of his career may reflect well on him as a scholar but is not relevant to the assessment of the overall program associated with his name.

31. Nagel, *The Structure of Science*, 57–59.

32. Hempel, *Aspects*, 293.

33. Hempel, *Aspects*, 274–76. Hempel's example is the explanation, which he considers valid,

T_1 = "$(x)[P(x) \supset Q(x)]$"
C_1 = "$R(a,b) \cdot P(a)$"
E_1 = "$Q(a) \cdot R(a,b)$"

for a general law T_1, antecedent condition C_1 and explanandum E_1. He admits that it seems counterintuitive to say that (T_1,C_1) potentially explains E_1, since the occurrence of the component "$R(a,b)$" of C_1 in the sentence E_1 amounts to a partial explanation of the explanandum by itself.

34. Hempel, "Aspects of Scientific Explanation," *Aspects*, 331–496, quote on 488.

35. In *Aspects* there are more references to Carnap's writings than to those of any other thinker, Hempel's own included. In his 240-page introduction to contemporary philosophy of science, Frederick Suppe credits Carnap and Hempel to-

gether with being the "main authors" of the "Received View"; see Frederick Suppe, ed., *The Structure of Scientific Theories* (1977), 50.

36. Hempel, "Formulation and Formalization of Scientific Theories," in Suppe, ed., *The Structure of Scientific Theories*, 253.

37. So Suppe on the "Received View" in Suppe, ed., *The Structure of Scientific Theories*, 50–52.

38. In his "Empiricist Criteria of Cognitive Significance: Problems and Changes," now in Hempel, *Aspects*, 101–19.

39. "Formulation," in Suppe, ed., *The Structure of Scientific Theories*, 244–65.

40. "Logical Positivism and the Social Sciences," in Achinstein and Barker, eds., *The Legacy of Logical Positivism* (1969), 163–94.

41. See Hempel, *Aspects*, 255 and 320. Hempel might respond that by "cognitive significance" or "empirical meaning" he means only to speak to their role in empirical science rather than to general questions of meaningfulness.

42. So most explicitly in "The Theoretician's Dilemma," in Hempel, *Aspects*, 178f.

43. See Nagel, *The Structure of Science*, chapter 5, e.g., 79–83.

44. "On the 'Standard Conception' of Scientific Theories," in M. Radner and Stephen Winokur, eds., *Analyses of Theories and Methods of Physics and Psychology* (1970), 162.

45. H. Putnam, "What Theories Are Not," in E. Nagel et al., eds., *Logic, Methodology and Philosophy of Science: Proceedings of the 1960 International Congress* (1962), 240–51. As far as I can tell, this was the first use of the term "the Received View" in the contemporary philosophy of science literature.

46. In Radner and Winokur, eds., *Analyses*, 163.

47. Hempel admits that the scope of lawlike sentences has not yet been adequately determined in the postscript to "Studies" (Hempel, *Aspects*, 293), and that questions remain about the meaning and reference of theoretical terms (Suppe, ed., *The Structure of Scientific Theories*, 264). Hempel's view also appears to need (and to lack) an adequate theory of confirmation; see Salmon, "Carl Hempel on the Rationality of Science."

48. See Hempel, "Deductive-Nomological vs. Statistical Explanation," in Feigl and Maxwell, eds., *Scientific Explanation*, 98–169, and "Aspects," *Aspects*, 331–496.

49. Hempel, *Aspects*, 402.

50. Wesley Salmon, Richard Jeffrey, and James Greeno, *Statistical Explanation and Statistical Relevance* (1971).

51. Wesley Salmon, "A Third Dogma of Empiricism," in R. E. Butts and J. Hintikka, eds., *Basic Problems in Methodology and Linguistics* (1977), 154. Salmon defines a property C as statistically relevant to a property B iff
$P(A \cdot C, B) \neq P(A, B)$. That is, C must not leave the initial probability of A given B unchanged.

52. Wesley Salmon, *Scientific Explanation and the Causal Structure of the World* (1984), 22. Achinstein's critique is contained in his *Nature of Explanation* (1983).

53. Salmon, "A Third Dogma," 162.

54. Salmon, *Scientific Explanation*, 278f.

55. See J. C. Forge, "Physical Explanation: With Reference to the Theories of Scientific Explanation of Hempel and Salmon," in Robert McLaughlin, ed., *What? Where? When? Why?* (1982), 211–29, esp. 227.

56. Mary Hesse, comment on Achinstein's paper, in S. Körner, ed., *Explanation* (1975), 45.

57. Popper, *Realism and the Aim of Science*, xxii.

58. Hempel, *Aspects*, 288; cf. Popper: "Every theoretical system can in various ways be protected from an empirical falsification" (*Grundprobleme*, 353); "It is always possible to find some way of evading falsification, for example by introducing *ad hoc* an auxiliary hypothesis" (*Logic*, 42).

59. It is thus simply absurd to suggest that Hempel's theory should be rejected because of its normative demands on explanation. See Forge, "Physical Explanation," who would "prefer a more liberal account" of explanation (223).

60. Obviously, the ongoing difficulties with the Received View, many of which we have already considered, also contributed to the shift of approach. That I treat the following school of thought more as a paradigm shift than as a falsification of what went before should hardly be offensive to the thinkers involved. However, it must not disguise the fact that many philosophers were dissatisfied with the formalist options for reasons internal to the program itself. For an excellent presentation of further difficulties with the Received View, see the relevant sections of Suppe's introduction in Suppe, ed., *The Structure of Scientific Theories*, 62–118.

61. The work of Alexandre Koyré, such as his three-volume *Études Galiléennes* (1939), deserves special mention. Ironically, Ludwik Fleck's important monograph on the role of historical development within science, *Entstehung und Entwicklung einer wissenschaftlichen Tatsache* (1935), appeared the same year as Popper's *Logic*, which defended conclusive falsifiability. See Fleck, *Genesis and Development of a Scientific Fact* (1979).

62. Indeed, Kuhn would be the first to admit this. In his preface to *Structure* (vi) he cites the influence on his thought of Piaget, Gestalt psychologists, B. L. Whorf's work on language and worldviews, and Quine's "Two Dogmas of Empiricism."

63. Stephen Toulmin, *The Philosophy of Science: An Introduction* (1953).

64. Norwood Russell Hanson, *Patterns of Discovery: An Inquiry into the Conceptual Foundations of Science* (1958), 2.

65. It would be unfair, however, to suggest a slavish borrowing from Wittgenstein. Hanson rejects, for instance, the identification of seeing with *seeing-as*, holding instead to the possibility of a "general perceptual case" of seeing (19). For him "seeing" lies somewhere *between* having a visual experience and seeing-as. There

are significant similarities between this position and the approach to the social sciences of Peter Winch, who also has been crucially influenced by Wittgenstein.

66. Stephen Toulmin, *Foresight and Understanding* (1961), 14.

67. See *The Lichtenberg Reader: Selected Writings*, ed. and trans. Franz Mautner and Henry Hatfield (1959).

68. Heinrich Hertz, *Principles of Mechanics* (1899), 1.

69. Ludwig Wittgenstein, *Tractatus Logico-Philosophicus* (1922; 1961), e.g., 4.04, 6.361. On the influence of these two thinkers on Wittgenstein see, e.g., Georg Henrik von Wright, "G. C. Lichtenberg," *Encyclopedia of Philosophy*, 6:461–65.

70. In the *Tractatus* the *Satz* has this holistic nature; it alone presents a complete picture of a state of affairs. Later it would be a whole paradigm or way of life that functions as a gestalt.

71. Wittgenstein, *Philosophical Investigations* (1953), par. 50.

72. Amazingly, Kuhn directly cites the *Investigations* only once in *The Structure of Scientific Revolutions*, 45n2, and that somewhat critically. Wittgenstein's influence is clear in a number of passages, e.g., 44f, 94, and wherever paradigms occur (and they are ubiquitous).

73. A good example is Toulmin's proposed philosophy of science in "Forecasting and Understanding," *Foresight and Understanding*, chap. 2.

74. Toulmin is occasionally somewhat unfair to Hempel, the chief proponent of the position in question, whom he never mentions by name. For instance, when he speaks of explanation as involving general laws, he is borrowing from the Hempelian (formalist) program, if only as a type of limit case or portion of the complete story. Moreover, the attack on prediction is more effective when directed at its more extreme, Laplacian forms. When Toulmin rejects the counterfactual version of prediction, accepted by many explanation theorists—"*if* y were added to x, z would result"—he only comments, without elucidation, "the term [prediction] has surely been excessively diluted" (37). Surely this major contemporary position deserves a more telling rebuttal; see, e.g., Bas van Fraassen, *The Scientific Image* (1980), 112–18.

75. Thomas S. Kuhn, *The Copernican Revolution: Planetary Astronomy in the Development of Western Thought* (1957).

76. See Bibliography. In fact, the insight and comprehensiveness of Blumenberg's more recent *Die Genesis der kopernikanischen Welt* (1975) has in many respects rendered Kuhn's early monograph obsolete.

77. We did note above, however, that Toulmin's references to "making sense" were a tacit reference to the coherential way of thinking about science.

78. Kuhn writes that space limitations of the *Encyclopedia of Unified Science* (*EUS*), within which his piece was to be published, made it necessary, against his original intentions, "to present my views in an extremely condensed and schematic form" (*Structure*, preface, viii). It is also ironically fitting that *Structure* should

appear in the *EUS*, since it has done more in the popular mind to reintroduce the notion of a unified philosophy of science than any work since the 1930s—though hardly along the lines anticipated by Neurath and Carnap.

79. We will find, however, that it was precisely this detailed account that most came under attack.

80. Helpful summaries can be found in Gary Gutting, ed., *Paradigms and Revolutions: Appraisals and Applications of Thomas Kuhn's Philosophy of Science* (1980) and in Ian Barbour, "Paradigms in Science," *Myths, Models, and Paradigms* (1974), chap. 6.

81. By 1980 at least seven dissertations and a number of monographs had been written on Kuhn's philosophy of science; see the massive list of secondary literature in Gutting, ed., *Paradigms and Revolutions*.

82. Margaret Masterman, "The Nature of Paradigm," in Imre Lakatos and Alan Musgrave, eds., *Criticism and the Growth of Knowledge* (1970), 59–89. Though her list contains a number of merely verbal variants, her basic point—that Kuhn equivocates—stands nonetheless.

83. Toulmin, "Does the Distinction Between Normal and Revolutionary Science Hold Water?" in Lakatos and Musgrave, eds., *Criticism and the Growth of Knowledge*, 39–47.

84. Galileo is discussed at length in Paul Feyerabend, *Against Method* (1975), M. Finocchiaro's publications *History of Science as Explanation* (1973) and *Galileo and the Art of Reasoning* (1980), and R. Westman, ed., *The Copernican Achievement* (1976). On Einstein see, e.g., Elie Zahar, "Why did Einstein's Programme Supersede Lorentz's?" *British Journal for the Philosophy of Science* 24 (1973):95–123, 223–62.

85. "Second Thoughts on Paradigms," in Suppe, ed., *Structure of Scientific Theories*, 459–82, quote on 460n4.

86. Kuhn, "Second Thoughts," 462–4.

87. Kuhn, "Reflections on My Critics," in Lakatos and Musgrave, eds., *Criticism and the Growth of Knowledge*, 231–78, quote on 234.

88. Kuhn, "Postscript—1969," in *Structure*, 174–210, quote on 199.

89. Cf. Toulmin, "Conceptual Revolutions in Science," in R. S. Cohen and M. W. Wartofsky, eds., *In memory of N. R. Hanson* (1967), 331–47.

90. Popper, *Conjectures*, 199.

91. Musgrave, "Kuhn's Second Thoughts," in Gutting, ed., *Paradigms and Revolutions*, 46.

92. Larry Laudan, *Progress and Its Problems* (1977), 5.

93. Feyerabend, "Consolations for the Specialist," in Lakatos and Musgrave, eds., *Criticism and the Growth of Knowledge*, 197–230, quote on 228.

94. Feyerabend, *Against Method* (1975), 21, 187n, 189, 296.

95. See Gerald Holton, *The Scientific Imagination: Case Studies* (1978), and Gerald Holton and William A. Blanpied, *Science and Its Public: The Changing Relationship* (1976).

96. Feyerabend, *Against Method*, 68.

97. Bas van Fraassen, *The Scientific Image* (1980), 87.

98. Van Fraassen admits that a brief survey "must of necessity be biased." Be that as it may, a "voluminous" literature does not justify, for example, criticizing a 1965 journal article by Mackie while neglecting to discuss his 1974 monograph on the subject with the lame excuse, "I must of necessity do less than justice to most authors discussed" (223n20).

99. Hanson, *Patterns of Discovery*, 54, in van Fraassen, *Scientific Image*, 125.

100. Van Fraassen, "The Pragmatics of Explanation," *American Philosophical Quarterly* 14 (1977):143–50. His *Scientific Image*, chap. 5, is taken, in many cases verbatim, from this article.

101. Van Fraassen, *Scientific Image*, 125.

102. Bengt Hannson, "Explanations—Of What?" cited by van Fraassen, "The Pragmatics of Explanation," 147.

103. John Passmore, "Explanation in Everyday Life, in Science, and in History," *History and Theory* 2 (1962):109, emphasis mine.

104. Coherence has also become the central criterion (and definition) for both rationality and truth according to a number of philosophers of science; see, e.g., Hilary Putnam, *Reason, Truth and History* (1981), and Nelson Goodman, *Ways of Worldmaking* (1978). Putnam writes, "'Truth'. . . is some sort of (idealized) rational acceptability—some sort of ideal coherence of our beliefs with each other and with our experiences" (49f). Or, more briefly: "Truth is ultimate goodness of fit" (64).

105. Cf. van Fraassen, "The Pragmatics of Explanation," 150.

106. This is especially clear in *Objective Knowledge*, where the term "basic sentence" appears on only two pages, as opposed to *The Logic of Scientific Discovery*, where, in addition to being the theme of two whole sections, it appears on 30 pages, not counting 11 additional subcategories in the index having to do with "basic statements."

107. Popper, *Objective Knowledge*, 7.

108. E. Harris, "Epicyclic Popperism," *British Journal for the Philosophy of Science* 23 (1972):55–67.

109. Wellmer notes in his *Methodologie*, 10, that "[Popper] has never admitted that decisive points in any of his earliest works have been 'refuted.'" The irony, for a theorist of "conjectures and refutations," is manifest.

110. Contained in Suppe, ed., *The Structure of Scientific Theories*; for the synthesis see especially Suppe's "Afterword—1977" (615–728). It is interesting to note, in light of the recent critiques of realism by, e.g., Mary Hesse and Hilary Putnam, that Suppe sees philosophy of science moving in the direction of realism; cf. "Toward a Metaphysical and Epistemological Realism," 716ff.

111. E.g., Popper, *Conjectures and Refutations*, 200.

112. See Kuhn, "Logic of Discovery or Psychology of Research," in P. A. Schilpp, ed., *The Philosophy of Karl Popper* (1974), 798–819.

113. See Imre Lakatos, "Falsification and the Methodology of Scientific Research Programmes," in Lakatos and Musgrave, eds., *Criticism and the Growth of Knowledge*, 91–196. The essay now appears in Lakatos's *Philosophical Papers*, vol. 1: *The Methodology of Scientific Research Programmes* (1977), chap. 1. The following citations are to the latter volume. Though the position was originally presented in 1965, its present form dates from 1969–70.

114. Actually, the term "protective belt" is probably an unfortunate one, despite the accuracy of its reference to the unfalsifiable elements in Kuhnian paradigms. The models and specific hypotheses that make up the "protective belt" are the meat of the scientist's daily fare; indeed, working scientists would tend to regard talk of a theory's "positive heuristic" as icing on the cake, a philosopher's game of only secondary interest during the bulk of their research. The intent of the protective belt is not to protect, but to do science. When, however, scientific attention is turned to the adequacy of an entire program of research, questions will inevitably be raised about how integral the link is between specific theories and correlations and the broader program which originally lay behind them.

115. Recall that Popper had also chosen Marxism as his prime instance of an unfalsifiable theory. There are obvious problems with treating a comprehensive social theory according to the same requirements that we use for theories in natural science.

116. Belief in the irrationality of science should also silence the attacks by scientists and philosophers of science on the irrationality of religion. People who live in glass houses are ill-advised to make stone-throwing a vocation.

117. Lakatos, "Why Copernicus's Programme Superseded Ptolemy's" (written 1972–73), in his *Philosophical Papers*, 1:179. Through the end of this chapter, all references in the text preceded by a volume number are to the *Papers*.

118. Feyerabend, "Consolations for the Specialist"; "Imre Lakatos," *British Journal for the Philosophy of Science* 26 (1975), 1–18; and "On the Critique of Scientific Reason," in R. S. Cohen, P. K. Feyerabend and M. W. Wartofsky, eds., *Essays in Memory of Imre Lakatos* (1976), 109–43.

119. Feyerabend, "Consolations for the Specialist," 229.

120. Feyerabend, "Imre Lakatos," 12.

121. Lakatos, "Replies to Critics," in Roger C. Buck and Robert Cohen, eds., *PSA 1970, In Memory of Rudolf Carnap* (1971), 174–82.

122. As, for instance, M. Hallett has done for mathematics; see his "Towards a Theory of Mathematical Research Programs," *British Journal for the Philosophy of Science* 30 (1979):1–25, 135–59. Economists have paid special attention to Lakatos's work. See Spiro Latsis, ed., *Method and Appraisal in Economics* (1976), esp. the essays by Hicks, Hutchinson, Latsis and Leijonhufvud. See also Mark Blaug, "Kuhn versus Lakatos, or Paradigms versus Research Programmes in the History of Economics," *Economic History and the History of Economics* (1986), chap. 13; Rod Cross, "The Duhem-Quine Thesis, Lakatos and the Appraisal of Theories in Macroeconomics," *Economic Journal* 92 (1982):320–40; and Joseph V.

Remenyi, "Core Demi-core Interaction: Toward a General Theory of Disciplinary and Subdisciplinary Growth," *History of Political Economy* 11 (1979):30–63. Applications of Lakatos's work outside economics include Douglas W. Hands, "The Methodology of Scientific Research Programmes," *Philosophy of the Social Sciences* 9 (1979):293–303; and Martin Fransman, "Conceptualising Technical Change in the Third World in the 1980s: An Interpretive Survey," *Journal of Development Studies* 21 (1984–85):572–652.

123. See Michael Mulkay and G. Nigel Gilbert, "Putting Philosophy to Work: Karl Popper's Influence on Scientific Practice," *Philosophy of Social Science* 11 (1981): 389–407.

124. Lakatos, for instance, would rather speak of the "power" than the coherence of a theory; see "Replies to Critics," 177.

125. See Lakatos, "History of Science and Its Rational Reconstructions," *Papers*, 1:102–38.

126. In conversation Peter Lipton has posited two additional requirements that must be assumed in order to employ the self-referential test: (1) the methodologies in question cannot be merely descriptive of particular disciplines; (2) they cannot be (L_2) methodologies that are expressly held to be valid only of scientific practice as their L_1, for, since such methodologies would not be a part of science, they would be designed precisely *not* to apply to themselves. However, it seems to me that it is fully justified to assume both stipulations as requirements for methodological theories. (1) The methodological debate in philosophy of science has never been merely descriptive; even our relativists insist on attacking some scientific practices and condoning others. (2) A nondescriptive theory that passes its own test is prima facie stronger than one that fails to do so—for what then *is* its warrant? If our normative stipulations necessarily go beyond mere descriptions of scientific activity, then they must be grounded in, or at least consistent with, broader standards of rationality— which is exactly the state of affairs expressed by the self-referential test.

127. Lakatos puts it, somewhat tongue-in-cheek, "One way to indicate discrepancies between history and its rational reconstruction is to relate the internal history *in the text*, and indicate *in the footnotes* how actual history 'misbehaved' in the light of its rational reconstruction" (1:120). Habermas has recently made a rather similar use of the notion of rational reconstruction, though apparently without knowledge of Lakatos's work.

128. The point is that one does not have to proceed through the process of abstraction precisely as Lakatos proceeds. Lakatos moves from science through methodologies of science to the level of metamethodologies, or from science through its historiography to the theory of the historiography of science. But one can just as easily move from an academic discipline as practiced, through methodological reflection about it, to the question of what the various academic disciplines share in common.

129. Indeed, Quine's web metaphor does essentially the same thing outside of a pure philosophy of science context. See W. V. O. Quine, "Two Dogmas of Empiricism," *From a Logical Point of View* (1961), 42–44.

Chapter 3

1. I continue to use the term *formalist*, in conscious opposition to the frequently employed label *positivist*. The latter term has been so overused in the philosophy of social science that it has become little more than a derogatory appellation suggesting everything and nothing. Worse, the formalists have argued in many cases *against* classical (Machian) positivism; the quest for formal parallels at the level of scientific methodology rather than empiricist prejudices often motivates their work.

The formalist-structuralist programs associated with Saussure and Levi-Strauss also approach the interpretation of a cultural object via an analysis of its structure (see, e.g., T. K. Seung, *Structuralism and Hermeneutics* [1982]). Obviously, this project has important affinities with the formalist efforts discussed here and in chapter 2. But one should note the difference of levels: structuralists look for structures in cultural objects or artifacts, formalists for a basic structure in all scientific explanations. All structuralists are formalists (to the extent that their structuralism gives to their explanations a unitary form); the converse does not hold.

2. Popper, *Unended Quest* (1974), 121. This confession is interesting in light of the fact that much economic theory assumes an ideally rational agent who seeks to maximize his financial gain, minimize risks, etc.

3. The book is not overly successful in this regard; as Popper admits in the 1957 preface, "I did not actually refute historicism" (*The Poverty of Historicism* [1960], v).

4. Popper, "Die Logik der Sozialwissenschaften" (1961), in Theodor Adorno et al., *Der Positivismusstreit in der deutschen Soziologie* (1969), 107. See Adorno et al., *The Positivist Dispute in German Sociology* (1976), 90f. I cite from the English edition, though the translations have been modified.

5. Adorno et al., *Positivist Dispute*, 95. With statements such as "objectivity and the avoidance of value-ladenness . . . are themselves *values*" and "without passion it [science] can't be done" (97), Popper sounds very little like the popular Popper stereotype.

6. Popper's clearest statement of this doctrine is that "all theoretical or generalizing sciences make use of the same method, whether they are natural sciences or social sciences" (*The Poverty of Historicism*, 130.)

7. Adorno et al., *Positivist Dispute*, 96.

8. Robert John Ackermann, *The Philosophy of Karl Popper* (1976), 158, emphasis mine.

9. Carl Hempel, *Aspects of Scientific Explanation* (1965), 449. Ernest Nagel offers a similar account in *The Structure of Science* (1961), 564–68, though with perhaps more insight into the actual problems of historical inquiry.

10. This model has been defended by William Dray; see his "'Explaining What' in History," in P. Gardiner, ed., *Theories of History* (1959), 403, and his *Laws and Explanation in History* (1957).

11. Hempel, *Aspects*, 454.

12. The influence of Weber's "ideal-typical" approach may perhaps be detected in Hempel's formulation. However, Hempel neglects the distinction between ideal-typical behavior and the actual behavior of the individual that is central in Weber's account.

13. Ernst Nagel, *The Structure of Science*. Including his consideration of explanation in biology, Nagel's discussion of the topic runs for four chapters and over two hundred pages (398–606).

14. I shall use the term *social science* for so-called empirical disciplines such as psychology, sociology, economics, political science, and anthropology. "Human sciences" will serve as a translation of the standard German term *Geisteswissenschaften*, which is decisively broader in scope than the English term *science*. Under the heading human sciences are thus included all the social sciences plus most of the humanities—everything from historiography to literary theory. For reasons that will become clear later, I exclude philosophy, which includes as part of its task second-order reflection on other disciplines. Whether theology should be included in this list will concern us in chapter 6.

15. In choosing separate labels for the disputants in the current debate (formalists versus antipositivists rather than, say, positivists versus antipositivists), I intend to imply that separate issues and complexes of concerns motivate the combatants. And indeed, anyone familiar with the literature will have recognized that Popper's proposal of a formal methodology of science does not stand in simple opposition to, e.g., Habermas's insistence on multiple knowledge interests.

16. Wilhelm Dilthey, *Gesammelte Schriften* (1927), 7:70–75; cf. 5:242–58. A translation project of Dilthey's collected works is underway. Some of the important sections are presently available in *Dilthey: Selected Writings* (1976); see esp. 168–245.

17. Collingwood, *The Principles of Art* (1955). See H. A. Hodges, *The Philosophy of Wilhelm Dilthey* (1952), 129ff, and Hodges, *Wilhelm Dilthey: An Introduction* (1944), 21ff, for a fuller discussion of these types.

18. This openness to the metaphysical implications of his methodology, reflecting perhaps Dilthey's romantic and idealist heritage, apparently survived the anti-metaphysical propensity that he inherited from the positivism of the Comtean tradition; see Ilse Bulhof, *Wilhelm Dilthey: A Hermeneutic Approach to the Study of History and Culture* (1980), 50, and Hodges, *The Philosophy of Wilhelm Dilthey*, 191. Dilthey's notion of life is always limited to the "world of man"; therefore, according to Diwald, "although life is not always identical with 'spirit,' it invariably includes it" (Hellmut Diwald, *Wilhelm Dilthey. Erkenntnistheorie und Philosophie der Geschichte* [1963], 124).

19. Bulhof, *Wilhem Dilthey: A Hermeneutic Approach*, 55; cf. Diwald, *Wilhelm Dilthey*, 121ff.

20. Not all, of course; other antipositivists employ arguments of later vintage. The appeal to the value-ladenness of the "idiographic" sciences, for instance, can be traced back to Windelband's 1894 rectorial address, "Geschichte und Natur-

wissenschaft," which became widely known through Rickert's *Die Grenzen der naturwissenschaftlichen Begriffsbildung* (1902).

21. Many of the articles have been collected in Adorno et al., *The Positivist Dispute*. The difficulty of achieving genuine dialogue between the two approaches is underscored by Popper's comment that none of the responses to his essay dealt with his concerns at all, such that he wondered why his essay had even been included in the volume. See his response to the German volume, "Reason or Revolution?" *Archives européennes de sociologie* 11 (1970):252–62, e.g. 262: "In fact, they were no more interested in my views than I am in theirs." Popper's response has been included in the English translation; see Adorno et al., *Positivist Dispute*, 288–300, quote on 300.

22. Adorno et al., *Positivismusstreit*, 97; cf. Adorno et al., *Positivist Dispute*, 83. The following references are to the English text, though I have modified the translations.

23. Adorno et al., *Positivismusstreit*, 90; cf. Adorno et al., *Positivist Dispute*, 76, which omits part of the German text. This statement is again evidence that the disputants are not fighting over the same issue: formalists like Hempel and Nagel proposed a unitary approach to social science while, ironically, Adorno accuses them of methodological pluralism.

24. Jürgen Habermas, *Erkenntnis und Interesse* (1968). See the translation, *Knowledge and Human Interests* (1968), 67–68.

25. Compare Habermas and N. Luhmann, *Theorie der Gesellschaft oder Sozialtechnologie?* (1971), 171.

26. Luhmann, *Theorie der Gesellschaft*, 171.

27. Habermas, *Knowledge and Human Interests*, 72ff.

28. Hans-Georg Gadamer, *Wahrheit und Methode. Grundzüge einer philosophischen Hermeneutik* (1975), 266f. English translation, *Truth and Method* (1975), 251. Citations are to the English text; some of the translations have been modified.

29. Paul Ricoeur, *Hermeneutics and the Human Sciences* (1981), 197–221.

30. The reference is to the major American opponent of Gadamer's hermeneutics, E. D. Hirsch; see especially his *Validity in Interpretation* (1967) and *The Aims of Interpretation* (1976).

31. See also Paul Ricoeur, *Interpretation Theory: Discourse and the Surplus of Meaning* (1976), esp. chap. 4, "Explanation and Understanding."

32. See, for example, the oft-cited discussions in William Dray, *Laws and Explanations in History* (1957); Dray, ed., *Philosophy of History* (1964); and A. C. Danto, *Analytical Philosophy of History* (1965).

33. John Kekes, "Rationality and the Social Sciences," *Philosophy of the Social Sciences* 9 (1979):105–113, quote on 105.

34. Anthony Giddens, *Central Problems in Social Theory: Action, Structure and Contradiction in Social Analysis* (1979), 234–37.

35. Anthony Giddens, "Reason Without Revolution? Habermas's *Theory of Communicative Action,*" *Praxis International* 2, no. 3 (Oct. 1982):318–38.

36. Jürgen Habermas, *The Theory of Communicative Action (TCA)*, translated by Thomas McCarthy from *Theorie des kommunikativen Handelns*, 2 vols. (1981). The volumes appeared separately in English as *Reason and the Rationalization of Society* (1984) and *Lifeworld and System: A Critique of Functionalist Reason* (1987). When I use the abbreviation *TCA*, unless otherwise noted, vol. 1 is implied.

37. Habermas himself points out how much his analysis "owes to investigations in the philosophy of language stemming from Wittgenstein" (96). Although I will not attempt a Wittgenstein critique here, it is important to note the extent to which Habermas has made his work dependent on the arguments advanced in the *Philosophical Investigations*.

38. Habermas, "Was heisst Universalpragmatik?" in Karl-Otto Apel, ed., *Sprachpragmatik und Philosophie* (1976), 174–272. English translation: "What Is Universal Pragmatics?" in Habermas, *Communication and the Evolution of Society* (1979).

39. *TCA*, 94ff. Similarly, the restrictiveness of Habermas's communicative theory is clear when he admits to the assumption "that with *every* speech act oriented to reaching understanding *exactly three* validity claims are raised" (310, emph. his).

40. See John B. Thompson and David Held, eds., *Habermas: Critical Debates* (1982). Note that the following dilemma parallels our discussion of the difficulties with evaluating theories of rationality at the end of the preceding chapter.

41. Dieter Misgeld, "Communication and Societal Rationalization" (1983), 438.

42. Habermas, "Wahrheitstheorien," in Helmut Fahrenbach, ed., *Wirklichkeit und Reflexion. Walter Schultz zum 60. Geburtstag* (1973).

43. An additional operator *B* could be introduced if belief is taken to be a primitive. This idea presented here stems from discussions with Lorenz Puntel.

44. Admittedly, on 25ff Habermas does present an analysis utilizing the three components process, procedure and product, where "product" is close in sense to Austin's locutionary acts. But (1) "product" is still discussed in behavioral terms (i.e., the "aim" of argumentation), and (2) the product aspect is virtually ignored in the rest of *TCA*.

45. Jürgen Habermas, *The Philosophical Discourse of Modernity* (1987). Obviously, communication-based approaches were not first introduced by Habermas. The Marxist, pragmatist, and linguistic analytic traditions contain similar strands, although Habermas's remains probably the most fully developed theory of rationality in this genre. It would be interesting to attempt an analogous project within these other major schools in social theory.

46. Dummett, "What is a Theory of Meaning?" cited in Habermas, *TCA*, 317.

47. John Kekes, *A Justification of Rationality* (1976), 115.

48. Habermas, "Was heisst Universalpragmatik?"

49. Hesse, in Thompson and Held, *Habermas*, 98–115, quotes on 105.

50. This argument has been developed by Lorenz Puntel in his "On Communicative Rationality: A Critique of Habermas," forthcoming. The following quote is from this paper.

51. Frisby, "The Popper-Adorno Controversy: The Methodological Dispute in German Sociology," *Philosophy of the Social Sciences* 2 (1972):105–119, quote on 114.

52. Mary Hesse, *Revolutions and Reconstructions in the Philosophy of Science* (1980), 225, emphasis mine.

53. Anthony Giddens, *New Rules of Sociological Method* (1976), 158.

54. See Peter Winch, *The Idea of a Social Science* (1958), and "Understanding a Primitive Society," in Bryan Wilson, ed., *Rationality* (1970), 78–111.

55. Alasdair MacIntyre, "The Idea of a Social Science," in Alan Ryan, ed., *The Philosophy of Social Explanation* (1973), 15–32.

56. MacIntyre, "Is Understanding Religion Compatible with Believing?" in Wilson, ed., *Rationality*, 62–77, quote on 69.

57. Habermas had in fact defended a similar approach in earlier essays, such as "Was heisst Universalpragmatik?"

58. See the "Afterword" to Habermas, *Knowledge and Human Interests*, and Habermas, "Universalpragmatik," 203.

59. Georg Henrik von Wright, *Explanation and Understanding* (1971), chap. 1. Note that the "galilean" tradition may have very little to do with the position of Galileo himself.

60. See Talcott Parsons, *The Structure of Social Action* (1961) and *Social Systems and the Evolution of Action Theory* (1977). Parsons' insistence on the indispensability of intentionality stems in part from the key role that language played for the social theory of G. H. Mead and E. Cassirer; see especially G. H. Mead, *Mind, Self and Society* (1934).

61. Obviously, these are ideal units employed here only for purposes of comparison. They need not be reified; at best they represent tendencies in the two discipline areas.

62. In nominating Weberian social theory for a central mediating role I follow the spirit if not the letter of Susan J. Hekmann's *Weber, the Ideal Type, and Contemporary Social Theory* (1983). Hekmann's thesis is that Weber's work can be updated to ground "a successful postpositivist synthesis" (149–51) that avoids the extremes of Popper et al. on the one hand and Winch and early Habermas on the other. Habermas's debt to Weber, though not uncritical, is also great; see his long chapter "Max Weber's Theory of Rationalization," *TCA*, 143–271.

63. Max Weber, "'Objectivity' in Social Science and Social Policy," *The Methodology of the Social Sciences* (1949), 49–112, quote on 81.

64. On the other hand, the natural sciences are also not value-neutral. It has often been pointed out that ecological concerns about the natural world, and especially potential ethical obligations toward animals and other life forms, render value

questions not inapplicable in the natural sciences as well. Habermas's chart (*TCA*, 238) and the discussion surrounding it do not do justice to this fact.

65. See Max Weber, "The Meaning of 'Ethical Neutrality' in Sociology and Economics," *Methodology*, 1–47. The contextual factors in scientific research described in chap. 2 perhaps require some weakening of Weber's notions of objectivity and neutrality, though they do not vitiate his broader point.

66. Of course, means/ends rationality (*Zweckrationalität*) represents only a portion of Weber's notion of "practical rationality." Although somewhat skeptical on the question, Weber is also willing to speak of the rationality of world-perspectives and spheres of value (*Wertrationalität*). See Weber, "The Social Psychology of the World Religions," in Hans H. Garth and C. Wright Mills, eds., *From Max Weber: Essays in Sociology* (1946), 267–301, esp. 293.

67. Habermas, *Knowledge and Human Interests*, e.g., 62–68.

68. This has been a major thesis of Winch's work; see "Understanding a Primitive Society," in Wilson, ed., *Rationality*, e.g., 99, 106–10. As already argued, I do not share Winch's tendency to specify coherence in terms of Wittgensteinian forms of life.

69. As, e.g., Steven Lukes maintains in "Methodological Individualism Reconsidered," in Ryan, ed., *The Philosophy of Social Explanation*, 119–29. A number of the articles in Ryan's collection are devoted to this question of whether social theory should start at the level of the individual or social structures.

70. Alfred Schütz, *Der sinnhafte Aufbau der sozialen Welt. Eine Einleitung in die verstehende Soziologie* (1932); see the translation, *The Phenomenology of the Social World* (1967), 13. The following page references are to the English text, though I have retranslated in many cases.

71. Is this movement of levels not similar to the separation of immediate scientific practice from the methodological reflection on its methods and rationality? Although this separation of levels is not found in Dilthey, it runs through much of the rest of interpretive sociology.

72. See Karsten Harries' critique of Schütz, *The Journal of Value Inquiry* 4 (1970):65–75, esp. 66f.

73. Peter Berger's *An Invitation to Sociology* (1963) provides a now classic manifesto of the sociologist's claim on this point.

74. See the criticisms in W. Pannenberg, "Sociology as an Understanding Science of Action," *Theology and the Philosophy of Science* (1976), 80–103.

75. So Harries (68–74), who likewise criticizes the naïve use of the term *objective* in Weber's theoretical work.

76. For a defense of the same point by a thinker in the Popperian tradition see J. W. N. Watkins, "Ideal Types and Historical Explanations," in Ryan, ed., *The Philosophy of Social Explanation*, 82–104. Watkins argues correctly that "we can apprehend an unobservable social system only by reconstructing it theoretically from what is known of individual dispositions, beliefs, and relationships."

77. Richard Bernstein alleges that it is precisely this effort at establishing general criteria that has been dismissed in what he takes to be the now ruling consensus in the philosophy of science; see his *Beyond Objectivism and Relativism* (1985), e.g., "The Development of the Philosophy of Science," 71–79.

78. Karl Popper, *Conjectures*, 199; Larry Laudan, *Progress and Its Problems* (1977), 5.

Chapter 4

1. Robert Nozick, *Philosophical Explanations* (1981), 8.

2. Alfred North Whitehead, *Process and Reality* (1978), 22–26. Whitehead argues that "every explanation should be a specific instance of [his] categories of explanation" (20).

3. In fact, Emerich Coreth has taken "questioning" as the point of entrance into his system of metaphysics in his *Metaphysik* (1964).

4. "Since the origins of philosophy, philosophical assertions have been justified by reflecting on other [second-order] assertions in which experience has already been articulated or in some other manner reflected upon" (Pannenberg, *Wissenschaftstheorie*, 221; Eng. trans., 221). Compare also the suggestions on evaluating theories of rationality in chap. 2.

5. For a similar requirement see John Kekes, *A Justification of Rationality* (1976), 118–32, whose work bears Popper's mark and has influenced the presentation here.

6. Larry Lauden, *Progress and Its Problems* (1977), 109.

7. Nozick, *Philosophical Explanations*, 13.

8. Wittgenstein, *Philosophical Investigations*, par. 123.

9. See Moltke S. Gram, "Transcendental Arguments," *Nous* 5 (1971):15–26; Gram, "Categories and Transcendental Arguments," *Man and World* 6 (1973):252–69; the essays (esp. Puntel and Körner) in S. Körner et al., *Zur Zukunft der Transzendentalphilosophie* (1978); and Peter Bieri et al., *Transcendental Arguments and the Philosophy of Science* (1979).

10. See the paradigmatic arguments of Hans Reichenbach in *The Rise of Scientific Philosophy* (1951).

11. Nozick, *Philosophical Explanations*, 19.

12. There are of course possible strategies. A "tu quoque" argument is often used against the skeptic: in arguing he generally makes use of precisely those standards whose normativity he is attempting to dispute. The metalevel of "practice" can also legislate some issues which cannot be resolved discursively from within philosophy; see Nicholas Rescher, *Methodological Pragmatism* (1977) and *The Primacy of Practice* (1973).

13. So Hans Albert, *Treatise on Critical Reason* (1985), 16–21.

14. Cited in Ian Barbour, *Issues in Science and Religion* (1966), 145.

15. See F. H. Bradley, *Essays on Truth and Reality* (1914), and Brand

Blanshard, *The Nature of Thought* (1969). Blanshard once admitted in a personal communication that he considered the problem of giving a more precise definition of coherence to be insoluble.

16. Rescher, *The Primacy of Practice* (1973), 1. The fullest statement to date of his coherence theory is *The Coherence Theory of Truth* (1973).

17. See, respectively, Rescher, *Methodological Pragmatism*, 121, and Hilary Putnam, *Reason, Truth and History* (1981), 64.

18. See, e.g., Stephen Ullman, *Semantics: An Introduction to the Science of Meanings* (1962), in which he distinguishes between "analytic" and "operational" meaning. That I focus on these two in no way denies that other meanings of meaning can be described: C. K. Ogden and I. A. Richards were able to list sixteen different definitions of the concept of meaning in their *The Meaning of Meaning* (1945).

19. Frege, "Über Sinn und Bedeutung" (1892), in his *Funktion, Begriff, Bedeutung*, ed. G. Patzig (1962), 38–63; English translation: "Sense and Reference," *Philosophical Review* 57 (1948):209–30.

20. Frege, *Grundlagen der Arithmetik* (1884), x and 71.

21. Anders Nygren, *Meaning and Method* (1972), 228.

22. F. Schleiermacher, *Gesammelte Schriften* (1938), 7:69.

23. See Nicholas Rescher, "Truth as Ideal Coherence," *Review of Metaphysics* 38 (1985):795–806. Incidentally, think of the self-application test developed at the end of chap. 2. The coherence theory of truth does not fail this test: if successfully developed in the sense here outlined, it would itself be consistent, comprehensive, etc.—in short, coherent.

24. Pannenberg, "Faith and Reason," *Basic Questions in Theology* (1971), 2:62. More recently, Pannenberg has distanced himself from this view. After admitting that his earlier position was close to Weischedel's belief that "if anything at all is claimed to have valid meaning, this implicitly presupposes absolute meaning," he proceeds to criticize at length the latter's views; see *Theology and the Philosophy of Science*, 217n435.

Chapter 5

1. To assist in distinguishing the levels of religious belief and the study of religion, I will consistently use masculine pronouns to refer to the religious believer and feminine pronouns for the student of religion in this chapter. I will do the same, but somewhat less consistently (perhaps because of the ambiguous status of the discipline of theology) in chap. 6.

2. Henry Duméry, *Phenomenology and Religion* (1958), vii; Duméry's reference at this point is to the institution of Christianity.

3. Merold Westphal has made an effective case for not beginning with the question of rational warrant in his *God, Guilt, and Death: An Existential Phenomenology of Religion* (1984), e.g., chap. 1.

4. Alvin Plantinga, "Reason and Belief in God," in Alvin Plantinga and Nicholas

Wolterstorff, eds., *Faith and Rationality* (1983), 16–93. Compare Richard Swinburne's stress on the role of basic propositions in his treatment of belief in *Faith and
Reason* (1981), 20ff. I have offered some criticisms of this approach in chap. 1.

5. As Swinburne does in *Faith and Reason*, chaps. 1–3. He later writes, "All the
kinds of faith which I have discussed involve attitudes towards, behavior in the light
of, *propositions*. They are not necessarily always so phased, but my claim is that talk
about believing in God or trusting God can without loss of meaning be analyzed in
one of these ways" (124).

6. The classic statement of this theory is L. Festinger, *A Theory of Cognitive
Dissonance* (1957); cf. J. Brehm and A. Cohen, *Explorations in Cognitive Dissonance* (1962). L. Festinger et al., *When Prophecy Fails* (1956) studied the rationalization processes in a religious cult after a prophesied flood failed to occur; much of
their theoretical work has since been replicated by other studies in the psychology
of religion.

7. In John Hick, *Faith and Knowledge* (1966), 98.

8. Recall Hick's famous parable of the two men traveling together along a road,
one believing the road leads to the Celestial City, the other that it does not (177–
78). In terms of *present* reality or facts Hick's parable is very similar to Wisdom's,
adapted by Flew in the University Debate; see "Theology and Falsification," in
Flew and McIntyre, eds., *New Essays in Philosophical Theology* (1955), 96–105. As
Mitchell pointed out in the same discussion, however, there is usually much greater factual disagreement than these parables would suggest. Hick seeks to mediate
Wisdom and Mitchell by means of his notion of "eschatological verification," the
imagined end of the journey when either the believer or unbeliever will turn out to
have been mistaken; see *Faith and Knowledge*, 176ff.

9. So M. C. D'Arcy, *The Nature of Belief* (1945), 130ff, cited in Hick, *Faith and
Knowledge*, 72, 91.

10. Hick's actual statement is that "while the object of religious knowledge is
unique, its basic epistemological pattern is that of all our knowing" (97). But, as I
have argued, the parallels are more naturally developed within a theory of meaning
than in a theory of knowledge.

11. G. van der Leeuw, *Religion in Essence and Manifestation*, vol. 2 (1963), 672.

12. Van der Leeuw has been influenced by the Diltheyan position in some of his
methodological comments, as when he speaks of phenomenology as proceeding via
"a second experience of the event, by a thorough reconstruction" (678). But, although he holds that "all science is hermeneutics" (676), his stress on the objectivity
of meaning, its dependence on structures, prevents an excessive subjectivization in
his phenomenology of religion.

13. Van der Leeuw, 679–80. There are clear parallels here with Heidegger's
concept of "world" that could be fruitfully explored.

14. Hick, *Faith and Knowledge*, 113; see chaps. 7–9 for a fuller exposition of his
understanding of these themes.

15. "Entwürfe der in aller einzelnen Erfahrung mitgesetzten Sinntotalität"

(Anders Nygren, *Sinn und Methode* [1979], 312). *Entwurf* should be taken in its three-fold German sense of sketch, proposal and draft.

16. Kekes, *A Justification*, 217f.

17. This phenomenon has been nicely described by Merold Westphal in *God, Guilt, and Death*, chap. 2, using the example of the ambivalence between attraction to and fear of the sacred.

18. Kekes, *A Justification*, 230f.

19. Stephen Pepper, *World Hypotheses* (1970). The notion of basic metaphors has more recently been given a central role in the analyses of theological method by Ian Barbour, *Myths, Models and Paradigms* (1974), and Sallie McFague, *Metaphorical Theology* (1982).

20. Paul Tillich, "The Philosophy of Religion," *What Is Religion?* (1969), 56.

21. Wolfhart Pannenberg, with reference to Schleiermacher, in "Meaning, Religion and the Question of God," in Leroy S. Rouner, ed., *Knowing Religiously* (1985), 162. Compare Wittgenstein's statement in the *Tractatus*: "*How* things are in the world is a matter of complete indifference for what is higher. God does not reveal himself *in* the world" (6.432).

22. Such as Max Müller, "Klassische und moderne Metaphysik oder Sinn als Sein," in Richard Wisser, ed., *Sinn und Sein* (1960). Contemporary hermeneutics in the tradition of Heidegger and his followers is another example.

23. John E. Smith, "Ultimate Concern and the Really Ultimate," in Sidney Hook, ed., *Religious Experience and Truth* (1961), 66, emphasis mine.

24. Anders Nygren, *Meaning and Method: Prolegomena to a Scientific Philosophy of Religion and a Scientific Theology* (1972).

25. It is true that Nygren is trying to avoid what he thinks are the vacuous questions asked by metaphysicians when no specific object is any longer in view. But "either autonomous contexts of meaning or classical metaphysics" is a false dichotomy. Much present philosophy of religion, especially in the phenomenological and symbolic traditions, argues that religion constitutes a synthetic perspective while disavowing metaphysical disputes. See, among others, Henry Duméry, *The Problem of God in the Philosophy of Religion* (1969), and the discussion of religious belief in the following section.

26. Ludwig Wittgenstein, *Lectures and Conversations on Aesthetics, Psychology and Religious Belief* (1966).

27. For a summary of the position and literature, see Louis Dupré, "Religious Experience Past and Present," *The Other Dimension* (1979), chap. 1.

28. Wittgenstein, *Tractatus*, 6.4

29. Eg.. Zen Buddhism's *koans*. See also Daya Krishna, "Religious Experience, Language and Truth," in Sidney Hook, ed., *Religious Experience and Truth*, 231–40.

30. One might also say: an encounter with what is believed to be the divine. Recall that a phenomenology of religious belief does not yet make commitments to the truth of these beliefs. Also, a long discussion would be needed to justify my use

of the term *divine*, a term which I believe still to be acceptable but which may be somewhat prejudicial in favor of the Western tradition. There are also difficulties with the other terms; Louis Dupré has, for example, questioned the contemporary usefulness of the notion of the sacred, defending *transcendence* as a more useful category. See his *Transcendent Selfhood* (1976), chap. 2, esp. 22–26.

31. Max Weber, *The Theory of Social and Economic Organization* (1947), 358f. It is intriguing to compare the founding of a new religious tradition with the process of a scientific revolution as described by Kuhn in *The Structure of Scientific Revolutions*, a comparison encouraged by Kuhn's talk of "conversion" to a new paradigm. Likewise, Weber's notion of the "institutionalization of charisma" in the next paragraph is reminiscent of Kuhn's description of the transition to "normal science," although there is no evidence that Kuhn has been influenced by Weber's work.

32. George Thomas, *Philosophy and Religious Belief* (1970), 62.

33. Perhaps this is to disagree with a caricature of Tillich's view. In *Dynamics of Faith* (1957), chap. 3, he does distinguish the "true ultimate" from "idolatrous" types of ultimate concern. But if a caricature, it is an influential one.

34. In its insistence on the fusion (*Verschmelzung*) of the horizons of tradition and interpreter in understanding, Hans-Georg Gadamer, *Truth and Method* (1975), offers a helpful corrective to such positions.

35. F. Schleiermacher, *On Religion: Speeches to Its Cultured Despisers* (1958), 219.

36. The use of "personal disclosure value" as a criterion has been advocated by Arthur Holmes in *Christian Philosophy in the Twentieth Century* (1969), ix-x, and *Faith Seeks Understanding* (1971), 5ff.

37. As the subtitle, "A Search for the Meaning of Religious Attitudes," suggests, this is the guiding project of Louis Dupré's *Other Dimension*.

38. An excellent example of such a failure is contained in Chinua Achebe's novel, *Things Fall Apart* (1959). The book chronicles the growing explanatory inadequacy of a religious tradition, drawn from the context of an African tribal religion.

39. Cf. Thomas, *Philosophy and Religious Belief*, 63–64, from whose work I here extrapolate. The terms *narrow* and *broad* are of course used in a nonevaluative sense.

40. For a summary of this tendency in the various mystical traditions see Dupré, "The Mystical Vision," *The Other Dimension*, chap. 9.

41. See W. Pannenberg et al., *Revelation as History* (1969).

42. See, for example, Raeburne Heimbeck, *Theology and Meaning* (1969), who argues that such claims often have entailments which are testable. A similar argument has recently been presented by Edward Schoen in his *Religious Explanations* (1985); see esp. chap. 5, "The Plausibility of Religious Explanations."

43. Hick, *Faith and Knowledge*, 151, 154. Hick is wrong, as we shall see, in treating *all* religious faith, for example the dispute between theism and atheism, as falling on this level.

44. T. S. Eliot, "Little Gidding," *The Four Quartets*, in *The Complete Poems and Plays* (1971), 138f.

45. This is arguably the motivating force behind Whitehead, *Process and Reality* (1978); the genre has become notorious through books like Fritjov Capra, *The Tao of Physics* (1975) and Gary Zukav, *The Dancing Wu-Li Masters* (1980). More sophisticated efforts can be found in David Bohm, *Wholeness and the Implicate Order* (1980) and Paul Davies, *God and the New Physics* (1983).

46. Thomas Luckmann, *The Invisible Religion: The Problem of Religion in Modern Society* (1967), 43.

47. So Charles Hartshorne, *A Natural Theology for Our Time* (1967).

48. Wayne Proudfoot, *Religious Experience* (1985), 196.

49. See D. Z. Phillips, *Religion Without Explanation* (1976).

50. The importance of preserving a place for internal redescription became clear to me in discussion with Hans Frei.

51. Ludwig Wittgenstein, *Lectures on Religious Belief* (1966), 53–54.

52. See Denis Diderot, *Addition aux Pensées philosophiques*, par. 1, in Diderot, *Oeuvres Complète* (1875), 1:158.

53. See Hans Frei, *The Eclipse of Biblical Narrative* (1974).

54. Ninian Smart, *The Phenomenon of Religion* (1973), 25.

55. Smart, *Phenomenon of Religion*, 21. A similar argument could be made using Gadamer's notions of historical horizons and the constantly new synthesis that results from the combination of the perspective of a given individual or historical horizon with the original story or account.

56. See Van Til's article in E. R. Geehan, ed., *Jerusalem and Athens* (1971), 14ff, and his *My Credo and In Defense of the Faith*.

57. Thomas, *Philosophy and Religious Belief*, 83f.

58. Gary Gutting, *Religious Belief and Religious Skepticism* (1982).

59. Ian Barbour, *Issues in Science and Religion* (1966), 185: "Our thesis [is] that science and religion may be placed in a spectrum of personal involvement." It is somewhat remarkable that Thomas F. Torrance uses precisely this factor of personal involvement to *deny* any significant epistemological distinction between theology and science in *Theological Science* (1969).

60. Gutting, *Religious Belief*, 106.

61. See William James, "The Will to Believe," *The Will to Believe and Other Essays* (1956). The objection concerning obedience was raised by Steven Knapp in conversation.

62. The rationality of religious belief so understood represents, I believe, the interpretation of religion and doctrine advocated by George Lindbeck in *The Nature of Doctrine* (1984).

63. Pannenberg, *Theology and the Philosophy of Science* (1976), 300. Because of the poor quality of the translation, most of the citations to this work have been

retranslated from *Wissenschaftstheorie und Theologie* (1973); all page references, however, are to the English text.

64. Think of Bonhoeffer's exhortation that one who doubts should continue in active church involvement, gradually dealing with his doubts there as a practicing member of the community; see Bonhoeffer, *Letters and Papers from Prison* (1972).

65. See Paul Helm, *The Varieties of Belief* (1973), 101ff, esp. 111–15.

66. Wolfhart Pannenberg, "Wahrheit, Gewissheit und Glaube," *Grundfragen systematischer Theologie*, vol. 2 (1980), 226–64, quote on 264. It must be emphasized that Pannenberg is in this article more concerned with the certainty of faith and its links to the holistic judgments of conscience than with the theoretical openness of its truth claims.

Chapter 6

1. The distinction between the three publics of church, academy, and society is made by David Tracy in his *Analogical Imagination* (1981).

2. As in Immanuel Kant, *Religion Within the Limits of Reason Alone* (1934). See, recently, Emil Fackenheim, "Immanuel Kant," in Ninian Smart et al., *Nineteenth Century Religious Thought in the West* (1985), 1:17–40 and, in the same excellent reference work on the nineteenth century, the background section of Gerrish's article on Schleiermacher, e.g., 1:140f.

3. See Hans Frei, "David Friedrich Strauss," in Smart et al., *Nineteenth Century Religious Thought*, 1:215–260.

4. The distinction between heuristic and probative contexts is due originally to Hans Reichenbach, in his *Experience and Prediction* (1938). It has played a central role (with modifications) in Popper's work, and has been more carefully expressed by Hans Albert in his *Treatise on Critical Reason* (1985), e.g. 48ff.

5. Popper, "The Logic of the Social Sciences," in Theodor Adorno et al., *The Positivist Dispute in German Sociology* (1976), 92–95, translation altered.

6. See A. R. Peacocke, ed., *The Sciences and Theology in the Twentieth Century* (1981), esp. part 4.

7. Heinrich Scholz, "Wie ist eine evangelische Theologie als Wissenschaft möglich?" *Zwischen den Zeiten* 9 (1931):8–53, esp. 49–53. Scholz's discussion of his three criteria—the postulates of propositionality, coherence, and "controlability" (*Kontrollierbarkeit*)—parallels the use of coherence and criticizability and the analysis of the assertion advanced in these pages.

8. Though I cannot offer an exposition of his views here, the work of Bernard Lonergan provides an instructive example of this approach; cf. esp. *Insight* (1957) and *Method in Theology* (1972).

9. In so doing, I bypass the issue of theology's responsibility to Tracy's third public, society. This additional responsibility would not invalidate any of the methodological points made here, though it would raise further methodological difficulties of its own.

10. That is, "sociological" in the sense of George Lindbeck's "cultural-linguistic" theory of religion in *The Nature of Doctrine* (1984), or the "interpretive anthropology" of Clifford Geertz in *The Interpretation of Cultures* (1973).

11. Stephen Pepper, *World Hypotheses* (1970), despite its antagonism toward religious world-pictures, remains one of the classic treatments of the nature and evaluation of such all-encompassing views about the world. Note that his use of the term *world hypotheses* avoids the connotations of finality and givenness associated with the term *Weltanschauung* since Herder. I have avoided employing the term *worldview* for the same reason.

12. Ninian Smart, *Worldviews: Crosscultural Explorations of Human Beliefs* (1983). Smart suggests that the categories of the Experiential, Mythic, Doctrinal, Ethical, Ritual and Social allow comparisons of various worldviews (chaps. 3–8).

13. I would, however, expect such a development in those cases where the beliefs of the religion are taught to or by believers in a university setting, or where debate between competing schools of thought has given rise to the notion of orthodoxy, heresy or apologetics (e.g., Patristic Christianity, Hinayana vs. Mahayana Buddhism).

14. I use the term *level one* to refer to the immediate beliefs, attitudes and practices of Christian communities and Christian tradition, and *level two* for any form of discourse that attempts to make systematic or abstracting statements about this belief and practice. Using these terms rather than, say, the terms *first order* and *second order* is meant to leave open the question of which form of discourse should have logical or theological priority.

15. One thinks of the deliberations as to whether a given position counted as heresy in earlier centuries, and arguably more recently in the cases of Küng and Schillebeeckx. It would be interesting to trace the sociological parallels between earlier heresy decisions and recent debates over liberation theologies, feminist revisions of Christian stories, or even the Presbyterian Inclusive Language Lectionary, in order to flesh out the variety of factors that are involved in the evaluation of material adequacy.

16. Brian Gerrish, *Tradition and the Modern World* (1978), 11: "the outsiders of a confessional tradition may sometimes, from their own standpoint, be viewed not as apostates but as true bearers or renovators of the heritage insofar as *its transmission can be interpreted as a process of revision and change*" (emph. mine).

17. B. Keckermann, *Systema logicae* (Hannover, 1600) and *Systema ss. theologiae* (Hannover, 1602); cited in W. Pannenberg, *Theology and the Philosophy of Science* (1976), 355n656. Again, I have retranslated passages from this book; page references are to the English text.

18. Pannenberg, *Theology and the Philosophy of Science*, 404ff.

19. G. J. Planck, *Einleitung in die theologischen Wissenschaften* (Leipzig, 1794), 113, cited in Pannenberg, *Theology and the Philosophy of Science*, 405f.

20. See P. Clayton, "Anticipation and Theological Method," in Carl E. Braaten and Philip Clayton, eds., *The Theology of Wolfhart Pannenberg: Twelve American Critiques* (1988), 142–50.

21. Once again, recall the role of understanding (or description) in chapters 3 and 4: it remains a precondition, a necessary but not sufficient condition, for theoretical explanations.

22. It is this point that T. F. Torrance has missed in his otherwise erudite work, *Theological Science* (1969), and which highlights more than any other the source of my difficulty with his work on scientific method.

23. Although his *Theological Science* appears to leave little room for this task, T. F. Torrance, *Ground and Grammar of Theology* (1980) contains some interesting suggestions. Torrance still wants to hold that natural science and theological science each have their own rationality and verification, since the one "inquires into the processes and patterns of nature," while the other "inquires of God the Creator of nature" (6). Yet—and this is the element I did not find clearly stated in his earlier *Theological Science*—as inquiry or "science" they share some commonalities. Torrance writes, "But since each of them is the kind of thing it is as a human inquiry because of the profound correlation between human knowing and the space-time structures of the creation, each is in its depth akin to the other" (6f). The question that concerns us here is exactly *what* they both share as "inquiries" or "sciences."

24. Paul Tillich, *Systematic Theology*; vol. 1: *Reason and Revelation, Being and God* (1951), 8–11, 17, 23.

25. Ernst Troeltsch, *Glaubenslehre* (1925). See also Brian Gerrish, "The Possibility of a Historical Theology: An Appraisal of Troeltsch's Dogmatics," *The Old Protestantism and the New* (1982), chap. 13.

26. Hans Frei, in his Shaffer Lecture, Yale University, 1983.

27. F. Schleiermacher, *Kurze Darstellung des theologischen Studiums zum Behuf einleitender Vorlesungen* (1961), par. 1.

28. F. Schleiermacher, *The Christian Faith* (1963), vol. 1, par. 2.

29. Brian Gerrish, "Friedrich Schleiermacher," in Smart et al., *Nineteenth Century Religious Thought*, 1:142.

30. No thinker has castigated Schleiermacher more strongly than Carl F. H. Henry. Bob E. Patterson writes correctly, "Schleiermacher represents to Carl Henry and contemporary evangelicals all that is wrong in theology. Schleiermacher did not believe the Enlightenment was fatal for Christianity." See Patterson, *Carl F. H. Henry* (1983), 28.

31. Ian Barbour, *Myths, Models and Paradigms: A Comparative Study of Science and Religion* (1974), 176.

32. See Pannenberg, *Theology and the Philosophy of Science*, 297ff. Interestingly, despite his debt to Barth not shared by Pannenberg, Thomas F. Torrance is also willing to define theology as "the science of God"; see his *The Ground and Grammar of Theology*, 112.

33. Pannenberg, *Theology and the Philosophy of Science*, 313; cf. *Wissenschaftstheorie*, 316. The English translation omits an entire line of the German and is incoherent as it stands.

34. For an exposition of his position, see Philip Clayton, "The God of History and

the Presence of the Future," *Journal of Religion* 65 (1985):98–108, and my "Being and One Theologian," *The Thomist* (October 1988):645–71.

35. W. V. O. Quine, "Ontological Relativity," in *Ontological Relativity and Other Essays* (1969), 47.

36. Bruce Hauptli, "Inscrutability and Correspondence," *The Southern Journal of Philosophy* 17 (1979):199–212; Hauptli, "Quinean Relativism: Beyond Metaphysical Realism and Idealism," *The Southern Journal of Philosophy* 18 (1980): 393–410, quote on 409n18.

37. Hilary Putnam, *Reason, Truth and History* (1981), esp. chap. 3, e.g., 49. For the many references to Quine see the index, and esp. 33ff. Putnam's 1985 Carus Lectures, published as *The Many Faces of Realism* (1987), continue his critique of classical realism and its doctrine of truth.

38. Mary Hesse, *Revolutions and Reconstructions in the Philosophy of Science* (1980), esp. chap. 2.

39. Typescript, Library of the Institute for the History and Philosophy of Science, Cambridge University.

40. For a presentation and critique of noncognitivist views of religious language such as expressivism and emotivism, see W. T. Blackstone, *The Problem of Religious Language* (1963).

41. A classic example of this approach is Filmer S. C. Northrop's treatment of the humanities, *The Logic of the Sciences and Humanities* (1947). Another entire line of inquiry not pursued here would be to consider the particular features of the historical sciences in order to use them as a model for theological method, as Pannenberg has done in *Theology and the Philosophy of Sciece*. Many of the differences between the position I have taken and Pannenberg's work can be traced to his privileging of the historical sciences.

42. I purposely avoid saying that they try to interpret a subject matter, since interpretation (as presented in chap. 3) implies a given meaning at which the interpretive endeavor is aimed. For effective arguments for this view of interpretation see Steven Knapp and Walter Benn Michaels, "Against Theory," in W. J. T. Mitchell, ed., *Against Theory* (1985), 11–30.

43. George Lindbeck, *The Nature of Doctrine*. My usage of the term here is not necessarily in conformity with Lindbeck's.

44. This is also the thesis of Nelson Goodman's influential *Ways of Worldmaking* (1978).

45. On this theme see Wolfgang Kayser, *Die Wahrheit der Dichter* (1959); Hans Sedlmayr, *Kunst und Wahrheit* (1978); and Kurt Hübner, *Wahrheit des Mythos* (1985). For samples of Heidegger's approach see "On the Essence of Truth" and "The Origin of the Work of Art," both of which have been translated in *Heidegger: Basic Writings* (1977).

46. There appears to be a subsumption of theology under the newly founded science of aesthetics in the work (esp. the 1735 dissertation) of Gottlieb Baumgarten. There the parallels between, for example, the theme of a poem and

God as the theme of the world suggest a reduction of theological truths to aesthetic truths, though I do not know that Baumgarten actually drew this conclusion. See Karsten Harries, "Copernican Reflections and the Tasks of Metaphysics," *International Philosophical Quarterly* 23 (1983): 235–50. The claim that theology has been reduced to existentialist philosophy is a common criticism of Bultmann's theology. See James Robinson and John Cobb, eds., *The Later Heidegger and Theology* (1962).

47. Hans Frei, *The Eclipse of Biblical Narrative* (1974). See now his "The Literal Reading of Biblical Narrative in the Christian Tradition: Does It Stretch or Will It Break?" (1986).

48. See Gadamer, *Truth and Method*, and his "Rhetorik, Hermeneutik und Ideologiekritik. Metakritische Erörterungen zu 'Wahrheit und Methode,'" in Karl-Otto Apel, ed., *Hermeneutik und Ideologiekritik* (1971), 57ff, esp. 76–77.

49. Emilio Betti, *Die Hermeneutik als allgemeine Methodik der Geisteswissenschaften* (1962), 47–48.

50. Pannenberg, *Theology and the Philosophy of Science*, 167.

51. A clear presentation of this approach to existential assertions in theology can be found in Raeburne Heimbeck, *Theology and Meaning* (1969).

52. In defense of this reading of Augustine, see Ronald H. Nash, *The Light of the Mind: St. Augustine's Theory of Knowledge* (1969), esp. 24ff. Aquinas uses the quoted phrase in the *Summa Theologica* I.1, q2 a3 respondeo, first argument.

53. The essay is reprinted in William James, *The Will to Believe and Other Essays* (1956), 1–31, quote on 3.

54. Pannenberg, *Theology and the Philosophy of Science*, 416–20.

55. Unless, of course, one could show that basic Christian terms (*prolepsis* or anticipation) are at the same time particular and universal, adequate to the specific historical events and acceptable in a systematic philosophical framework. Pannenberg addressed the former pole in *Jesus—God and Man* (1977) and the latter in *Metaphysik und Gottesgedanke* (1988).

56. The following concluding comments are admittedly extremely speculative, and would require a much fuller treatment than they receive here. Nonetheless, their inclusion may be justified as indicating a line of approach worthy of further consideration.

57. See, e.g., Pannenberg, *Theology and the Philosophy of Science*, 41ff.

58. And there is at least some reason to think that it may; see my "Anticipation and Theological Method," in Braaten and Clayton, eds., *The Theology of Wolfhart Pannenberg*, e.g., 136–42.

59. See the various publications of Nicholas Rescher, from *The Coherence Theory of Truth* (1973) to "Truth as Ideal Coherence," *Review of Metaphysics* (1985). A useful summary of many of the positions is provided in Lorenz Bruno Puntel, *Wahrheitstheorien in der neueren Philosophie* (1978); see also his forthcoming *Grundlagen einer Theorie der Wahrheit*. An important defense of the (related) coherence theory of justification can be found in Laurence Bonjour, *The Structure of Empirical Knowledge* (1985).

Bibliography

Abraham, William J., and Steven W. Holtzer, eds. *The Rationality of Religious Belief: Essays in Honor of Basil Mitchell*. Oxford: Clarendon Press, 1987.

Achebe, Chinua. *Things Fall Apart*. New York: McDowell, Obolensky, 1959.

Achinstein, Peter. *The Nature of Explanation*. New York: Oxford University Press, 1983.

Achinstein, Peter, and Stephen F. Barker, eds. *The Legacy of Logical Positivism: Studies in the Philosophy of Science*. Baltimore: The Johns Hopkins University Press, 1969.

Ackermann, Robert John. *The Philosophy of Karl Popper*. Amherst: University of Massachusetts Press, 1976.

Adorno, Theodor W., et al. *Der Positivismusstreit in der deutschen Soziologie*. Berlin: Hermann Luchterhand, 1969. [*The Positivist Dispute in German Sociology*. Trans. Glyn Adey and David Frisby. London: Heinemann, 1976.]

Albert, Hans. *Das Elend der Theologie. Kritische Auseinandersetzung mit Hans Küng*. Hamburg: Hoffmann und Campe, 1979.

———. *Plädoyer für kritische Rationalismus*. Munich: R. Piper, 1971.

———. *Theologische Holzwege. Gerhard Ebeling und der rechte Gebrauch der Vernunft*. Tübingen: J. C. B. Mohr, Paul Siebeck, 1973.

———. *Traktat über kritische Vernunft*. Tübingen: J. C. B. Mohr, Paul Siebeck, 1978. [*Treatise on Critical Reason*. Trans. Mary V. Rorty. Princeton: Princeton University Press, 1985.]

———. *Transzendentale Träumereien. Karl-Otto Apels Sprachspiele und sein hermeneutischer Gott*. Hamburg: Hoffmann und Campe, 1975.

Anselm. *Basic Writings*. Trans. S. N. Deane. LaSalle: Open Court, 1962.

Apel, Karl-Otto. *Transformation der Philosophie*. 2 vols. Frankfurt: Suhrkamp, 1973. [*Towards a Transformation of Philosophy*. Trans. Glyn Adey and David Frisby. 2 vols. London: Routledge and Kegan Paul, 1980.]

Apel, Karl-Otto, ed. *Sprachpragmatik und Philosophie*. Frankfurt: Suhrkamp, 1976.

Apel, Karl-Otto, et al. *Hermeneutik und Ideologiekritik*. Frankfurt: Suhrkamp, 1971.

Augustine. *Confessions*. Trans. Edward B. Pusey. New York: Collier, 1972.

Ayer, Alfred Jules. *Language, Truth and Logic*. New York: Dover, 1952.

Barbour, Ian G. *Issues in Science and Religion*. London: SCM Press, 1966.

————. *Myths, Models and Paradigms: A Comparative Study in Science and Religion*. New York: Harper and Row, 1974.

Barnes, Barry. *Interests and the Growth of Knowledge*. London, 1977.

————. *Scientific Knowledge and Sociological Theory*. London: Routledge and Kegan Paul, 1974.

Barth, Karl. *Die Christliche Dogmatik im Entwurf*. Munich: C. Kaiser, 1927.

————. *Church Dogmatics*. Trans. and ed. G. W. Bromiley. Edinburgh: T. and T. Clark, 1961.

————. *The Word of God and the Word of Man*. Trans. Douglas Horton. New York: Harper Torchbooks, 1957.

Bartley, W. W. *The Retreat to Commitment*. New York: Alfred A. Knopf, 1962.

Bechermann, A. "Die realistischen Voraussetzungen der Konsensustheorie von J. Habermas." *Zeitschrift für allgemeine Wissenschaftstheorie* 3 (1972):63–80.

Benn, S. I., and G. W. Mortimore. "Rationality and the Social Sciences—A Reply to John Kekes." *Philosophy of the Social Sciences* 9 (1979):175–80.

Benn, S. I., and G. W. Mortimore, eds. *Rationality and the Social Sciences*. London: Routledge and Kegan Paul, 1976.

Benoist, Jean-Marie. *The Structural Revolution*. London: Weidenfeld and Nicolson, 1978.

Berger, Peter. *An Invitation to Sociology*. Garden City, N.Y.: Doubleday, Anchor, 1963.

Bernstein, Richard J. *Beyond Objectivism and Relativism: Science, Hermeneutics, and Praxis*. Philadelphia: University of Pennsylvania Press, 1985.

————. *The Restructuring of Social and Political Theory*. New York: Harcourt Brace Jovanovich, 1976.

Betti, Emilio. *Die Hermeneutik als allgemeine Methodik der Geisteswissenschaften*. Tübingen: J. C. B. Mohr, Paul Siebeck, 1962. ["Hermeneutics as the General Methodology of the *Geisteswissenschaften*." In *Contemporary Hermeneutics: Hermeneutics as Method, Philosophy and Critique*, by Josef Bleicher. London: Routledge and Kegan Paul, 1980.]

Bieri, Peter, et al. *Transcendental Arguments and the Philosophy of Science*. Dordrecht: D. Reidel, 1979.

Blackstone, W. T. *The Problem of Religious Knowledge: The Impact of Philosophical Analysis on the Question of Religious Knowledge*. Englewood Cliffs, N.J.: Prentice-Hall, 1963.

Blanshard, Brand. *The Nature of Thought*, 2d ed. 2 vols. London: George Allen and Unwin, 1969.

Blaug, Mark. "Kuhn vs. Lakatos, or Paradigms versus Research Programmes in the History of Economics." Chap. 13. *Economic History and the History of Economics*. New York: New York University Press (1986).

Bloor, David. *Knowledge and Social Imagery*. London: Routledge and Kegan Paul, 1976.

Blumenberg, Hans. *Die Genesis der kopernikanischen Welt*. Frankfurt: Suhrkamp, 1975.

————. *Die Legitimität der Neuzeit*. Frankfurt: Suhrkamp, 1966. [*The Legitimacy of the Modern Age*. Trans. Robert M. Wallace. Cambridge: MIT Press, 1983.]

Bohm, David. *Wholeness and the Implicate Order*. London: Routledge and Kegan Paul, 1980.

Bonhoeffer, Dietrich. *Letters and Papers from Prison*. Ed. Eberhard Bethge. New York: Macmillan, 1972.

Bonjour, Laurence. *The Structure of Empirical Knowledge*. Cambridge: Harvard University Press, 1985.

Braaten, Carl E., and Philip Clayton, eds. *The Theology of Wolfhart Pannenberg: Twelve American Critiques*. Minneapolis: Augsburg, 1988.

Bradley, F. H. *Essays on Truth and Reality*. Oxford: Clarendon Press, 1914.

Braithwaite, Richard Bevan. *Scientific Explanation: A Study of the Function of Theory, Probability and Law in Science*. Cambridge: Cambridge University Press, 1953.

Brehm, Jack, and Arthur R. Cohen. *Explorations in Cognitive Dissonance*. New York: Wiley, 1962.

Brody, Baruch A., ed., *Readings in the Philosophy of Religion: An Analytic Approach*. Englewood Cliffs, N.J.: Prentice-Hall, 1974.

Buck, Roger C., and Robert Cohen, eds. *PSA 1970: In Memory of Rudolf Carnap*. Vol. 8, *Boston Studies*. Dordrecht: D. Reidel, 1971.

Bulhof, Ilse N. *Wilhelm Dilthey: A Hermeneutic Approach to the Study of History and Culture*. The Hague: Martinus Nijhoff, 1980.

Bunge, Mario. *The Critical Approach to Science and Philosophy*. New York: Free Press, 1964.

Burtt, Edwin A. *The Metaphysical Foundations of Modern Science*. Rev. ed. New York: Humanities Press, 1951.

Butts, Robert, and Jaakko Hintikka, eds. *Basic Problems in Methodology and Linguistics*. Dordrecht: D. Reidel, 1977.

Calvin, Jean. *Institutes of the Christian Religion*. Ed. John T. McNeill. Trans. F. L. Battles. 2 vols. Philadelphia: Westminster, 1960.

Capra, Fritjov. *The Tao of Physics*. New York: Random House, 1975.

Carnap, Rudolf. *Der logische Aufbau der Welt*. Berlin: Welkreis Verlag, 1928. [*The Logical Structure of the World: Pseudoproblems in Philosophy*. Trans. Rolf A. George. Berkeley: University of California Press, 1967.]

Carnell, Edward John. *An Introduction to Christian Apologetics.* Grand Rapids: Eerdmans, 1948.

Casper, Bernard, et al. *Theologie als Wissenschaft. Methodische Zugänge.* Freiburg: Herder, 1970.

Chomsky, Noam. *Reflections on Language.* New York: Pantheon, 1975.

Clayton, Philip. "The God of History and the Presence of the Future." *The Journal of Religion* 65 (1985):98–108.

———. "Being and One Theologian." *The Thomist* (October 1988):645–71.

Cobb, John B., Jr., and David Ray Griffin. *Process Theology.* Philadelphia: Westminster, 1976.

Cohen, R. S., and M. W. Wartofsky, eds. *In Memory of R. N. Hanson.* Vol. 3, *Boston Studies.* Dordrecht: D. Reidel, 1967.

Cohen, R. S., P. K. Feyerabend, and M. W. Wartofsky, eds. *Essays in Memory of Imre Lakatos.* Vol. 39, *Boston Studies.* Dordrecht: D. Reidel, 1976.

Collingwood, Robin George. *The Principles of Art.* Oxford: Clarendon Press, 1955.

Connolly, William E. Review of *The Critical Theory of Jürgen Habermas,* by Thomas McCarthy. *History and Theory* 18 (1979):397–417.

Coreth, Emerich. *Metaphysik. Eine methodisch-systematische Grundlegung.* 2d ed. Innsbruck: Tyrolia, 1964.

Cross, Rod. "The Duhem-Quine Thesis, Lakatos and the Appraisal of Theories in Macroeconomics." *Economic Journal* 92 (1982): 320–40.

Dallmayr, W. "Critical Theory Criticized: Habermas' *Knowledge and Human Interests* and Its Aftermath." *Philosophy of the Social Sciences* 2 (1972):211–29.

Dallmayr, W., ed. *Materialien zu Habermas' "Erkenntnis und Interesse."* Frankfurt: Suhrkamp, 1974.

Danto, A. C. *Analytical Philosophy of History.* Cambridge: Cambridge University Press, 1965.

Davies, Paul. *God and the New Physics.* New York: Simon and Schuster, 1983.

Delaney, C. F., ed. *Rationality and Religious Belief.* Notre Dame: University of Notre Dame Press, 1979.

Dilthey, Wilhelm. *Gesammelte Schriften.* Ed. Bernhard Groethuysen. Leibzig: B. G. Tuebner, 1927. [Selections translated in *Dilthey: Selected Writings.* Ed. H. P. Rickman. Cambridge: Cambridge University Press, 1976.]

Diwald, Hellmut. *Wilhelm Dilthey: Erkenntnistheorie und die Philosophie der Geschichte.* Göttingen: Musterschmidt, 1963.

Dray, William. *Laws and Explanations in History.* London: Oxford University Press, 1957.

———. *Philosophy of History.* Englewood Cliffs, N.J.: Prentice Hall, 1964.

Duméry, Henry. *Phenomenology and Religion: Structures of the Christian Institution.* Berkeley: University of California Press, 1975.

———. *The Problem of God in Philosophy of Religion.* Trans. Charles Courtney. Evanston: Northwestern University Press, 1969.

Dupré, Louis. *The Other Dimension: A Search for the Meaning of Religious Attitudes.* New York: Seabury, Crossroad, 1972.

————. *Transcendent Selfhood: The Loss and Rediscovery of the Inner Life.* New York: Seabury, Crossroad, 1976.

Ebeling, Gerhard. *Theologie und Verkündigung. Ein Gespräch mit Rudolf Bultmann.* Tübingen: J. C. B. Mohr, 1962.

Eliot, T. S. *The Complete Poems and Plays.* New York: Harcourt, Brace and World, 1971.

The Encyclopedia of Philosophy. Ed. Paul Edwards. 8 vols. New York: Macmillan, 1967.

Ewing, A. C. *Idealism: A Critical Survey.* 2d ed. London: Methuen, 1974.

Fahrenbach, Helmut, ed. *Wirklichkeit und Reflexion. Walter Schultz zum 60. Geburtstag.* Pfullingen: Neske, 1973.

Feigl, Herbert, and Grover Maxwell, eds. *Scientific Explanation, Space, and Time.* Vol. 3, *Minnesota Studies in the Philosophy of Science.* Minneapolis: University of Minnesota Press, 1962.

Festinger, Leon. *A Theory of Cognitive Dissonance.* Evanston: Row, Peterson, 1957.

Festinger, Leon, et al. *When Prophecy Fails.* Minneapolis: University of Minnesota Press, 1956.

Feyerabend, Paul. *Against Method: Outline of an Anarchistic Theory of Knowledge.* London: NLB, 1975.

————. "Imre Lakatos." *British Journal for the Philosophy of Science* 26 (1975):1–18.

Finocchiaro, Maurice. *Galileo and the Art of Reasoning.* Vol. 61, *Boston Studies.* Dordrecht: D. Reidel, 1980.

————. *History of Science as Explanation.* Detroit: Wayne State University Press, 1973.

Fleck, Ludwik. *Entstehung und Entwicklung einer wissenschaftlichen Tatsache.* 1935. [*Genesis and Development of a Scientific Fact.* Eds. T. J. Trenn and P. K. Merton. Trans. F. Bradley and T. J. Trenn. Chicago: University of Chicago Press, 1979.]

Flew, Anthony, and Alasdair MacIntyre, eds. *New Essays in Philosophical Theology.* London: SCM Press, 1955.

Fransman, Martin. "Conceptualising Technical Change in the Third World in the 1980's: An Interpretive Survey." *Journal of Development Studies* 21 (1984–85):572–652.

Frege, Gottlob. "Über Sinn und Bedeutung." *Zeitschrift für Philosophie und philosophische Kritik* N. F. 100 (1892):25–50. (Reprinted in *Funktion, Begriff, Bedeutung. Fünf logische Studien.* Ed. Günther Patzig. 2d ed. Göttingen: Vandenhoeck und Ruprecht, 1962). ["Sense and Reference." *Philosophical Review* 57 (1948):209–30.]

————. *Die Grundlagen der Arithmetik*. Breslau, 1884.

Frei, Hans. *The Eclipse of Biblical Narrative*. New Haven: Yale University Press, 1974.

————. "The 'Literal Reading' of Biblical Narrative in the Christian Tradition: Does It Stretch or Will It Break?" In *The Bible and the Narrative Tradition*. Ed. Frank McConnell. New York: Oxford University Press, 1986.

Freundlieb, D. "Zur Problematik einer Diskurstheorie der Wahrheit." *Zeitschrift für allgemeine Wissenschaftstheorie* 6 (1975):82–107.

Frisby, David. "The Popper-Adorno Controversy: The Methodological Dispute in German Sociology." *Philosophy of the Social Sciences* 2 (1972):105–19.

Gadamer, Hans-Georg. *Philosophical Hermeneutics*. Berkeley: University of California Press, 1976.

————. *Wahrheit und Methode. Grundzüge einer philosophischen Hermeneutik*. 4th ed. Tübingen: J. C. B. Mohr, Paul Siebeck, 1975. [*Truth and Method*. Ed. and trans. Garrett Barden and John Cumming. New York: Crossroad, 1975.]

Gardiner, Patrick, ed. *Theories of History*. Glencoe: Free Press, 1959.

Geehan, E. R., ed. *Jerusalem and Athens: Critical Discussions on the Theology and Apologetics of Cornelius Van Til*. Nutley, N.J.: Presbyterian and Reformed Publishing, 1974.

Geertz, Clifford. *The Interpretation of Cultures*. New York: Basic Books, 1973.

Geraets, Theodore F., ed. *Rationality To-day*. Ottawa: University of Ottawa Press, 1979.

Gerrish, Brian A. *The Old Protestantism and the New: Essays on the Reformation Heritage*. Chicago: University of Chicago Press, 1982.

————. *A Prince of the Church: Schleiermacher and the Beginnings of Modern Theology*. Philadelphia: Fortress, 1984.

————. *Tradition and the Modern World: Reformed Theology in the Nineteenth Century*. Chicago: University of Chicago Press, 1978.

Giddens, Anthony. *Central Problems in Social Theory: Action, Structure and Contradiction in Social Analysis*. Berkeley: University of California Press, 1979.

————. *New Rules of Sociological Method: A Positive Critique of Interpretive Sociologies*. London: Hutchinson, 1976.

————. "Reason Without Revolution? Habermas's *Theory of Communicative Action*." *Praxis International* 2, no. 3 (1982):318–38.

Glymour, Clark. "Explanation and Realism." In *Scientific Realism*, ed. Jarrett Leplin. Berkeley: University of California Press, 1984.

Goodman, Nelson. *Ways of Worldmaking*. Indianapolis: Hackett, 1978.

Gutting, Gary. *Religious Belief and Religious Skepticism*. Notre Dame: University of Notre Dame Press, 1982.

Gutting, Gary, ed. *Paradigms and Revolutions: Appraisals and Applications of Thomas Kuhn's Philosophy of Science*. Notre Dame: University of Notre Dame Press, 1980.

Habermas, Jürgen. *Erkenntnis und Interesse*. Frankfurt: Suhrkamp, 1968. [*Knowledge and Human Interests*. Trans. Jeremy J. Shapiro. Boston: Beacon Press, 1968.]

―――. *Der philosophische Diskurs der Moderne*. Frankfurt: Suhrkamp, 1985. [*The Philosophical Discourse of Modernity: Twelve Lectures*. Trans. Frederick G. Lawrence. Cambridge: MIT Press, 1987.]

―――. *Theorie des kommunikativen Handelns*. 2 vols. Frankfurt: Suhrkamp, 1981. [*The Theory of Communicative Action*. Trans. Thomas McCarthy. 2 vols. Boston: Beacon Press, 1984 and 1987.]

―――. "Was heisst Universalpragmatik?" In *Sprachpragmatik und Philosophie*, ed. Karl-Otto Apel. Frankfurt: Suhrkamp, 1976. ["What Is Universal Pragmatics?" In *Communication and the Evolution of Society*. Trans. Thomas McCarthy. Boston: Beacon Press, 1979.]

―――. *Zur Logik der Sozialwissenschaften*. In *Philosophische Rundschau* 14. Tübingen: J. C. B. Mohr, Paul Siebeck, 1967. Reprint. Frankfurt: Suhrkamp, 1970.

Habermas, Jürgen, and N. Luhmann. *Theorie der Gesellschaft oder Sozialtechnologie—Was leistet die System-Theorie?* Frankfurt: Suhrkamp, 1971.

Hacking, Ian. "Imre Lakatos's Philosophy of Science." *British Journal for the Philosophy of Science* 30 (1979):381–402.

Hallett, M. "Towards a Theory of Mathematical Research Programs." *British Journal for the Philosophy of Science* 30 (1979):1–25, 135–59.

Hands, Douglas W. "The Methodology of Scientific Research Programmes." *Philosophy of the Social Sciences* 9 (1979):293–303.

Hanson, Norwood Russell. *Patterns of Discovery: An Inquiry into the Conceptual Foundations of Science*. Cambridge: Cambridge University Press, 1958.

Harries, Karsten. "Copernican Reflections and the Tasks of Metaphysics." *International Philosophical Quarterly* 23 (1983):235–50.

―――. Review of *The Phenomenology of the Social World*, by A. Schutz. *The Journal of Value Inquiry* 4 (1970):65–75.

Harris, Errol E., "Epicyclic Popperism." *The British Journal for the Philosophy of Science* 23 (1972):55–67.

Hartshorne, Charles. *A Natural Theology for Our Time*. La Salle: Open Court, 1967.

Hauptli, Bruce. "Inscrutability and Correspondence." *The Southern Journal of Philosophy* 17 (1979):199–212.

―――. "Quinean Relativism: Beyond Metaphysical Realism and Idealism." *The Southern Journal of Philosophy* 18 (1980):393–410.

Heidegger, Martin. *Basic Writings from Being and Time to the Task of Thinking*. Ed. David Farrell Krell. New York: Harper and Row, 1977.

Heimbeck, Raeburne. *Theology and Meaning*. Stanford: Stanford University Press, 1969.

Hekman, Susan J. *Weber, the Ideal Type, and Contemporary Social Theory*. Notre Dame: University of Notre Dame, 1983.

Helm, Paul. *The Varieties of Belief*. London: George Allen and Unwin, 1973.

Hempel, Carl. *Aspects of Scientific Explanation and Other Essays in the Philosophy of Science*. New York: Free Press, 1965.

———. "Some Remarks on 'Facts and Propositions,'" *Analysis* 2, no. 6 (1935):93–6.

Hertz, Heinrich. *Principles of Mechanics*. Trans. D. E. Jones and J. T. Walley. New York: Macmillan, 1899.

Hesse, Mary. *Revolutions and Reconstructions in the Philosophy of Science*. Bloomington: Indiana University Press, 1980.

Hick, John. *Faith and Knowledge*. 2d ed. Ithaca: Cornell University Press, 1966.

Hirsch, E. D., Jr. *The Aims of Interpretation*. Chicago: University of Chicago Press, 1976.

———. *Validity in Interpretation*. New Haven: Yale University Press, 1967.

Hodges, H. A. *The Philosophy of Wilhelm Dilthey*. Westport: Greenwood Press, 1952.

———. *Wilhelm Dilthey: An Introduction*. London: Routledge and Kegan Paul, 1944.

Holmes, Arthur F. *Christian Philosophy in the Twentieth Century*. Nutley, N.J.: Craig, 1969.

———. *Faith Seeks Understanding*. Grand Rapids: Eerdmans, 1971.

Holton, Gerald. *The Scientific Imagination: Case Studies*. Cambridge: Cambridge University Press, 1978.

Holton, Gerald, and William A. Blanpied. *Science and Its Public: The Changing Relationship*. Vol. 33, *Boston Studies*. Dordrecht: D. Reidel, 1976.

Hook, Sidney, ed. *Religious Experience and Truth: A Symposium*. New York: New York University Press, 1961.

Hübner, Kurt. *Wahrheit des Mythos*. Munich: C. H. Beck, 1985.

James, William. *The Varieties of Religious Experience: A Study in Human Nature*. New York: Mentor, New American Library, 1958.

———. *The Will to Believe and Human Immortality*. New York: Dover, 1956.

Kant, Immanuel. *Religion Within the Limits of Reason Alone*. Trans. T. M. Greene and H. H. Hudson. New York: Harper and Row, 1934.

Kayser, Wolfgang. *Die Wahrheit der Dichter. Wandlung eines Begriffes in der deutschen Literatur*. Hamburg: Rowohlt, 1959.

Kegley, Charles W., ed. *The Philosophy and Theology of Anders Nygren*. London: Feffer and Simons, 1970.

Kekes, John. *A Justification of Rationality*. Albany: State University of New York, 1976.

———. "The Rationality of Metaphysics." *Metaphilosophy* 4, no. 2 (1973):124–39.

———. "Rationality and the Social Sciences." *Philosophy of the Social Sciences* 9 (1979):105–13.

————. "Rationality and the Social Sciences—A Reply to Benn and Mortimore." *Philosophy of the Social Sciences* 9 (1979):181–84.

Kierkegaard, Søren. *Concluding Unscientific Postscript.* Ed. W. Lowrie. Trans. D. F. Swenson. Princeton: Princeton University Press, 1941.

Knapp, Steven, and Walter Benn Michaels. "Against Theory." In *Against Theory: Literary Studies and the New Pragmatism,* ed. W. J. T. Mitchell. Chicago: University of Chicago Press, 1985.

Körner, Stephan, ed. *Explanation.* New Haven: Yale University Press, 1975.

Koller, John M. *Oriental Philosophies.* New York: Charles Scribner's Sons, 1970.

Koyré, Alexandre. *Études Galiléennes.* 3 vols. Paris: Hermann, 1939. Reprint. 1966.

Kuhn, Thomas S. *The Copernican Revolution: Planetary Astronomy in the Development of Western Thought.* Cambridge: Harvard University Press, 1957.

————. *The Structure of Scientific Revolutions.* 2d ed. Chicago: University of Chicago Press, 1970.

Lakatos, Imre. *Philosophical Papers.* 2 vols. Eds. John Worrall and Gregory Currie. 2 vols. Vol. 1, *The Methodology of Scientific Research Programmes.* Vol. 2, *Mathematics, Science and Epistemology.* Cambridge: Cambridge University Press, 1978.

Lakatos, Imre, and Alan Musgrave, eds. *Criticism and the Growth of Knowledge.* Cambridge: Cambridge University Press, 1970.

Latsis, Spiro, ed. *Method and Appraisal in Economics.* New York: Cambridge University Press, 1976.

Laudan, Larry. *Progress and Its Problems: Toward a Theory of Scientific Growth.* Berkeley: University of California Press, 1977.

Lewis, Gordon L. *Testing Christianity's Truth Claims.* Chicago: Moody, 1976.

Lichtenberg, Georg Christoph. *The Lichtenberg Reader: Selected Writings.* Ed. and trans. Franz Mautner and Henry Hatfield. Boston: Beacon Press, 1959.

Lindbeck, George. *The Nature of Doctrine: Religion and Theology in a Post-Liberal Age.* Philadelphia: Westminster Press, 1984.

Lonergan, Bernard. *Insight: A Study of Human Understanding.* New York: Philosophical Library, 1957.

————. *Method in Theology.* New York: Herder and Herder, 1972.

Luckmann, Thomas. *The Invisible Religion: The Problem of Religion in Modern Society.* New York: Macmillan, 1967.

McCarthy, Thomas. *The Critical Theory of Jürgen Habermas.* London: Hutchinson, 1978.

McFague, Sallie. *Metaphorical Theology.* Philadelphia: Fortress, 1982.

McLaughlin, Robert, ed. *What? Where? When? Why? Essays on Induction, Space and Time, Explanation.* Dordrecht: D. Reidel, 1982.

Mead, George Herbert. *Mind, Self and Society from the Standpoint of a Social Behaviorist.* Ed. Charles W. Morris. Chicago: University of Chicago Press, 1934.

Misgeld, Dieter. "Communication and Societal Rationalization: A Review Essay of Jürgen Habermas's *Theorie des kommunikativen Handelns.*" *Canadian Journal of Sociology* 8 (1983):433–53.

———. "Critical Theory and Sociological Theory." *Philosophy of the Social Sciences* 14 (1984):97–105.

Mitchell, Basil. *The Justification of Religious Belief.* New York: Seabury, 1973.

Mitchell, Basil, ed. *Faith and Logic: Oxford Essays in Philosophical Theology.* London: George Allen and Unwin, 1957.

Moser, Simon, and Eckhart Pilick, eds. *Gottesbilder heute. Zur Gottesproblematik in der säkularisierten Gesellschaft der Gegenwart.* Köningstein, Ts: Hanstein, 1979.

Mulkay, Michael, and G. Nigal Gilbert. "Putting Philosophy to Work: Karl Popper's Influence on Scientific Practice." *Philosophy of the Social Sciences* 11 (1981):389–407.

Nagel, Ernest. *The Structure of Science: Problems in the Logic of Scientific Explanation.* London: Routledge and Kegan Paul, 1961.

Nagel, Ernest, Patrick Suppes, and Alfred Tarski, eds. *Logic, Methodology and Philosophy of Science: Proceedings of the 1960 International Congress.* Stanford: Stanford University Press, 1962.

Nash, Ronald H. *The Light of the Mind: St. Augustine's Theory of Knowledge.* Lexington: University Press of Kentucky, 1969.

Newton-Smith, W. H. *The Rationality of Science.* Boston: Routledge and Kegan Paul, 1981.

Northrop, Filmer S. C. *The Logic of the Sciences and the Humanities.* New York: Macmillan, 1947.

Nozick, Robert. *Philosophical Explanations.* Cambridge: Harvard University Press, Belknap Press, 1981.

Nygren, Anders. *Meaning and Method: Prolegomena to a Scientific Philosophy of Religion and a Scientific Theology.* Trans. Philip S. Watson. Philadelphia: Fortress, 1972. [*Sinn und Methode. Prolegomena zu einer wissenschaftlichen Religionsphilosophie und einer wissenschaftlichen Theologie.* Trans. Gerhard Klose. Göttingen: Vandenhoeck und Ruprecht, 1979.]

Oelmüller, Willi, ed. *Transzendentalphilosophische Normenbegründungen.* Paderborn: Ferdinand Schöningh, 1978.

Ogden, C. K., and I. A. Richards. *The Meaning of Meaning,* 8th ed. New York: Harcourt, Brace, 1945.

Pannenberg, Wolfhart. *Basic Questions in Theology.* Trans. George H. Kehm. 2 vols. Philadelphia: Fortress, 1971.

———. *Grundfragen systematischer Theologie.* 2 vols. Göttingen: Vandenhoeck und Ruprecht, 1967 and 1980.

———. *Jesus—God and Man.* Trans. Lewis L. Wilkins and Duane Priebe. 2d ed. Philadelphia: Westminster, 1977.

————. "Meaning, Religion and the Question of God." Trans. Philip Clayton. In *Knowing Religiously*, ed. Leroy S. Rouner. Notre Dame: University of Notre Dame Press, 1985.

————. *Metaphysik und Gottesgedanke*. Göttingen: Vandenhoeck und Ruprecht, 1988.

————. "Was Ist Wahrheit?" In *Vom Herrengeheimnis der Wahrheit, Festschrift for Heinrich Vogel*, ed. Karl Scharf. Berlin: Lettner, 1962.

————. *Wissenschaftstheorie und Theologie*. Frankfurt: Suhrkamp, 1977. [*Theology and the Philosophy of Science*. Trans. Francis McDonagh. Philadelphia: Westminster, 1976.]

Pannenberg, Wolfhart, and Gerhard Sauter. *Grundlagen der Theologie—ein Diskurs*. Ed. S. M. Daecke and H. N. Janowski. Stuttgart: W. Kohlhammer, 1974.

Pannenberg, Wolfhart, et al. *Revelation as History*. Trans. David Granskou. New York: Macmillan, 1968.

Parsons, Talcott. *Social Systems and the Evolution of Action Theory*. New York: Free Press, 1977.

————. *The Structure of Social Action*. 2d ed. New York: Free Press, 1961.

Passmore, John. "Explanation in Everyday Life, in Science, and in History." *History and Theory* 2 (1962):105–23.

Patterson, Bob E. *Carl F. H. Henry*. Waco, Texas: Word Books, 1983.

Peacocke, A. R., ed. *The Sciences and Theology in the Twentieth Century*. Stocksfield, England: Oriel Press, 1981.

Pepper, Stephen. *World Hypotheses: A Study in Evidence*. Berkeley: University of California Press, 1970.

Pettit, Philip. *The Concept of Structuralism: A Critical Analysis*. Dublin: Gill and Macmillan, 1975.

Peukert, Helmut. *Science, Action and Fundamental Theology: Toward a Theology of Communicative Action*. Trans. James Bohman. Boston: MIT Press, 1984.

Phillips, D. Z. *Faith and Philosophical Inquiry*. New York: Schocken, 1970.

————. *Religion and Understanding*. New York: Macmillan, 1967.

————. *Religion Without Explanation*. Oxford: Basil Blackwell, 1976.

Plantinga, Alvin, and Nicholas Wolterstorff, eds. *Faith and Rationality: Reason and Belief in God*. Notre Dame: University of Notre Dame Press, 1983.

Popper, Karl. *Die beiden Grundprobleme der Erkenntnistheorie*. Ed. Troels Eggers Hansen. Tübingen: J. C. B. Mohr, Paul Siebeck, 1979.

————. *Conjectures and Refutations: The Growth of Scientific Knowledge*. London: Routledge and Kegan Paul, 1969.

————. *The Logic of Scientific Discovery*. 2d. ed. London: Hutchinson, 1980.

————. *Objective Knowledge: An Evolutionary Approach*. 2d ed. Oxford: Clarendon Press, 1979.

————. *The Open Society and Its Enemies*. 2d ed. 2 vols. London: Routledge and Kegan Paul, 1952.

————. *Postscript to the Logic of Scientific Discovery.* 3 vols.: *Realism and the Aim of Science, The Open Universe: An Argument for Indeterminism,* and *Quantum Theory and the Schism in Physics,* ed. W. W. Bartley. Totowa, N.J.: Rowman and Littlefield, 1983.

————. *The Poverty of Historicism.* 2d ed. London: Routledge and Kegan Paul, 1960.

————. "Reason or Revolution?", *Archives européennes de sociologie* 11, no. 2 (1970):252–62.

————. *Unended Quest: An Intellectual Autobiography.* Glasgow: Fontana, Collins, 1974.

Proudfoot, Wayne. *Religious Experience.* Berkeley: University of California Press, 1985.

Puntel, L. Bruno. "On Communicative Rationality: A Critique of Habermas." Forthcoming.

————. *Grundlagen einer Theorie der Wahrheit.* Forthcoming.

————. *Wahrheitstheorien in der neueren Philosophie. Eine kritisch-systematische Darstellung.* Darmstadt: Wissenschaftliche Buchgesellschaft, 1978.

Putnam, Hilary. *The Many Faces of Realism.* La Salle: Open Court, 1987.

————. *Realism and Reason.* Cambridge: University Press, 1983.

————. *Reason, Truth and History.* Cambridge: University Press, 1981.

Quine, Willard van Orman. *From a Logical Point of View.* 2d ed. Cambridge: Harvard University Press, 1961.

————. *Ontological Relativity, and Other Essays.* New York: Columbia University Press, 1969.

Radner, Michael, and Stephen Winokur, eds. *Analyses of Theories and Methods of Physics and Psychology.* Vol. 4, *Minnesota Studies.* Minneapolis: University of Minnesota Press, 1970.

Radnitzky, Gerard, and Gunnar Andersson, eds. *Progress and Rationality in Science.* Vol. 58, *Boston Studies.* Dordrecht: D. Reidel, 1978.

Ramm, Bernard. *Varieties of Christian Apologetics.* Grand Rapids: Baker Book House, 1961.

Ray, L. J. "Critical Theory and Positivism: Popper and the Frankfurt School." *Philosophy and the Social Sciences* 9 (1979):149–73.

Reichenbach, Hans. *Experience and Prediction: An Analysis of the Foundations and the Structure of Knowledge.* Chicago: University of Chicago Press, 1938.

————. *The Rise of Scientific Philosophy.* Berkeley: University of California Press, 1951.

Remenyi, Joseph V. "Core Demi-core Interaction: Toward a General Theory of Disciplinary and Subdisciplinary Growth." *History of Political Economy* 11 (1979):30–63.

Rescher, Nicholas. *The Coherence Theory of Truth.* Oxford: Clarendon, 1973.

————. *Methodological Pragmatism: A Systems-Theoretic Approach to the Theory of Knowledge*. New York: New York University Press, 1977.

————. *The Primacy of Practice: Essays Towards a Pragmatically Kantian Theory of Empirical Knowledge*. Oxford: Basil Blackwell, 1973.

————. "Truth as Ideal Coherence." *Review of Metaphysics* 38 (1985):795–806.

Rickert, Heinrich. *Die Grenzen der naturwissenschaftlichen Begriffsbildung*. 2d ed. Tübingen, 1913.

Ricoeur, Paul. *Hermeneutics and the Human Sciences*. Ed. and trans. John B. Thompson. Cambridge: Cambridge University Press, 1981.

————. *Interpretation Theory: Discourse and the Surplus of Meaning*. Fort Worth: Texas Christian University Press, 1976.

Robinson, James, and John Cobb, eds. *The Later Heidegger and Theology*. New York: Harper and Row, 1962.

Ryan, Alan, ed. *The Philosophy of Social Explanation*. Oxford: Oxford University Press, 1973.

Salmon, Wesley C. "Carl G. Hempel on the Rationality of Science." *Journal of Philosophy* 80 (1983):555–62.

————. *Scientific Explanation and the Causal Structure of the World*. Princeton: Princeton University Press, 1984.

Salmon, Wesley, Richard Jeffry, and James Greeno. *Statistical Explanation and Statistical Relevance*. Pittsburgh: University of Pittsburgh Press, 1971.

Sauter, Gerhard. *Theologie als Wissenschaft. Aufsätze und Thesen*. Munich: Chr. Kaiser, 1971.

————. *Wissenschaftstheoretische Kritik der Theologie. Die Theologie und die neuere wissenschaftstheoretische Diskussion*. Munich: Chr. Kaiser, 1973.

Schilpp, Paul Arthur, ed. *The Philosophy of Karl Popper*. Vol. 14, *The Library of Living Philosophers*. 2 vols. La Salle: Open Court, 1974.

Schleiermacher, Friedrich. *The Christian Faith*. Ed. and trans. H. R. Mackintosh and J. S. Stewart. New York: Harper and Row, 1963.

————. *Kurze Darstellung des theologischen Studiums zum Behuf einleitender Vorlesungen*. Ed. Heinrich Scholz. Hildesheim: Georg Olm, 1961.

————. *On Religion: Speeches to Its Cultured Despisers*. Trans. John Oman. 3d ed. New York: Harper and Row, 1958.

————. *Sämtliche Werke*. Berlin: G. Reimer, 1834–64.

Schoen, Edward. *Religious Explanations*. Durham: Duke University Press, 1985.

Scholz, Heinrich. "Wie ist eine evangelische Theologie als Wissenschaft möglich?" *Zwischen den Zeiten* 9 (1931):8–53.

Schütz, Alfred. *Der sinnhafte Aufbau der sozialen Welt. Eine Einleitung in die verstehende Soziologie*. Vienna: Julius Springer, 1932.

Sedlmayr, Hans. *Kunst und Wahrheit. Zur Theorie und Methode der Kunstgeschichte*. Itzelsberger: Mäander, 1978.

Segundo, Juan Luis. *The Liberation of Theology*. Trans. John Drury. New York: Orbis Books, 1976.

Seung, T. K. *Structuralism and Hermeneutics*. New York: Columbia University Press, 1982.

Siemans, Helge and Reuter, eds. *Theologie als Wissenschaft in der Gesellschaft. Eine Heidelberger Experiment*. Göttingen: Vandenhoeck und Ruprecht, 1970.

Smart, Ninian. *Doctrine and Argument in Indian Philosophy*. London: George Allen and Unwin, 1964.

———. *The Phenomenon of Religion*. New York: Herder and Herder, 1973.

———. *Worldviews: Crosscultural Explorations of Human Beliefs*. New York: Charles Scribner's Sons, 1983.

Smart, Ninian, John Clayton, Patrick Sherry, and Steven T. Katz, eds. *Nineteenth Century Religious Thought in the West*. 3 vols. Cambridge: Cambridge University Press, 1985.

Suppe, Frederick, ed. *The Structure of Scientific Theories*. 2d ed. Urbana: The University of Illinois Press, 1977.

Swinburne, Richard. *Faith and Reason*. Oxford: Clarendon Press, 1981.

Thomas, George F. *Philosophy and Religious Belief*. New York: Charles Scribner's Sons, 1970.

Thompson, John B., and David Held, eds. *Habermas: Critical Debates*. London: Macmillan, 1982.

Tillich, Paul. *Dynamics of Faith*. New York: Harper and Row, 1957.

———. *Gesammelte Werke*. 14 vols. Stuttgart: Evangelisches Verlagswerk, 1959. Reprint. 1975.

———. *Systematic Theology*. Vol. 1, *Reason and Revelation, Being and God*. Chicago: University of Chicago Press, 1951.

———. *What Is Religion?* Ed. James Adams. New York: Harper and Row, 1973.

Torrance, Thomas F. *The Ground and Grammar of Theology*. Charlottesville: University Press of Virginia, 1980.

———. *Theological Science*. London: Oxford University Press, 1969.

Toulmin, Stephen. *Foresight and Understanding: An Enquiry into the Aims of Science*. Bloomington: University of Indiana Press, 1961.

———. *The Philosophy of Science: An Introduction*. London: Hutchinson, 1953.

Tracy, David. *The Analogical Imagination: Christian Theology and the Culture of Pluralism*. London: SCM Press, 1981.

Troeltsch, Ernst. *Gesammelte Schriften*. 3 vols. Tübingen: J. C. B. Mohr, 1913.

———. *Glaubenslehre*. Munich: Duncker und Humblot, 1925.

Ullmann, Stephen. *Semantics: An Introduction to the Science of Meanings*. 2d ed. Oxford: Basil Blackwell, 1970.

van Fraassen, Bas C. "The Pragmatics of Explanation." *American Philosophical Quarterly* 14 (1977):143–50.

———. *The Scientific Image*. Oxford: Clarendon Press, 1980.

Van der Leeuw, G. *Religion in Essence and Manifestation*. Trans. J. E. Turner. 2 vols. New York: Harper and Row, 1963.

Van Til, Cornelius. *The Defense of the Faith*. Philadelphia: Presbyterian and Reformed Publishing, 1955.

von Wright, Georg Henrik. *Explanation and Understanding*. Ithaca: Cornell University Press, 1971.

Watkins, J. W. N. "Confirmable and Influential Metaphysics." *Mind*, n.s. 67 (1958):344–65.

Weber, Max. *From Max Weber: Essays in Sociology*. Ed. and trans. H. H. Gerth and C. Wright Mills. New York: Oxford University Press, 1946.

———. *The Methodology of the Social Sciences*. Ed. and trans. Edward A. Shils and Henry A. Finch. New York: Free Press, 1949.

———. *The Theory of Social and Economic Organization*. Trans. A. M. Henderson and Talcott Parsons. New York: Free Press, 1947.

Wellmer, Albrecht. *Methodologie als Erkenntnistheorie. Zur Wissenschaftslehre Karl R. Popper*. Frankfurt: Suhrkamp, 1967.

Wendt, Hans Hinrich. *System der christlichen Lehre*. 2d ed. Göttingen: Vandenhoeck und Ruprecht, 1920.

Westman, R., ed. *The Copernican Achievement*. Los Angeles: University of California Press, 1976.

Westphal, Merold. *God, Guilt, and Death: An Existential Phenomenology of Religion*. Bloomington: Indiana University Press, 1984.

Whitehead, Alfred North. *Process and Reality*. Eds. David Ray Griffin and Donald W. Sherburne. Corrected ed. New York: Free Press, 1978.

———. *Science and the Modern World*. New York: New American Library, 1925. Reprint. 1948.

Wilkins, Burleigh Taylor. *Has History Any Meaning? A Critique of Popper's Philosophy of History*. Ithaca: Cornell University Press, 1978.

Wilson, Bryan, ed. *Rationality*. Oxford: Basil Blackwell, 1979.

Winch, Peter. *The Idea of a Social Science and Its Relation to Philosophy*. London: Routledge and Kegan Paul, 1958.

Wisser, Richard, ed. *Sinn und Sein: Ein philosophisches Symposium*. Tübingen: M. Niemeyer, 1960.

Wittgenstein, Ludwig. *Lectures and Conversations on Aesthetics, Psychology and Religious Belief*. Ed. Cyril Barrett. Oxford: Basil Blackwell, 1966.

———. *Philosophical Investigations*. Trans. G. E. M. Anscombe. 3d ed. New York: Macmillan, 1953. Reprint. 1968.

———. *Tractatus Logico-Philosophicus*. Trans. D. F. Pears and B. F. McGuinness. London: Routledge and Kegan Paul, 1922. Reprint. 1961.

Zahar, Elie. "Why did Einstein's Programme Supersede Lorentz's?" *British Journal for the Philosophy of Science* 24 (1973):95–123, 223–62.

Zukav, Gary. *The Dancing Wu-Li Masters: An Overview of the New Physics*. New York: Bantam, 1980.

Index

DATE DUE